S0-CCL-501

GUERRILLA TACTICS IN THE JOB MARKET

This book is dedicated to the thousands of job seekers who have the ability to do the job they want but who won't get a decent job offer if they tell the truth.

GUERRILLA TACTICS IN THE JOB MARKET

HOW TO WIN THE JOB OF YOUR LIFE

GARTH BROCKMAN, Ph.D.

PALADIN PRESS
BOULDER, COLORADO

Guerrilla Tactics in the Job Market
How to Get the Job of Your Life
by Garth Brockman, Ph.D.

ISBN 0-87364-420-4
Printed in the United States of America

Published by Paladin Press, a division of
Paladin Enterprises, Inc., P.O. Box 1307,
Boulder, Colorado 80306, USA.
(303) 443-7250

Direct inquiries and/or orders to the above address.

Contents

Introduction

Let's get one thing straight right from the start: this is a book about full-blown, deliberate, and planned lying. It's intended for job seekers who want to misrepresent one, some, or all aspects of their qualifications and experiences so they'll be hired by someone who might not give them a job if the truth were known. You are going to learn about *serious lying.* Serious lying goes beyond the mild little white lies (such as, "Oh, yes, I love to work lots of extra hours") and the slight exaggerations of the truth ("My past bosses have always told me that I was the one they could count on") which are a vital and expected part of resumes, interviews, and thank-you letters. These sickly, anemic little lies, while critical to any job search, aren't sufficient to deal with the big problems faced by many job seekers. It takes more than a spontaneous, off-the-cuff exaggeration to hide an unsightly gap in your job history. Little fibs aren't going to compensate for educational credentials which you never earned. These types of problems require not only big, but also carefully planned lies. If that's what you're looking for, you won't be disappointed.

In order to conduct a successful job search utilizing lies, you must learn deliberately planned, thoroughly practiced, and boldly executed job-search deceits which rend the very fabric of actual qualifications and experience. This type of lying can't be done on the spur of the moment in an interview, and it doesn't come naturally to any but a select few. Here's how to plan, organize, and conduct everything from a small goose of the truth to a full blown gang rape of reality.

Why is it difficult for most people to lie well? What are the subtle body language and voice cues which people associate with both lies and the truth? How do people learn how to practice their face-to-face lying so they don't give themselves away when they drop the big one? Why in the world would most interviewers want to believe your most outrageous lies? You'll learn the answers to these questions and more.

Put together a complete job-search campaign which smoothly blends your finely crafted lies with reality. Or enhance the execution all of your routine, day-to-day lying ("Yessir, Mr. Legree, your speech was a real inspiration!" and "Yes, honey, that dress looks great!"). Strange as it may seem, you'll discover that a well rounded understanding and appreciation of the technology of lying will make you more effective socially; you'll "read" people with more insight and you'll have a better handle on projecting the social impression you want to project in situations outside of the job search arena.

The information on employers' strategies, what

goes on behind the scenes, and the employers' expectations is invaluable to any job seeker, liar or not. This book presents the most detailed and complete treatment of the critical skill of job-search lying that you'll ever encounter. Whether you simply need to put a little polish on slightly off-white job search lies which even ministers use without guilt, or if you're going to lie about every aspect of a twenty year employment history, you'll come away with a more complete understanding of what to do and a knowledge of how to do it. If you plan carefully, practice diligently, and show a little courage, your job search lies will work well for you. Better yet, you'll have the satisfaction of knowing that you rose to the occasion and used your wits and daring to take control of a desperate job search situation. Over the years, your successful job search lies will be a source of happy and proud reflection. Few nonliars will ever have that type of pleasure.

THE MORALITY OF JOB-SEARCH LYING

Let's not beat around the bush; a lie is a lie. Most of us are at least momentarily disturbed when we tell small, harmless lies, not to mention the large, carefully planned lies. In later chapters, we'll discuss why we feel that way, and how the feeling manifests itself. What we're concerned with here is keeping things in perspective. I don't want you compromising the effectiveness of your very large and carefully planned job-search lies by getting mired down in a swamp of false morality, guilt feelings, and subsequent subtle displays of behavioral cues that scream, "Yes, yes. I admit it, I'm a liar."

I'm not going to try to convince you that lying is always okay or that there's no moral difference between lying and telling the truth. Some lying is immoral and, moreover, won't do you any good. For example, while a married man may wisely choose not to be completely honest with his wife in response to the question, "Honey, do you still think I'm beautiful?" he owes it to her and to himself to be honest with her about things that are important to maintaining a mutually beneficial relationship. In the above example, it's not helping anyone to point out to one's wife what she already knows: She's not as beautiful as she used to be. What she's seeking is a personal statement from her husband that he still finds her desirable.

Shared, candid, and trusted information on the important issues is the only basis for establishing lasting and meaningful relationships. If we don't give it, we won't get it. Therefore, since we all require at least one close, personal relationship in order to be emotionally healthy, significant lying in a relationship is "bad" because it breeches an established trust and hurts everyone involved. If you're doing that type of lying, you should feel bad about it; you're betraying a trust and the lies will gain you little value for the amount of suffering you're inflicting on others and, ultimately, yourself.

Job-search lying is another story. You don't owe anything at all to prospective employers. Most of the time, there's no relationship, no shared trust, no common and shared values; there's no established trust to breach. Nobody owes anyone anything. In fact, companies "ask for it" by lying to job seekers about everything.

First, the companies lie about their status in the industry.

They say: "This organization is on the cutting edge of our industry's technology." But the truth is: the latest technology in the organization is their fifteen-year-old phone system.

Then, they lie about the working conditions. They say: "All of our employees work in tastefully decorated, ergonomically designed work areas." But the truth is: everyone except the brass gets dropped at an army surplus desk next to a chili addict with a chronic gas problem in a small, unventilated cubicle.

Face it, they lie about everything. This lying by employers enables them to compete with all of the other lying employers for available talent. No one can afford to hinder his recruiting effort with the truth. In fact, no organization would want the kind of person who would willingly work there if he did know the truth about the company. In the words of one personnel director, "I wouldn't want a bunch of losers who are so hard up they'd take a job here if they knew what a dump it was."

Employers attempt to get the best people they can, as quickly and as cheaply as possible. They know they couldn't get what they need by telling the truth, so they lie. They don't feel bad about it because they believe, "I don't have any choice. Besides, I didn't make the rules." As a result, the entire recruiting process is rife with employers' lies of commission (telling you blatant falsehoods like "There's a lot of room for advancement" when nobody's going anywhere) and omission (not mentioning the fact that your new boss is considered the laughing stock of the entire company).

Given the above, there's no reason on earth why you should believe that you owe a potential employer anything at all in advance of your first day at work. You owe him nothing. He owes you nothing. He's lying shamelessly about everything, intentionally and unintentionally. He's trying to get the most for his effort and money, and you're trying to get the best job you can as fast as you can. What he tells you about the job is only remotely related to what you'll get, and most employers could care less. In their eyes, your career is your problem. That's all the morality you're going to find in a job search.

All you owe potential employers in return is an equally distorted view of who you are and what you can do for them so that they'll be inclined to give you a shot at the job. If it doesn't work out for them, it's their problem. So let's not hear anything about worrying about the morality of lying until you start working. If you get to the point where you're working for a new employer, you'll then have an established trust: you'll owe him a decent day's work for your pay, nothing more, nothing less.

It's Your Life

Of course, the bottom line of this whole discussion revolves around your need for a job. If you're out of work long enough, you run the risk of losing your home and car. In that case, you may need to lie, even if you must take a chance on jail or shamelessly violate a trust. It's your life, your family, and your problem. There's nobody out there who's going to take care of you because you "played fair." There's nobody out there counting who's been naughty and nice.

You'll find that there's little justice or fairness in job searching (or business or life in general, for that matter). You're not going to get the job simply because you could do it best. In fact, few companies have any objective way to determine who is best for a job; the entire selection process is a morass of subjective opinions (which is one reason why lies work so well).

If you should lose everything because of your scruples, nobody will care. If you have to declare bankruptcy because you're out of work, nobody will be understanding and extend you credit, even many years later. It's up to you to fix your situation any way you can. You've got to do what you must do to survive.

Lying is a tool which will help you fight harder to save what's yours. It's up to you as to when and how you lie. When you decide to lie, I want you to lie in the most effective and intelligent manner; anything less is just plain stupid.

Good luck with your lies and your job search. I hope you find what you're looking for.

Chapter One

Elements of an Honest Job Search

Lying is not a panacea for all job-search problems. There's no doubt that an effective lie can do a lot to cover up a problem and make you appear to be a more attractive candidate. At the same time, no lie, however crafty, can compensate for the damage you'll do to your chances by conducting a job search that is organized and executed poorly. There's no sense lying if you're not taking care of the basics first. Most job seekers, liars or not, don't know the first thing about putting together an effective job search. Most can't put together a decent resume, don't know what should go into a cover letter, and don't even know where to find good job ads or where to locate lists of headhunters.

If you're not getting first-class job-search materials out to the right people in sufficient volume, you're not going to get many chances to practice your lies on employers; they'll be turned off by (or never afforded an opportunity to see) your materials.

There are a great many elements to a successful job search. This book is primarily concerned with job-search lying, and will not cover all aspects of the job-search process in great detail. You will learn the bare essentials, with a little of the rationale behind my recommendations. If you require more detailed information on the honest aspects of a job search, there are many additional books on the subject. There's a lot of bad advice out there, but you can learn a little something from every book you pick up.

RESUMES

Your resume is the most important part of your job search. Yes, it's even more important than your lies! The only purpose a resume serves (along with its accompanying cover letter) is to get you into interviews. If the resume is substandard in appearance or preparation, confusing, not hard-hitting, or too long, it'll be lost in the sea of resumes which are submitted in response to ads or sent by job seekers who are conducting a direct-mail campaign. Using a poor resume will mean that you'll get fewer face-to-face opportunities to lie.

If your resume is shoddy in appearance or poorly organized in presenting your achievements, readers will feel less secure about you, and perhaps a little suspicious. Then you're in trouble because they'll start to look for subtle bits of information and behavior which will vindicate their initial negative feelings about you.

If you're lying, an outstanding resume is even more critical. Properly prepared and organized, your resume will lead readers to believe your claims of experience and knowledge. If your resume is professional and businesslike, readers will assume that you're a well-balanced professional even before they meet you. In fact, an outstanding resume actually leads them to look for evidence to support their expectations. A great resume will not only get you the critical interviews you must have, it'll get your lies off on the right foot.

The Purpose of a Resume

The only purpose of a resume is to get you an interview. A resume won't get you a job unless you already have great connections; since you're reading a book about job-search lying, you're obviously not in that very small, privileged category. Your resume, whether it's a pack of well-designed lies or (please excuse my language) the truth, has only one aim: to impress the reader enough to make him want to interview you over the phone or in person. Only five to ten people, and usually no more than seven, will get interviewed on the phone for most jobs. No matter what all the resumes said, no matter what the qualifications of the hundreds who responded, once the calls are made, all of the folks who don't get called are out of the running. Once the calls have been made, the person who gets hired will come from the small number who get interviewed. Once you get into that select number, you've got a 10- to 20-percent shot at the job just on the face of the odds themselves.

In order to induce a prospective employer to call you, your resume must do several things to the reader in a short time.

1. The resume must impress the interviewer that you're an organized, efficient applicant who'll prob-

ably exhibit these qualities on the job. This is achieved by the careful format and organization of the resume's layout. Appearance is important.

2. The resume should describe achievements that show you can get the job done, using action words to describe what you did (for example, "reduced costs" and "increased sales" present your experience in terms of separate responsibilities and achievements sections), and citing accomplishments with lots of numbers in them (for example: "cut overhead 23 percent," "completed project three months early").

3. The resume must demonstrate that you're an astute businessperson who understands the conventions of the business world. This is achieved by using proper wording, perfect presentation (for example, expert typing of resume, perfect spelling), correct stationery, proper cover letters with resume, and subtle boasting, if any.

4. Arouse the reader's curiosity so he'll want to see the real-life version of the magnificent job candidate the resume describes. You accomplish this by never providing any personal information, never all the information, and by *never giving any hint of any problems* (e.g., gaps in job history, mentioning why you left, making unreasonable demands).

5. Develop an expectation through the resume that you can solve their problems (filling the job, doing the work) so that the interviewer will be ready to believe whatever you say on the phone or in person. If he has serious doubts when he reads the resume, he won't call; he'll turn to another of the hundreds of resumes received. Once the interviewer calls, he's

ready to swallow the hook. *This is an overall effect achieved by executing all of the above actions.*

What the Resume Must Look Like

A sample of the recommended format for your resume is shown in Figures 1 and 2. This is a variant of resume format which most "resume books" label as the "professional" resume format. The format presented in Figures 1 and 2 was carefully designed to do all of the right things to the people who read it. Because this suggested format satisfies all of the earlier-cited objectives which a resume must achieve, it's the single best resume format for everyone. Don't alter the format unless you've a good reason. This resume has the following physical characteristics:

Format and General Appearance

1. The resume should consist of one page, with copy on one or both sides, *never* longer.

2. It should be expertly typed on a word processor with right justification. If you don't have a word processor and a letter-quality printer (daisy wheel or typewriter element; dot matrix is the kiss of death to a resume), get it typed by a secretarial service. *Do not let them design your resume* (they don't know what they're doing).

3. Use only white, off-white or extremely light tones of tan or beige 8 1/2 x 11-inch good quality stationery with some texture. Use the same paper for cover letters and matching business-size (4 1/8 x 9 1/2-inch) envelopes. *Never* use business stationery from your job.

4. Use only black printing -- *never* two colors of

ink, nor any colored inks or colored photocopiers. Use only standard, business-correspondence typefaces, never script styles. It's OK to have your resume offset-printed (see below) but don't have it typeset, using all sorts of fancy fonts; the resume then starts to look like a mail-order brochure for encyclopedias and not an item of business correspondence.

5. Have the people who type your resume give you several master copies on plain, smooth, white paper. Use these copies for photocopying or printing onto your selected stationery. If you attempt to copy or print from textured, off-white letterhead, you won't get very good results. A very good, well-maintained photocopier can make copies which are acceptable. Offset printing gives better quality, but with a good copier, it's too close to make a big difference.

FIGURE 1. PAGE 1 OF RECOMMENDED RESUME FORMAT

126 Forsythia Drive
Glenside, CA 91307
(818) 555-5555

RESUME
of
JACK STOUTHEART

SUMMARY OF QUALIFICATIONS

Resourceful, Take-Charge, Sales Professional. Exceptional skills in organizing and executing aggressive territory development campaigns. Have developed new territories and have increased sales in well-developed markets.

Planning and Analysis. Skilled in the use of marketing information for identifying and qualifying leads and formulating sales strategies and individual client development programs.

Communications. Excellent verbal and written communications skills. Extensive experience in the design and preparation of written and verbal marketing analyses, sales reports and presentations, and client-briefings.

Client Relations. Successful experience in handling customer relations, including the following: service/adjustments, requests for technical assistance/training, and account maintenance activities.

Office Systems. Thoroughly experienced in the use of personal computers for maintaining and generating sales reports and records.

PERSONAL DATA
DOB: 5/21/60, single, excellent health.

EDUCATION
B.S., Marketing, GLENSIDE UNIVERSITY
Los Angeles, CA, 1982
Certificate, Industrial Sales, UCLA
Los Angeles, CA, 1984

FOR FURTHER DATA, PLEASE SEE REVERSE SIDE .

FIGURE 2. PAGE 2 OF RECOMMENDED RESUME FORMAT

Jack Stoutheart Page 2

EXPERIENCE
June 1984 to Present
WORLDBEATERS EXTRUDERS, INC.
Los Angeles, CA

Account Executive
Responsibilities: Identify and develop industrial accounts for a $75M per year manufacturer of extruded plastics. Maintain existing sales accounts and identify and resolve customer technical and service problems. *Achievements:* Identified and landed four new accounts (total: $560K per annum). Recovered three previously lost accounts and maintained second-lowest (of seven account executives) rate of closed accounts.

July 1982 to May 1984
DENSEPACK PACKAGING, INC.
Orange, CA

Sales Representative
Responsibilities: Call upon and service existing industrial accounts in order to maintain order levels, resolve problems, provide support, and develop orders for new product lines. *Achievements:* Serviced 37 large industrial accounts. Increased average orders for current lines by 7 percent per client after inflation. Developed orders for previously not used products with 21 of the 37 accounts, which increased total sales from the 37 accounts by $345K per annum. Did not lose one account.

September 1978 to June 1982
GLENSIDE UNIVERSITY
Los Angeles, CA

<u>Student - Marketing</u>
Responsibilities: Attended four-year university with major in marketing and minor in accounting. *Achievements:* Attained 3.2 GPA in solid business course load while working 25 hours per week (see below) to support myself. Also took courses in business programming, personal computers, and marketing research.

September 1978 to June 1982
BOILEROOM SALES, INC.
City of Commerce, CA

<u>Telephone Sales Supervisor</u>
Started as telemarketing salesperson. Promoted to evening supervisor in November 1980. *Responsibilities:* Train and supervise 15 salespersons on evening shift in contract telemarketing sales. *Achievements:* Met 17 out of 18 campaign goals. Overhauled training program and reduced order-taking errors by 22 percent.

REFERENCES AND FURTHER DATA UPON REQUEST

Contents

1. The front side of the resume should have your name, address, and home telephone number at the top. Most of the front page should be taken up by separate sections presenting a summary of your qualifications, your personal data, and your educational, technical, and professional training.

2. The back side should present your employment history. Each job should be presented separately as shown in Figure 2. It's an exceptional idea to present each job's data by means of separate responsibilities and achievements sections. Use the exact format suggested by the Figure 2 example. The

specific achievements and responsibilities sections for each job are particularly important if you're going to be doing any more than the routine and expected amount of job-search lying. When you lie with specific statements, it's much more believable because most poorly skilled liars use easily spotted and unconvincing sweeping generalities.

3. Never use the pronoun "I" in a resume. The reader knows who it's about. Rather than using full sentences such as, "I was responsible for supervising accounts payable," use hard-hitting clauses such as "successfully managed the operations of a dynamic, high-volume accounts-payable section (or department)."

4. For every job, present at least one achievement (two or three are better) which have specific number or dollar amounts in them. For example, use "reduced invoice backlog by 18 percent" rather than "improved invoicing processing." When employers see the numbers, they think about what such benefits could mean to their operations.

5. Never give any information on what any of your jobs paid or why you left. If you must provide earnings information, write it on the resume with a pen, giving approximate amounts only, such as "$18K per annum" rather than "$345.15 per week."

ANSWERING CLASSIFIED ADS

The best source of job leads for most people in most situations is classified employment advertising. This advertising is most commonly associated with Sunday newspapers in big cities, as that's the place where most employers spend their advertising funds.

If you're earning (or seeking to earn) more than $20K per year and you're willing to relocate, you've got to use more than your local newspaper to find ads. Several other sources are critical to an aggressive search. These are:

1. *National Business Employment Weekly* (NBEW). The NBEW is published by Dow Jones and Company, Inc., the firm which produces *The Wall Street Journal* (WSJ). There are four regional weekday editions of the WSJ, each of which runs it own classified job ads. The heaviest day for WSJ advertising is Tuesday. The NBEW is published once a week and presents all of the previous week's employment advertising from all four regional editions. It's the single best source of high-quality job leads in the country. Because regional editions of the WSJ are not sold outside their regions, it's otherwise almost impossible to get all of the ads from the various editions of the WSJ. Many employers advertise in only one region, knowing that many job seekers will see the ad all over the country the next week when the ads from all editions of the WSJ are printed in the NBEW. You can order a subscription to the NBEW by calling (800) JOB-HUNT or (212) 808-6791. The minimum subscription is eight weeks and runs about five dollars a week. The NBEW runs quite a few "filler" articles about job searching. Accept their advice with caution; many are written by self-serving personnel types who don't know what they're talking about.

2. *National Job Market* (NJM). The NJM is one of the largest in terms of the ads it presents from major papers across the country. Subscribers are

included in a mailer which the publishers send to executive recruiters, and are given a federal jobs kit as well as a free resume kit (be careful of any resume advice which differs from mine). The publication comes out every two weeks and costs about $30 for six issues. You can order by calling (800) 323-7702.

3. *National Ad Search* (NAS). This paper publishes approximately 2,000 classified ads from major newspapers each week. Subscribers are offered a free resume service (be careful!). Various subscription periods are available at about six dollars an issue. Orders may be placed at (800) 992-2832.

The NJM and NAS are outstanding sources of the types of ads which you'll never see in the NBEW. If you're looking for something in the $15,000 to $30,000 range, you'll find a lot of appropriate jobs in the NAS and NJM which you'll never spot in the WSJ; many smaller employers can't afford to use the WSJ or don't think they need to (and for many jobs, they're correct). You'll also spot a lot of much-higher-paying positions which you wouldn't spot otherwise. Of course, if you're not willing to relocate, there will be few additional jobs you'll be able to go after in the NJM and NAS which won't also be in your local newspaper. For most searches, I'd recommend that you subscribe to the NBEW and one of the other two, perhaps alternating between them after you've tried them both for a minimum subscription.

How To Answer an Ad

What you send in response to an ad is mandated by what you're trying to do: have your letter and resume reach and be read by the right person. Each response to an ad *absolutely must* consist of a cover letter and a copy of your resume. Don't even think of sending a resume without a cover letter; your odds of having it read with any degree of attention are five times worse than if it arrives with a cover letter, even a bad one. It must appear to be a custom-typed letter; you've got to make it look like you thought enough about the ad to answer it personally. Whether you actually compose and type each letter individually is beside the point. A secretarial or word-processing service can use a computer to generate custom-appearing letters which are little more than form letters. Regardless of how you do it, be sure to send only perfectly spelled, perfectly typed letters (no type-overs, no erasures, no Liquid Paper, *no* hand-writing, no weak ribbons, and no shoddy old typewriters with the capitals raised above the line).

What You're Up Against

Your response to each ad will have to fight it out with hundreds, or perhaps a thousand or more responses for most jobs. Anything less than a perfect letter and resume will look like garbage compared to the dozen or so good-looking replies they'll get among all the other trash. If you can make it into the small pile of responses they'll read in detail, your lies will have a chance to work for you. If you send a sloppy letter with poor content (or worse, no letter at all), your finely honed lies will never get a chance to roll off the tip of your magnificently forked tongue.

What a Cover Letter Must Do

A good cover letter does several things for you.

Among them are:

1. It increases your odds that the resume will get to the correct person. Remember, most personnel offices and executive recruiters (more on them later) are actively seeking candidates for many positions. In a given day, each receives hundreds of letters and resumes, some in response to the ads and some sent in the course of direct-mailing campaigns (more on this later also). This avalanche of mail is opened, sorted, and routed by the youngest, lowest-paid, and least-motivated employees. If you don't state exactly what position you're after in your cover letter, you're assuming that the sorter will be able to figure it out. You don't need to lower your odds like that.

2. It gives you a chance to repeat many of your great qualifications (or lies). If you present them in the cover letter in order to entice the readers to read the resume and then lay the qualifications out in detail in the resume, the readers will be more impressed because they will have read them twice; it'll seem like more just because it was repeated.

3. The use of a cover letter demonstrates that you're aware of proper business and job-search etiquette. This will reinforce their expectation that you'll "work out" if the employer hires you.

4. A properly designed cover letter will make them want to read the resume. You'll pique the readers' curiosity so they'll want to see where you got all those great qualifications. Moreover, since they'll be faced with so many poorly designed letters and resumes, your materials will be a refreshing and rare respite from the rest; they'll see your attractive letter and want to continue the experience by reading a

similarly superb resume.

5. Finally, a well-organized cover letter makes it easy on the reader. He can quickly and easily determine whether you've got the qualifications they're looking for (and shame on you if you can't show the readers what they want to see, one way or another!). An organized presentation will save them time and aggravation and they'll feel more favorable about the considerate professional who provided a moment of clarity in a day of confusion and idiocy (all of the poorly designed resumes and letters).

What a Good Cover Letter Looks Like

Let's take a look at a series of cover letters which might be used to respond to a classified ad. Figure 3 presents an actual ad taken from a major Sunday paper (only the name of the company has been changed).

The contents of the most basic cover-letter response to the Figure 3 ad are shown in Figure 4. Paragraphs 1, 2, and 3 represent the absolute minimum acceptable letter content which will get your resume into the "will read" pile (the paragraph numbers are included only for your reference; exclude them when you write your letters). This type of cover letter can be used for almost every ad you answer.

FIGURE 3. REPRESENTATIVE CLASSIFIED JOB ADVERTISEMENT

INDUSTRIAL SALES REPRESENTATIVE

National injection mold, plastics company is seeking a highly motivated Sales Representative in the Atlanta area. Plastic-selling experience a plus but not required. Candidates should possess a B.S. degree and knowledge of the packaging industry. This position offers extensive travel and attractive compensation (Sal. + bonus). Qualified applicants should forward a resume in confidence to:

Mr. Mallable
Sales Manager
PLASTIC INJECTION CORP.
1111 Smokestack Road
Beverly Hills, CA 91307

It's extremely easy to have a word-processing service set up a form letter which permits them to generate custom-appearing letters by simply substituting the important bits of information shown in italic letters.

Note that paragraph 1 of Figure 4 states the job title and the specific publication in which you read the ad. Your presentation of this information demonstrates that you're very businesslike and also ensures that your letter will get to the correct person. The statements that your "qualifications are an ideal match" and "resume is enclosed" begin to orient the reader to expect that you are a good candidate (Chapter Two deals in detail with the important subject of expectations).

FIGURE 4. RECOMMENDED MINIMUM CONTENTS OF A COVER LETTER SENT IN RESPONSE TO A CLASSIFIED AD

Jack Stoutheart
126 Forsythia Drive
Glenside, CA 91326
(818) 555-5555

October 22, 1990

Mr. Mallable
Sales Manager
Plastic Injection Corp.
1111 Smokestack Road
Beverly Hills, CA 91307

Dear Mr. Mallable:

[1] I am responding to your October 23, 1990, advertisement in *The Wall Street Journal* in which you solicited candidates for the position of *industrial sales representative.* My qualifications are an ideal match to those which you outlined in the advertisement. My resume is enclosed.

[2] My qualifications include two years of Industrial Sales experience in the highest volume office of a successful plastics molding company. I earned a B.S. in marketing from Glenside University and have taken numerous sales development seminars. I am seeking more stimulating sales challenges.

[3] I would be pleased to discuss my potential sales contributions with you in detail at your convenience. I look forward to hearing from you. Thank you for your attention.

Respectfully,

Jack Stoutheart

Paragraph 2 of Figure 4 is a rather general, all-purpose presentation of those strong points which will be relevant for most of the positions you're after. Clearly, if you're going to be lying, this is the place to start packing them in. If you're working on several dramatically different types of lies, or even if you're not lying, but you're pursuing markedly different types of positions, one general-purpose paragraph such as the one shown might not be appropriate for all ads. You might have to have several "standard" paragraphs which each outline a different range of credentials. For example, if you're an engineer, you might have one version which highlights your management experience and another which highlights your technical knowledge and project experience. Both could be the truth, but for each specific job, you'd want to emphasize the set of qualifications which would be most appropriate to the employer's needs as outlined in the ad.

Many times, you'll want to do more than the standard paragraph 2 shown in Figure 4. If you're getting desperate and need to pull out all the stops, or if you spot an ad that seems "perfect," you should take a little more time and generate a more "customized" response. Figures 5 and 6 show, respectively, correspondingly more detailed and effective alternatives to the standard paragraph 2. Figure 5 demonstrates an approach in which highlighted qualifications are presented for each of the stated qualifications in the ad.

The qualifications paragraph shown in Figure 5 is extremely effective with letter/resume screeners. First of all, simply the appearance of having taken that much trouble will make you look like a fire-eater! Secondly, there's the impression that you really do have all the qualifications; after all, since you're responding in such detail, how could there be any doubt? Lastly, they're going to be extremely curious about what the resume says. You'll note that the qualifications paragraph in Figure 5 doesn't specifically state each qualification mentioned in the ad. This technique is particularly effective when there's a specific qualification or two which you don't have. You first state, "in terms of the requirements you stated in the advertisement, I offer the following qualifications," and then you list what you do have in detail, as well as putting in any other information which looks impressive but perhaps wasn't asked for in the ad. It doesn't matter whether the ad asked for those qualifications or not; by simply listing those qualifications, you're subtly influencing the employer to view all of the items as important to him and something that other candidates may not have. Remember, the only purpose of your cover letter is to get the right people to read your resume, whether or not you have all the qualifications. Few job seekers manage to get their resumes read in detail. If you can do that, both your lies and the truth will have a chance to work for you.

FIGURE 5. MORE DETAILED TREATMENT OF PARAGRAPH 2 FOR A RESPONSE TO A CLASSIFIED AD LETTER

In terms of the requirements you stated in the advertisement, I offer the following qualifications:

I am a highly motivated sales professional who has excelled in every sales job I've had. My account development, retention, and service statistics have always been excellent.

I possess a B.S. in marketing (minor in accounting) and have attended many additional sales, marketing, and management seminars.

My experience includes four years of industrial sales experience, including two years of successful sales experience as an account executive with an extruded plastics manufacturer. I also possess four years of additional telemarketing sales experience.

Figure 6 presents the ultimate approach to qualifications-paragraph design. Each required qualification stated from the ad is actually presented in quotes and is then followed by a statement of your corresponding qualification. For obvious reasons, this type of technique was referred to as the "drag 'em face-down through the cactus" method in a recently popular job-search book.

This technique is tremendously effective with employers. For one thing, it's easy to read and figure out. Nobody will have any trouble figuring out exactly how you meet each of their requested qualifications (trying to separate the lies from the truth is something else!). Another plus is that everyone likes to read their own writing; it makes them feel reassured and flattered. By quoting their own words, you're flattering them and showing that you accept what they say as the literal requirement. All employers prefer the subservient posture this implies.

Finally, since you're using their words, there's no doubt in their minds that you understand exactly what they want. This technique, if you respond to each of the employers' required qualifications, guarantees that your resume will be carefully read; this means that you're already in the top 10 percent of the competition.

FIGURE 6. MOST AGRESSIVE AND IMPRESSIVE PRESENTATION OF QUALIFICATIONS VERSUS STATED REQUIREMENTS FOR A RESPONSE TO A CLASSIFIED AD

In terms of your stated requirements, I offer the following corresponding qualifications:

". . .highly motivated Sales Representative. . ."

I am a highly motivated sales professional who has excelled in every sales job I've had. My account development, retention, and service statistics have always been excellent.

"Candidates should possess a B.S. degree . . . "

I possess a B.S. in marketing (minor in accounting) and have attended many additional sales, marketing, and management seminars.

"Candidates should possess knowledge of the packaging industry."

My sales experience includes two years with a diversified manufacturer of corrugated plastic, and paper containers for industrial and commercial packaging.

"Plastic selling experience a plus."

My experience includes four years of industrial sales experience, including two years of successful sales experience as an account executive with an extruded plastics manufacturer. I also possess 4 years of additional telemarketing sales experience.

EXECUTIVE RECRUITERS

Executive Recruiters, commonly referred to as "headhunters," locate job candidates for employers for a fee. Depending upon their level of skill, abilities, and the wishes of the employer, they may simply screen resumes and forward the resumes to employers, or they may screen, interview, assess, and recommend candidates for hire. As in every profession, there are hordes of incompetent headhunters who don't know what they're doing. The shoddy operators don't care if they recommend a poor candidate for a position and they don't care if a candidate gets placed in a bad job. All they want is the fee (which the employer *always* pays, unlike the manner in which personnel agencies operate). There are, on the other hand, a great many headhunters who are responsible and who have outstanding contacts with potential employers. If one of these headhunters recommends you to an employer, you're almost as good as hired.

The headhunter works on a fee basis which is always paid by the employer. Employers give him job orders which outline the requirements of the job and the qualifications they're looking for. "Contingency" recruiters get the fee only if they fill the job. "Retainer" recruiters are paid a retainer for conducting a given number of searches or for merely being on standby. If they make more placements than the retainer will cover, they submit a bill for more. The fees are quite impressive, ranging up to as much as 30 percent of the first-year salary of the job. From your point of view, there's little difference between contingency and retainer headhunters.

Many headhunters work alone, out of their homes or from small offices. While many of the shoddy operators fall into this category (as this is how many people try to break into the business), many top flight headhunters prefer to work alone, having built up loyal customers over the years. Many other headhunters work in small, two-to-five-person offices or as employees of large headhunting firms or franchises. Generally, headhunters who work as someone's employees are paid either straight commission or a draw against commission. Keep this in mind as you deal with any headhunter. They only get paid if they get you hired. They don't care who gets the job as long as the client is happy and they get their money; headhunters aren't trying to help you any more than the plumber cares about you personally while he is fixing your toilet. Keep this in mind at all times, as it determines much of your headhunters' strategies.

Headhunters locate candidates for jobs in several ways. They would like employers to believe that they maintain huge research files in which choice candidates are carefully tracked. Forget this nonsense. Headhunters locate their candidates primarily through three means. The first is through third-party connections, associates, former clients, and friends. The hope is that someone who knows somebody can give them a name. Often, after you've sent out a headhunter mailing, you'll get a call in which the headhunter tries to get you to help him out with another search.

The headhunter will tell you that he has something for you which might work out in the near future and/or "wants to see if you're still looking." Then, the real purpose of the call comes to the surface. "Oh, by the way, you wouldn't know anyone who might be interested in a position as Systems Manager for a Fortune 500 outfit, would you?" The headhunter is under pressure to find someone and is calling *everyone* he knows or has had contact with in the last few months.

The second technique is much the same as that used by businesses: place ads in the classified sections of the paper. These are the ads which read, "Our client is looking for . . ." In these cases, the employers are paying the headhunters to not only locate people but to screen them as well. When you respond to these ads, treat them exactly like any other classified ad.

The third technique is the most exciting, as it's a variant of lying. As such, it's a technique for which personnel types and headhunters alike have a natural affinity. Headhunters steal employees from one company which isn't a client of theirs for another company which is. For example, one of my friends was working as a headhunter and needed to find a female controller for a client. He called dozens of companies and told the secretary in the controller's department, "I hope you can help me. I was at a regional financial conference about three months ago and a very im- pressive woman financial officer was there, from your company I believe, who gave a speech. I'd like to invite her to our next national conference but I lost her card. Do you know who that might be?" After only 30 calls, he came up with six names who he then called and told that he had heard of them due to their reputation. He could then present the job to them and ask if they were interested.

The fourth way that headhunters locate candidates is through unsolicited resumes which are sent to them by job seekers.

How To Use Headhunters

Using headhunters is an established job-search strategy which is used by thousands of job seekers. This means that headhunters get hundreds of resumes every day from all sorts of people who located them in a list of headhunters (the next section discusses where to get this list) and sent out large numbers of resumes. At the same time, the headhunter is getting hundreds of responses each week to ads which he placed in *The Wall Street Journal, The New York Times, The Los Angeles Times,* and other Sunday papers. When this deluge of daily mail hits, it's sorted out by the lowest-paid, least-motivated member of the staff.

The responses to ads placed by the headhunters are given first priority and are routed to the appropriate person for review. All of the unsolicited letters and resumes are directed to whomever seems appropriate, based upon what the cover letter says and upon the sorter's knowledge. Each headhunter reviews responses to his ads and then quickly scans all of the remaining unsolicited mail to see if any of the resumes appear to match an open job order or a particular client's upcoming plans, or appear interesting in terms of a chronic need that a particular client may frequently have.

Each unsolicited resume is screened for 10 to 30 seconds (MAXIMUM!) to see if it "fits." If not, 99 times out of 100, it goes immediately into the trash. You may get an acknowledgment letter, but that's just a courtesy; believe it, your resume is in a landfill by the time you get the letter. No headhunting firm can afford to pay someone to catalog or computerize all of the unsolicited stuff they receive. It's more sensible for them to pay for an ad when they need someone and then receive hundreds of current, fairly on-target resumes.

Occasionally, a resume may attract a headhunter's attention because it fits an upcoming or immediately past need and he thinks it might come in handy in the near future. In that case, the resume is stuffed in an "If I remember it's there later file" and may or may not be retrieved at a later date.

Where to Locate Headhunters

The single best source of reasonably up-to-date lists of headhunters is a small softcover book entitled *Directory of Executive Recruiters.* This directory is published each year by Consultants News, Templeton Road, Fitzwilliam, NH 03447. You can order by phone at (603) 585-2200 and (603) 585-6544. The cost is about $20. The *Directory* lists over 2,000 headhunters, indexed by industry, state, and city, and areas of specialization. The *Directory* is very much superior to the short, badly out-of-date lists of headhunters which are published in many job-search books.

How Many Headhunters to Contact

If you're going to use headhunters, you have to

play the numbers. There's no point in contacting 10 to 50 of them. You have to send mailings of at least 100 as you're playing the odds. You've got to use a lot of them or you're wasting your time. You're gambling your printing and postage expense that there's going to be open job orders on their desks which match your qualifications. That's a small probability affair for any one headhunter, so you've got to go after a lot of them in order to maximize your odds of success. Further compromising your search is the fact that your materials have a short lifespan. You're not registering with them for life. If they don't have a job which matches your qualifications on their desk the day your resume arrives, you're out of luck. Therefore, you have to do repeat mailings to the same headhunters every four to six months of your search. Every two months is ideal, but the cost is prohibitive.

What You Should Send

As you've probably surmised by now, it's essential to send an impressive cover letter with your resume. In terms of designing your materials for use with headhunters, the above constraints mean that you must make it perfectly clear to everyone from the secretary to the headhunter *exactly* what you're looking for so that your resume at least gets a chance to be thrown out by the right person. Figure 7 presents a cover letter which would be sent with the resume shown in Figures 1 and 2.

The main difference between the headhunter letter and the ad response letter shown in Figure 4 is the listing of titles in the first paragraph. This listing is extremely important. The support personnel who sort the letters will be able to easily determine which headhunter should receive your materials.

Just as critically, when the headhunter scans over your letter, he will be able to tell in an instant whether your list of job titles matches any open job searches. If so, you're in luck. Without such a listing of titles, it's a little more work for the headhunter to see "what" you are; if he is a little tired, angry, not particularly desperate that day, or rushed, he might not take the trouble to read through your materials carefully.

There are several other critical differences between what you say when you're responding to a specific ad (even if it's to a headhunter's ad) and what you disclose in a "shotgun" mailing to headhunters. For the same reasons you supply a list of job titles, it's important to state the approximate levels of compensation that you're looking for. If you don't, you're making the headhunter have to think a little more, he may have some doubts, and maybe it'll all be too much trouble. The same goes for stating your geographical preferences; don't make the headhunters have to wonder about any aspect of what you want. Your cover letter must make everything easy to process, must answer all their unspoken questions, and must create no worries or leave any doubts. A cover letter such as the one in Figure 7 will serve these purposes well.

If you don't have the money to pay a secretarial service to produce custom-appearing letters with the inside address of each headhunter on the letter itself, there's another way. It's not as good, but it's a lot cheaper. Simply prepare a letter with the same contents as those shown in the Figure 7 letter but without space for the headhunters' names and addresses beneath the date. Use "Gentlemen" as your salutation. Then, print (or photocopy) as many copies as you need. All you've got to do then is type out the envelopes. They'll know it's not a custom job but if they've got an open job order, they won't care (as long as you've got a great resume).

FIGURE 7. RECOMMENDED COVER LETTER FOR USE IN UNSOLICITED MAILINGS TO HEADHUNTERS

Jack Stoutheart
126 Forsythia Drive
Glenside, CA 91326
(818) 555-5555

October 28, 1990

Mr. B. L. Oodsucher
Oodsucher and Associates
22 Park Avenue, N.E.
New York, NY 10001

Dear Mr. Oodsucher:

I am seeking to make a positive career move. My experiences and skills qualify me for the following types of positions:

DISTRICT SALES MANAGER
SENIOR SALES REPRESENTATIVE
INDUSTRIAL SALES REPRESENTATIVE
ACCOUNT EXECUTIVE
SALES CONSULTANT

I am currently employed (last two years) as an Account Executive with a large industrial plastics manufacturer where I have excelled in new accounts and servicing existing clients. Prior to my current position, I was in industrial sales for a packaging manufacturer and supervised a telemarketing operation.

My qualifications include a B.S. in marketing from Glenside University and completion of numerous sales development seminars.

I am seeking a compensation package in the $30K per annum range. I am willing to relocate for an appropriate opportunity. I have no geographical preferences.

I would be pleased to discuss my potential contributions with you in detail at your convenience in the event that you have an open search for someone with my credentials. My resume is enclosed.

I look forward to hearing from you. Thank you for your attention.

Respectfully,

Jack Stoutheart

Enclosures

One final word about headhunters. Don't bother to call them unless you're returning a call from them. If you haven't sent them a resume, they won't want to take the time to talk with you because it'll take too long to determine if you match any of their open job orders by questioning you on the phone; they can scan 50 resumes in the amount of time it'll take to brush you off. And, even if they're interested, they'll ask you to send a resume anyway. If you have sent a resume, it doesn't do any good to call (and even hurts, as they don't want to be bothered) as they'll either call you if they need you or toss the resume in the trash if they don't. Checking by phone doesn't impress headhunters like it might with some employers who will admire the tenacity (although even most of them don't want to be bothered).

DIRECT-MAIL CAMPAIGNS: THE APPROACH

A direct-mail campaign consists of sending a cover letter and a resume to a selected group of potential employers in the hopes that one of them will be impressed with your credentials or will need you for a current or upcoming opening. This strategy isn't as good as it sounds for reasons which are similar to the limitations of using headhunters. Unless you're in a field which is in short supply and heavy demand, the chances are low that any one employer is going to have an opening for which you're qualified. For example, there may be 15 ads for Data Processing Managers in your city's Sunday paper, but there are probably another 200 to 300 companies which have a Data Processing Manager but who aren't looking. If you were to mail a resume to all of these organizations, only the 15 who are looking would have any interest. And with those employers, your direct-mail solicitation would have to fight it out with the hundred of responses to the ad. So, on the surface of it, direct mail is a low-probability approach.

However, direct-mail campaigns can be useful and shouldn't be overlooked in some situations. If you're in a field or industry which is highly specialized and if you can very selectively identify the specific individuals to whom you would report, direct mail campaigns can be worthwhile.

The chances are still low that any one individual will have anything for you, but that disadvantage is offset by the fact that if they do have, or are about to have an opening, you'll be contacting the correct person. An advantage of direct mail campaigns is that you bypass the personnel department and therefore lower your chances of being "filed," misrouted, or rejected by the personnel officer who isn't as worried about upcoming openings as the hiring manager has to be.

An additional plus is that your cover letter to the hiring manager can be a little less bland than an "ad response" letter. The hiring manager is always going to be more open to slight deviations from standard qualifications which might worry a personnel officer. If the hiring manager thinks you can do the job, the battle is won without having to egg-suck your way through the personnel department.

Locating Targets

If you don't send your letters and resumes to the right people, it won't matter how good they are; you'll be wasting your time and money. You've got to put in a little research time at the library. Check with the reference librarian of a public or university library and tell them what you're trying to do: "I'm trying to find a job in the [your field of interest] field/industry and I need to locate the names, addresses, and phone numbers of companies and specific individuals who I can contact." Standard resources include the *Poors*

Register of Corporation Directors and Executives, the *Million Dollar Directory,* and the *Thomas Register.*

Each state typically publishes directories of manufacturers, service companies, etc. Each profession usually publishes its own. Use the latest editions available. Depending upon your profession (the real one or the one you're lying about), you're going to need a list of about 100 to 200 companies and the hiring managers to whom you'd report. It doesn't do any good to address letters to general job titles such as "Director of Data Processing," "Purchasing Manager," etc. That type of letter ends up in the trash. You've got to have the name of a real person (and the right person) on the letter. If you're in the same town as the addressee, you should call and verify the names and titles you've got or create your own list from scratch. Call and ask, "What is the title of the person who is in charge of [the department you want] and what is his or her title?" If you're in a different city than the employer, it'll cost a lot to make all the calls so you'll just have to make sure your list is as accurate as possible.

The Cover Letter

Figure 8 presents an example of a cover letter that Jack Stoutheart might send with his resume (Figures 1 and 2) in a direct-mail campaign to sales managers. The direct-mail campaign letter should not mention anything about geographical preferences or compensation issues; you don't want to risk getting rejected before you talk to them in person. Always give them at least three accomplishments which have numbers in them. Numbers make your achievements appear "hard" and businesslike. Always be completely candid about the fact that you're seriously looking for a job. Everybody knows why you're writing; if you beat around the bush or act coy, you're going to seem like a spineless egg-sucker and they'll toss your resume (unless they have an opening in personnel and are actively seeking egg-suckers).

It's very important for you to follow up with a phone call. If the expense makes it totally out of the question (as when you'd have to make 100 cross-country phone calls), don't worry about calling but always put the statement in the letter anyway.

FIGURE 8. RECOMMENDED COVER LETTER FOR DIRECT-MAIL CAMPAIGN

Jack Stoutheart
126 Forsythia Drive
Glenside, CA 91326
(818) 555-5555

November 8, 1990

Ms. Martha Ironmaiden
Sales Manager
Acme Plastics Corporation
Plastics Park
Hoboken, NJ 08765

Dear Ms. Ironmaiden:

I am currently employed as an Account Executive with a large industrial plastics manufacturer where I have excelled in opening new accounts and servicing existing clients. Prior to my current position, my experience included industrial packaging sales and supervision of a telemarketing operation.

I am seeking a more demanding and challenging sales position involving state-of-the-art technology represented by a diversified product line. In short, I want to be selling for a winner, where my success is limited only by my hard work and creativity.

The contributions I've made to my current and prior employers include:

Maintained highest new-account closing rate and lowest lost-account statistics in the highly competitive Southern California plastics market. Was able to recover three large, previously lost accounts through extensive account servicing and consulting support to the client's technical staff.

Serviced 37 large accounts and increased adjusted orders by 7 percent through account support and servicing. At the same time, cross-sold additional product lines to 21 of the 37 accounts which resulted in an additional 14 percent in billings. Met sales goals in 17 out of 18 sales campaigns while supervising telemarketing sales force.

Given the foundation provided by these successful experiences and my desire to excel as a sales professional, I am confident that I could make the same types of contributions to your organization.

My qualifications include a B.S. in marketing from Glenside University and completion of numerous sales development seminars.

I would be pleased to discuss my potential contributions with you in detail at your convenience. I will call your office next week to determine whether we have any common interests. My resume is enclosed.

I look forward to speaking with you. Thank you for your attention.

Respectfully,

Jack Stoutheart

Enclosures

If they think you'll call, they'll look at the resume a little closer for a few more seconds simply because they'll be a little worried about the call and what they'll say if they haven't looked at it and you manage to get by the secretary. Of course, some tough guys won't care, but there's a lot more guilt floating around out there than you might think. If they do look at it a little closer, maybe they'll make a connection with a need they have or they'll be impressed enough to call you if they've got a current or near-term need. If they don't have a need, your resume and letter will get trashed (or sent to the personnel department, which amounts to the same thing) so it doesn't matter if you don't call back when you said you would.

Don't worry about making a bad impression by not calling. Three weeks later, they'll never remember your name and the odds are that you'll never contact them again in your whole life. If you are in the same city as the target, it makes sense to call, if only to pump them for data on other openings around town which they may know about (see the next section on telephone campaigns). The fact that you're in the same town and you said you'll call may help your resume stay in their minds for a few more days.

JOB-SEARCH TELEMARKETING

Telemarketing is a popular buzz word in many business circles these days. It's also known as "networking" in the broader sense of using friends, acquaintances, and current/former business associ-ates as sources of leads. Telemarketing consists of making telephone calls to numerous contacts and trying to get them to hire you, give you a lead on someone else who might, or give you the name of someone else who may be able to help you. This technique is not as useful as the jargon masters would have you believe.

The biggest problem with the telephone is the one we have even when we're only calling to get an appliance fixed or make a date: the person you want to talk to is never there. The situation is even worse when you're trying to locate job leads. Not only are people "in meetings," "out of the office," and "not in," but even if they are there, there's always a secretary who's screening their calls and who has instructions not to let job seekers (or customers or employees who work there) bother them. On top of all that, it's often difficult to find out exactly who is the hiring manager for the types of jobs you're after. And that's not all the bad news about job-search telemarketing!

The main problem, even if you handle all of the above difficulties, is that there's a very low chance that any one hiring manager or organization is going to need someone with your skills. And, miracle of miracles, if they do have an opening, they've probably already got personnel working on it and you'll have to fight it out with all of the people who are responding to the ad. And many of those job seekers (and direct solicitors like yourself) will be contacting the hiring manager by phone and mail, trying to gain a leg up on all of the competition for the job. The only time you'll have even a hope of scoring is when you happen to get through to the hiring manager just as he is about to get moving on filling a position that's not yet vacant and on which personnel isn't yet working. And then you've got to have just the right set of qualifications and be able to impress the manager that you can do the job, all in a brief telephone conversation. Those are long odds.

Over and above all of the above limitations, job-search telemarketing must be ranked as a minimally effective technique for one additional reason, which is the most important drawback of all: very few people can endure the rejection, disappointment, and hard work which an effective job-search telemarketing campaign requires. Our society focuses on immediate gratifications. Unlike many Eastern cultures, most Westerners have no patience for the long, implacable struggle; we prefer to think we can always save the day by substituting a flash of insight for days of mundane work. In situations where the problem is one which calls for a creative solution, our impatient Western approach works well (these characteristics also make it much easier to get away with some of the boldest lies ever devised; more on this in Chapter Two). But often, there's no substitute for putting in the time and taking the abuse. Using the phone to "network" your way to a job lead is one of those "put in the time" situations. Few people can handle it properly.

Properly means sitting at the phone for hours at a crack, making at least 50 calls a day, perhaps 500 or more a week, never taking no for an answer, never getting swallowed up by the rejection or rudeness, never showing your anger, always remaining polite, and writing down every scrap of information you get so you can make further "networking" calls to the people whose names you're given. Sounds like fun, huh?

Don't misread my intentions; I'm not trying to imply that telemarketing isn't a useful technique. It is. When used properly, it can be very effective. Yet, it's a hard fact that few people have what it takes to do it right. I don't want you to waste time and divert energy from other critical job-search strategies for a half-baked telemarketing campaign which won't get you results. Do it right or don't do it at all.

HOW TO DO IT

There are a number of basic rules to successful telemarketing for any purpose, whether you're selling magazines or looking for a job. They are:

1. You're dealing in volume. You've got to make as many calls as you can, never pretending that quality makes up for quantity. It takes both.

2. Get something from every call. You've got to obtain at least some information from every call to use as a basis for another call. You can't afford to waste even one call. If you let one get by without getting something from it, soon you'll be taking the easy way out and not putting the pressure on. Then you'll be "rolling over" every time someone gives you a little

resistance. You've got to stay tough and calculating on every call.

3. Don't take anything personally, no matter how rude. You're using them as a tool, nothing more. You're not trying to make friends or get them to like you. You want information and that's all you care about.

4. Never try to outsmart them or get clever with them. Never try to ad lib your way through a call. *Always* work from a telemarketing script (more on this in a minute) and never deviate from it.

5. *Always* be unfailingly courteous and polite but never give in until you get some information or they hang up on you.

6. Never get emotionally involved with a call or the way it's going. Stick to your plans, don't get angry, and just make the calls. If you make enough of them, they'll pay off.

Putting Together A Script For Your Calls

As I mentioned above, you can't hope to handle your calls with objectivity if you take things personally, get discouraged, or give up in trying to pump something out of them, even if it's only a watered-down lead. The best way to handle things is to have a script ready to handle any contingency. All you have to do is generate a list of the various excuses or dodges that'll be used to get rid of you and then comeup with a reply. Once you have a pretty good list, you're ready to make your first phone call. If you get a reply you haven't heard, write it down and follow it with a new reply which doesn't take no for an answer, or use one of your existing replies from another excuse.

It really doesn't matter what you say as long as you agree with them, don't accept "no" for an answer, and keep asking them for what you want. After you refuse to be brushed off with the standard excuses, you'll find that very few people will either hang up or tell you to get lost. Most will give you something simply because they've been conditioned by our society to feel guilty. Let's look at an example.

Let's suppose you're Joe Snaketongue and you're just starting your telemarketing campaign. Your first call is to Mr. Jones, a Management Information Systems manager.

You: "Good morning, Mr. Jones. My name is Joe Snaketongue and I'm looking for a position as a lead programmer. I was wondering when it would be convenient for you to see me." *(Notice that you don't ask if you can see him.)*

Mr. Jones (attempting the brush-off): "Oh, I'm sorry. I'd love to talk with you but I'm very busy. Besides, we don't have any openings." *(Mr. Jones waits for you to say you understand and then give up.)*

You (not giving up): "I understand that you're very busy. I only need 10 minutes of your time. I'd like to tell you about my qualifications in case something comes up in the near future."

Mr. Jones (attempting the brush-off again): "I don't anticipate any openings in the near future. We have a very stable staff here. And I just don't have time for a meeting."

You (not giving up): "I understand. Look, I'm willing to get together any time you say and I promise not to take any more than 10 minutes. Suppose I meet you for breakfast or lunch? Anytime you say." *(Notice how you continue to agree and continue to ask for the same thing, making it harder and harder for Mr. Jones to say no nicely.)*

Mr. Jones (getting desperate because he can see that you're not going to give up): "Look, I'm extremely busy and I just don't know what my schedule will be for the next few weeks."

You: "I understand that you're very busy. Look, suppose I promise to take no more than five minutes, just five minutes. I really need your help and I realize it's an inconvenience but I promise not to take more than five minutes. And we can meet anytime you want. How about helping me out?"

Few people can handle that type of begging without giving in. The problem is that you've got to be able to do the begging, time after time, without flinching. Suppose in the above example that Mr. Jones still wouldn't meet you, seems to be on the verge of getting very angry, but hasn't yet hung up. What do you do next? No problem. You go for the next best thing when you begin to sense that the guy just won't see you in person. You go after a name or names that can be used for the next call. Observe the technique in action:

You: "I understand that you're too busy to get together in person. Since we're already talking on the phone, can you give me the name of someone who might know of an opening as a programmer?"

Mr. Jones (feeling relieved that he won't have to see you): "Well, I can't think of anything offhand. I'm not too active in professional circles."

You (not giving up): "Yes, I understand that you're

too busy for that sort of thing. Just one name would be a great help. I really need your help. Can you think of one person who might be able to help me? Perhaps someone in your own company?"

At this point, you're assured of getting a name. Only one in 100 people could resist at that point. One problem is that you'll get a lot of worthless names which will be offered just to get rid of you. That's part of the game. Each time you make a call, write down everything you get on a piece of paper. As soon as you get a good name (someone with any status at all), use it as an introduction. For example:

You: "Good morning, Mr. Jones. Mrs. Betty Hiroller, President of Hiroller Industries, spoke with me yesterday and said that you might be able to give me the names of a few people who might be able to help me find a job as a programmer. When would it be convenient for us to get together this week for a few minutes?" *(And you're off again!)*

When you're putting your script together, list the excuse/brush-off and then follow it with two or three replies. When you get a brush-off, simply read the next reply. If you use all of your replies, no problem; simply start back at the top.

If you run into secretaries who give the proverbial stone wall, simply use the same techniques as above: agree with them, suggest an alternative, and don't take no for an answer. With support staff, it's effective to flatter them a lot, thank them a lot, and emphasize your need for their help and influence in getting assistance from Mr. Big. Those who are closest to power are the ones who respond most effusively to such groveling and flattery. Use it extensively. If you absolutely can't get through, don't get angry; thank them profusely and say you'll call again. A good ploy is to call and tell the secretary that you're returning Mr. Jones' call from last week. Often, the secretary won't relay the message but will simply put you through. Even if she tells Mr. Jones that it's a return call and he says he doesn't remember, chances are that you'll get through. If you don't, move on to the next tactic.

The best times to reach high level people are early in the morning, from 7:00 a.m. to 9:00 a.m. and late in the day, after 5:30 p.m. Very often, the help is out of the office at these times and the brass will answer their own phones. Then you've got a chance. It's also helpful to call on Saturday mornings as many executives like to demonstrate their dedication by dropping by the office for an hour or so before playing golf. If you decide to try the early-late-Saturday ploy, you're going to have to get the direct-dial extensions of the brass because many of the switchboards will be closed and nobody will be there to transfer you. If the big shot's help won't give out the extension number to you during the week, simply call another department in the company, claim that you made a mistake and ask them for it. It may take a call or two but you'll get it from some good samaritan.

As you're no doubt beginning to appreciate, telemarketing for jobs (or anything else) is dirty, hard work. But, if you stick to it, you'll get results. If you decide to try it, make a pact with yourself that you'll go at it hard for at least four weeks. Set a goal for yourself of at least 50 calls per day.

It should be clear that the time demands almost

eliminate this strategy for people who are employed.

THANK-YOU LETTERS

Each job lead must be treated like a precious commodity. By lead, I'm referring to any sign of interest by an employer or headhunter. Since you'll get very few (statistically speaking) calls from employers or headhunters, it's essential that you leave no stone unturned in your attempts to impress them with your business savvy and courtesy. One very important way to do this is to follow up all phone and in-person interviews with a short thank-you letter.

A thank-you letter serves several purposes:

1. It demonstrates that you're one of the very few who know enough about business to realize that it's expected.
2. It demonstrates that you're organized and hard-working enough to put in the required effort to follow up with them.
3. It demonstrates to them that you are very interested, much more than the other candidates who might say they're interested but who didn't take the time to write.
4. It maintains a positive image of you in their minds as they interview and evaluate other candidates.

Once you've gotten to the point where you've talked with them, it's ridiculous not to take a few more minutes to solidify the impression you've made. Figure 9 shows an example of a standard thank-you letter after a phone interview. The letter should be written on the same type of stationery which was used for the earlier cover letters and resumes. Keep it short, businesslike, and formal. Don't get overly informal and don't refer to any personal information.

FIGURE 9. RECOMMENDED CONTENTS OF A THANK-YOU LETTER SENT AFTER A PHONE INTERVIEW

Jack Stoutheart
126 Forsythia Drive
Glenside, CA 91326
(818) 555-5555

December 2, 1990

Mr. Mallable
Sales Manager
Plastic Injection Corp.
1111 Smokestack Road
Beverly Hills, CA 91307

Dear Mr. Mallable:

I thoroughly enjoyed our phone conversation yesterday in which we discussed my qualifications for the position of Industrial Sales Representative. The future plans of Plastic Injection Corporation and the opportunities which you outlined are very exciting and I would like to be a part of them.

I look forward to our interview on December 14 at your offices. Thank you once again for your interest and courtesy.

Respectfully,

Jack Stoutheart

Chapter Two

The Psychology of Lying

The biggest enemy of job-search lies is not the truth itself. To the accomplished job-seeking liar, the truth is a seldom-encountered, distant consideration. Few job-search lies are discovered in part or in whole. Most of the time, absolute, hard facts aren't available when the lie is delivered. If a job-search lie is well executed and convincingly supported by the liar's resume and telephone performances as well as the face-to-face interview, the lie will be accepted before any contrary information could possibly be available to expose it.

For example, let's suppose that you don't have the minimum required education for the types of jobs you want. Instead of crippling your job search by admitting this deficit, you simply apply one of the techniques from Chapter Ten and claim that you possess the appropriate degrees from a reputable school. If you answer an ad with a well-prepared resume (containing the false educational credentials), support the story in the phone interview (and perhaps with fraudulent references), and then give a great, convincing in-person interview, you'll probably get a job offer. If you get away with the initial lie, you'll be on the job for many weeks and maybe months before the employer might get a reply from the school, if he bothers to check at all. In this situation, the truth itself (you never earned the education) isn't a major obstacle to the initial lie. That's typically the case in most instances of job-search lying; nobody can discover the "actual" truth during the interview or even within a week or so.

Yet, despite the fact that the truth isn't the enemy, thousands of job-seeking lies about education, job experience, employment dates, and compensation fail every day. Even though the job seeker may not be denounced as a liar and chased from the personnel office, and even though most interviewers may not even realize they've been lied to, the lies fail. For some reason, they don't "go over" and the chance at the job is lost. In the majority of cases, the interviewer doesn't even know why he is uneasy about the liar; things "just don't seem right" and the job seeker is considered unfit for the job for one or more of any number of secondary reasons which have nothing to do with the fact that a lie occurred. What's going on?

Simply put, the lies are compromised by the liar's own guilty behavior. Even though the liar wants to lie, may desperately need to lie, and may even enjoy lying, he often ruins the entire performance by displaying stress responses which are caused by guilt feelings. While the stress responses may not be interpreted by the interviewer as having been motivated by guilt feelings, they are observed and attributed to some unfavorable characteristic.

Let's suppose, for example, that the job seeker is lying about his or her responsibilities in a prior position. When the job seeker makes a claim of having "prepared a great many speeches for the company president" (actual truth: he proofread one or two of them), the interviewer asks if it might be possible to see a work sample or two. If the liar isn't well prepared, hasn't thought about work samples, or didn't expect the question, he might be somewhat surprised and a bit anxious as the threat of the question becomes apparent (the threat being what happens if he can't come up with a work sample). As a result of the anxiety, the lying job seeker stammers a little, perhaps flushes a bit, and doesn't answer the next few questions smoothly. Most interviewers wouldn't equate the nervousness with lying because they encounter many nervous job applicants. However, you can lose an interview just as quickly by appearing anxious and uncertain as you can by not having the proper credentials. The interviewer may conclude that the applicant is satisfactory but not quite as self-assured as another less-fidgety candidate. Nobody is going to hire the most flighty or nervous candidate if another applicant is Mr. Cool. There goes the job offer.

Whether you're lying or telling the truth, your success in interviewing depends almost entirely upon sending the correct verbal and nonverbal signals to the interviewer. The most important part of the verbal signals are not the content of what you say but how you say it. If you speak with confidence, with sincerity, and with a smile in your voice, almost anything you say will be accepted. At the same time, the nonverbal signals you send must be consistent and positive. You must not give off any indication of tension, anxiety, uncertainty, or cunning. If the interviewer senses any one of these, verbally or nonverbally, your chances will be dramatically reduced. Unfortunately for job-seeking liars, they are most at risk for inadvertently sending these damaging signals.

ADULT HONESTY FROM CHILDHOOD CONDITIONING

It's hard to accept, but our parents and teachers are the ones who are responsible for the main part of our difficulties in performing convincing lies. They wanted you to have a great career so they could be proud of you, and yet they were the ones who compromised your greatest weapon. Talk about irony! The actions they took years ago, under the guise of raising us properly, have conditioned us to fail when we tell a creative lie.

Yes, it's shocking, but (excuse my language) true! Your finely honed and cleverly schemed lies are most often rendered impotent by the time bomb of early childhood education and conditioning which was primed to go off when we tell a lie or do something else that's "bad." When unpracticed liars tell a lie, their guilt over being naughty causes them to have an emotional stress response. The conditioning of all of those, "No, no Johnny, you must never tell a lie to Mommy. Bad, bad, bad!" is present in a powerful way. It's important for you to understand how this training operated so that you'll know what you're up against as you work to be a proficient job-seeking liar.

If it weren't for the way most of us have been

raised in a standard home environment, we'd be natural and adept liars. Most people lie badly because they've been taught by parents and teachers that lying is "bad." As a result, they carry around an internal belief system (which some psychologists call the superego) which monitors their behavior. When the superego detects a "bad" behavior or the intention to commit one, it activates feelings of guilt which usually stop the bad behavior and/or make the person feel guilty. In a job-search lying situation, this guilty feeling creates stress which activates the sympathetic nervous system to increase heart rate, blood pressure, etc. These changes are often observed, and the liar might be suspected of lying or, more likely, perceived to be lacking in confidence, "fidgety," or otherwise "not quite right for the job."

In effect, each of us carries around a set of guilt mechanisms which monitor our behavior almost as effectively as if our parents and teachers were right there in the job interviews with us. This internal guilt system is conditioned into each of us in ways that make it difficult to modify it without conscious effort. A brief review of how these guilt systems are conditioned will demonstrate how they operate and how they can be defeated by a job-searching liar.

Consider an infant in terms of what it knows and how it behaves. A small baby knows almost nothing about anything, and has no morality or guilt. If you could magically teach it to interview, it would be an incredibly good liar; the truth or a huge lie would all be just words, with no guilt responses, no worries, no conscience -- a lying job seeker's dream. A baby's only concerns are the avoidance of discomfort. If something uncomfortable happens (hunger, a dirty diaper, and so on), the baby cries until the situation gets better. If the baby feels the need to defecate or urinate, it just lets it rip whenever the urge arrives. While the baby is small, nobody expects anything different and no demands are placed on the baby. As the baby begins to get bigger and begins to crawl around, the situation changes.

The baby can now get into trouble by eating plants, hitting its head on the corner of the table, tormenting the dog, and so on. Now the parents begin to place some limits on the baby. When it does something they don't want it to do, they tell it "no" very firmly and make it stop whatever it was doing. The child doesn't want the parents to be angry at it (because they're the source of food and comfort) and the child doesn't like to be yelled at or spanked. Over a period of time, with many repetitions, the child begins to associate the prohibited activity with the parental admonitions not to do the behavior. For example, if the child is continually scolded for pulling on the cat's tail, eventually it will hesitate to pull the cat's tail even when it's alone with the cat. The thought of pulling the cat's tail will be associated with remembered negative feelings which were associated with all of the scolding it received on prior occasions. The child will worry about this association and will feel guilty if he is thinking about doing it anyway. And if the child does pull the cat's tail, he will feel a bit guilty, perhaps demonstrate a few stress-related behaviors (such as perspiring more, looking around nervously), and will hope the parents don't find out. Such are the beginnings of a superego or conscience and the development of guilt mechanisms (and problems for liars).

Once the child begins to learn to talk, the internalization of the guilt mechanisms speeds up. Now the child can learn concepts to feel guilty about. Each time the child thinks about or does something that's not "good," it now associates the discomfort of the parental displeasure with the circumstances of the situation and its own feeling of self-worth. In effect, each child begins to tell itself, whenever it gets into trouble, "Here I am, doing something bad and making these nice people angry. Maybe I'm not such a nice person if I keep doing it. On top of that, I may get caught and get in trouble." This is the beginning of true, adult guilt mechanisms. Once these types of thoughts are internalized, the child begins to monitor many of its own behaviors, including ideas and opinions about what's right.

The above situation describes one aspect of how physiological reactions to stress occur; the child associates certain types of situations (not doing what he has been told to do) with the possible consequences and feels bad. As a result of the guilt, self-reproach, and/or worry, the child feels stressed and may appear anxious. This is the basic mechanism which creates "guilty" behaviors. It's these guilt-motivated stress responses which are the target of lie detectors and voice analyzers which are sometimes used to investigate criminals and job candidates (which shows you what employers think of you). Chapter Thirteen will discuss the operation of such devices and methods which you can use to thwart them.

The preceding discussion almost makes it appear

as if the appearance of stress responses is casual and amenable to self-control. As you may have guessed, given all of the other obstacles which a liar must face, this assumption is not valid. Physiological stress responses that have been conditioned to cognitive feelings of guilt are extremely resistant to manipulation. A brief explanation of what's going on physiologically will convince you that a successful liar must work hard on controlling these stress responses.

The Nervous System of a Liar

Our stress responses are monitored and created by our central nervous system; they're part of our hardware. The part of our nervous system which is involved is called the autonomic nervous system. Unlike our skeletal muscles, which we can control very easily, we have very little direct control over the two divisions of our autonomic nervous system. One portion of the autonomic system is called the sympathetic nervous system and the other is called the parasympathetic nervous system.

When the sympathetic nervous system is activated, through something that we see or feel or think, a number of things happen automatically, without any action on our part. The sympathetic nervous system sends out nerve impulses which contract arteries, and inhibit the stomach secretions and contractions which help digest food, change heart rate, dilate pupils, and produce sweating. These responses are part of what's referred to as the "fight or flight response": the body is energized to fight or run from a perceived danger or threat. It's assumed that evolution developed the sympathetic nervous system because it increased the odds of survival when outrunning or outfighting threats.

We've all experienced the power, speed, and involuntary nature of these responses, even if we haven't been in a life-or-death situation. Consider what happens when you're at a restaurant and you feel for your wallet and it's not where you thought it was. The instant your hand doesn't touch the expected wallet, you think, "Oh, no, my wallet's lost!" You have visions of trying to replace credit cards, standing in long lines to get another license, worries about how you'll pay for the dinner, etc. In the same instant, you perspire more, your blood pressure goes up, your heart rate increases, and you feel flushed, nervous, and maybe a little sick to your stomach. As you desperately search your pockets or purse, you find your wallet and you're saved. Yet, you feel wrung out and a little wasted. It takes a while for your heart rate to slow down, you'll need a few minutes to stop perspiring, you don't feel as hungry, and it'll take about ten minutes before you stop thinking about all of the bad things that could have happened. These are the same types of responses, in varying degrees of severity, which poorly practiced liars experience in a job-interview situation. You know how hard it is to appear calm and at ease when you're looking for your lost wallet. You're up against the same challenge when you deliver your job-search lies.

The parasympathetic nervous system reacts in the opposite manner, slowing down the heart rate, increasing flow of blood to the arteries, and speeding up digestion, all activities which build up energy reserves and slow things down. When you're feeling content and relaxed, it's your parasympathetic nervous system which is in charge. The fact that it takes two separate sets of wiring in our nervous systems to do these things should impress you with the deep-seated, physiological basis for the stress responses which foil so many liars.

Classical Conditioning

Stress responses caused by lying can manifest themselves in many ways. Some poorly skilled liars may sweat, others may blush, and still others may become nervous and hyperactive. Each person has a unique pattern of responses to stressful situations including those generated when they're lying. The particular way a given person physiologically responds to stress is determined by genetic predispositions and by a mechanism called "classical conditioning." An understanding of classical conditioning is important for two reasons: first, you'll appreciate the powerful link between your autonomic nervous system responses and external stimuli (such as being asked for references), and second, you'll understand the importance of the relaxation and rehearsal techniques recommended in Chapters Twelve and Thirteen.

Classical conditioning was first recognized by a Russian physiologist by the name of Ivan Pavlov in the early part of this century. In his most famous set of experiments, he demonstrated that it was possible to condition a seemingly neutral stimulus (such as the sound of a bell or buzzer) so that the neutral stimulus could cause a physiological reaction to occur. Pavlov succeeded in conditioning dogs to salivate (drool) at the sound of a bell. In the course of performing research on digestion, he had noticed that the dogs would drool when they heard the food carts coming every day. He discovered that if he repeatedly rang a bell (or shone a light in a dog's eye) and then quickly showed the dog the food, he could eventually (after maybe 20 pairings of the bell or light and the food) make the dog drool with just the bell or the light. The dog had no choice, it would have to drool. The external stimulus (the bell or light) which before had absolutely no meaning to the dog had become associated with a physiological response in such a way that the dog had no control over it. The same type of classical conditioning can be done on humans. You can do it yourself. If you sound a bell or buzzer and then immediately blow in someone's eye enough to make him blink (or tap his patellar tendon in the knee so that his leg "jumps"), you can condition him to blink to the buzzer (or move his leg reflexively) after only 20 to 30 pairings of the bell and the breeze (or the knee tap).

Classical conditioning exerts its influence in all sorts of ways in everyday life. Most phobias (fear of elevators, fear of snakes, and so on) are classically conditioned stress responses. The person whose stomach gets knotted up, and who might eventually develop ulcers has classically conditioned himself to release stomach acids when certain stimuli are present (most often unpleasant, work-related stimuli). The man who is impotent or the woman who is frigid has very often been inadvertently conditioned by parents or by unpleasant prior sexual experiences to react physiologically to some of the stimuli which are associated with sexual encounters. Once the conditioning is established, it's no longer possible to control it by merely trying to stop it (or start it, in the case of sexual problems).

If you've been classically conditioned to react to the stress of lying by sweating or speaking in a high voice, it's going to take more than a wish for it to go away. You're going to have to work at it because you'll be fighting conditioned responses over which you have little conscious control. If you display extreme stress responses such as profuse sweating or blushing when you're under pressure, you'll have to take definite steps to counter these classically conditioned responses. Fortunately, there are several easy and straightforward techniques presented in Chapter Thirteen which can eliminate the greater part of classically conditioned stress responses.

Perceptions of Stress

Fortunately for liars, a large part of stress responses is not inexorably tied to classically conditioned responses. While classical conditioning may determine the exact type of physiological stress responses which will occur to certain stimuli for a given individual, there's still a large component of subjective interpretation involved. A person's subjective assessments and evaluations of a situation have quite a lot to do with the amount of stress he will feel in a given situation. To a large extent, if an event occurs which someone believes is going to be stressful, the chances are that whatever happens will be at least partially perceived as a stress-producing event, much as a self-fulfilling prophecy. One research experiment demonstrates the power of these preconceptions about the perceived effects of stressful events.

A sample of carefully selected, healthy male college students was given a drug which caused their temperatures to go up slightly and which made them feel just a little agitated and hyperactive. One group of the students was shown pictures of attractive naked women, another group of the students was shown pictures of dead people, and a third group was told that it would have to sit and "wait" for the researcher with a group of students who were "troublemakers" (these troublemakers were working with the researchers and did nothing but sit in the room and wait). In each group were "controls" who were treated exactly the same except that the drug they were given was a placebo, a phony which had no effect.

In experiment after experiment, those who were given the real stimulant, compared to the controls, always reported that the pictures of the naked women were more exciting, the pictures of the dead people were more disturbing, and the "troublemakers" were more annoying (even though they only sat there). The arousal caused by the stimulant was attributed to the situation in which it was experienced, not to the drug itself. In effect, we've learned to associate emotional responses with external circumstances, whether the external cues cause them or not. Thus, naked women were seen as more exciting, dead people were more disturbing, and silent people were seen as more irritating, simply because of physiological arousal.

This experiment has important implications for job-seeking liars. If an interview situation is anticipated to be one that'll be stressful, the liar will react to any arousal, whether it's from the anxiety of lying or healthy excitement, by feeling guilty and then displaying preconditioned, guilt-generated stress responses. It's normal for anyone, even an honest saint, to feel some degree of healthy excitement during a job interview. After all, it's an important event with significant consequences if handled properly. If the arousal is interpreted by the liar to be the sole result of guilt or worries about being discovered, the stress responses and behaviors will generate more stress and worry and the entire interview performance will appear stilted and tense at best, or a sweaty, agitating disaster at worst. Once a job-seeking liar realizes that not all physiological responses to job interviewing are necessarily connected to worries about lying, a great deal of potential anxiety is eliminated. A more important factor involves a liar's control over the amount of stress which is generated by lying in an interview. If the liar practices and carefully prepares contingencies for all anticipated events (requests for work samples, references, transcripts, etc.), he will anticipate less stress, will experience less stress, and will be less likely to interpret any general arousal as being anxiety. As a result, a great deal of the normal, "it's an important interview" excitement will be favorably evaluated by the liar and will result in the display of behaviors which will most likely be correctly interpreted by the interviewer as healthy enthusiasm.

If this discussion sounds a bit too arcane and somewhat irrelevant to your applied lying concerns, be very careful. Believe me, more lies fail as a result of subtle behavioral cues caused by the stress of interviewing alone, not to mention lying, than for any other single cause. It's absolutely essential that you appreciate what you're up against, not only in terms of the schemes and plots of the employers but in terms of your own ingrained reactions to stress.

Personally, I'm one of the great, all-time, job seeking liars. Among my circle of friends, many of whom are outstanding job-seeking and general business liars in their own right, I am a legend. Yet, even I, who love to lie and who can lie with exceptional skill, even without extensive preparation, always have some feelings of anxiety when I drop the really big ones during a job interview. I'm probably more sensitive to these feelings than are most people, but I've studied video-tapes of myself and I can tell when I'm not quite comfortable with what I'm saying. Most interviewers wouldn't notice, but some might. For those of you who are just starting out in the world of serious job-search lying, your reactions will be more readily observable. Take heed, my lying friends, your greatest obstacle to effective job-search lying is the person holding this book in front of you right now.

WHAT EMPLOYERS EXPECT OF YOU

Much of your lying strategy and technique must be based on the anticipated behavior of the people you'll be lying to. Fortunately, people in general and employers and personnel officers in particular are remarkably trusting. Better yet, employers have a variety of expectations and stereotypical behaviors and reactions which play right into the hands of a clever and skilled liar. A review of these expectations and behaviors will help you understand why so many job-search lies continue to be effective, even when they're well known. A better understanding of interviewers' expectations and assumptions will also demonstrate why it's so important to control stress responses in an interview; more than a little anxiety, especially that which generates fidgety behavior, violates interviewers' expectations and sets them on a search for clues to substantiate their suspicions.

You're probably thinking that employers are naturally suspicious about lying on the part of job seekers. But this isn't true, at least insofar as most job seekers and the majority of employers are concerned. Your interest in the subject of lying (the fact that you're reading this book) sensitizes you to the issue of lying in general.

If you were to interview a job candidate tomorrow, you'd be a bit more on guard for signs of lying simply because many of the points made in this book would be fresh in your mind. Fortunately for you not every interviewer in this country will purchase a copy of this book. Unless they've just uncovered a job-seeking liar themselves (a very rare occurrence), they'll have no predetermined reason to be more than normally suspicious. "Normally" suspicious of liars means hardly suspicious at all. While any interviewer will contend that he is constantly on guard to detect the deceits of job seekers, the majority of them accept a great portion of what they hear from candidates at face value. Of course, if the applicant has poor interviewing skills and is attempting unpracticed lies, the performance will most likely fail. But if the lies are delivered with finesse, and if the applicant's one-to-one technique is fair to good, there's almost no way that he will be suspected of lying, much less caught.

There are three factors working to influence the perceptions of interviewers in your favor and render them so easy to lie to:

1. Few interviewers are ever faced with evidence that they have been lied to. While everyone has an apocryphal story or two about the organization uncovering fake degrees and the like, most interviewers have never been involved in the catch. Since they don't usually get any feedback about whether they've been lied to, they naturally make the most flattering assumption possible: they didn't spot a lie so there must not have been one.

2. The second reason why it's easy to get away with lies is that so few people tell really bold lies. Sure, everyone attempts to "pump up" his resume a little, but that's a common, accepted practice. The really big stuff, the lies which we're talking about in this book, are, statistically speaking, hardly ever attempted. If more people did try really big lies, the odds are that a small percentage of them would be careless and unskilled and would make a mess out of it and be discovered as liars. If this was happening on a regular basis, employers and interviewers would be much more cautious and suspicious. Luckily for you, this is not the case.

3. The third expectation works even more powerfully in your favor. Employers interview so many candidates who have incredibly bad interview technique that they expect the average candidate to be nervous or illiterate or pushy or afraid to talk. In the few instances when the poor signals are the result

of lying-induced anxiety, it's never suspected to be anything more than interview stress. Better yet, if you lie with confidence and an easygoing manner, you'll be viewed not as a smooth-talking liar but as a skilled, at-ease professional. They want you to be a skilled, relaxed professional because they're so sick of interviewing complete losers and/or arrogant snobs. When the interviewer meets the master of job-search lying, he's ready to believe anything.

What Employers Expect of Liars

While the average interviewer has little experience in dealing with liars (known liars, as opposed to all those who are working there and haven't been discovered), most of them have a fairly consistent set of expectations about how liars act and behave. If you're a poorly practiced liar, you'll be playing right into their hands. If you have any skills as a liar at all, their expectations will lead them to view you as a saint, even as the vilest lies drop from the magnificent forks of your well-practiced, artful tongue.

The very fact that it's so difficult for most people to tell a lie also makes them believe that most other people are telling the truth most of the time. Since they can't lie easily, they assume, quite correctly, that most others can't either. In general, they're correct; most people don't lie well without extensive preparation. The few natural liars who are self-taught (or raised by parents with cunning insight into the child's future job-search needs) are always able to get away with the most shameful lies because people generally accept what others say as the truth. That's why con men can continually defraud old people of the people's savings and Hollywood movie stars of their investment funds. It's one thing to read about these cons in the paper and say, "Boy, how could anybody fall for a stupid scheme like that? It'd never happen to me!" and it's quite different to be talked into it face-to-face by someone who smiles at the right time and looks to be every inch the sincere, professional, helpful person we all trust. Believe it; everyone is just sitting out there, expecting to be told the truth, believing that it's extremely difficult to tell a lie, and eagerly waiting to lap up the most outrageous lies as long as they're presented sincerely and candidly. They expect the truth, they want the truth, and, most of the time, they're convinced that they're hearing it.

You almost have to go out of your way to lead people to suspect you of lying when you're doing it in a job search. Even though most personnel professionals will talk a cynical line about how many job-search liars there are, they don't really believe it.

Interviewers' expectations of the behavior and motivations of liars are taken almost completely from the media. Most people are not trained psychologists and observers of behavior (and most psychologist/psychiatrists aren't extensively trained in behavioral analysis and the reading of subtle behavioral cues). Their perceptions of behavior and motivation are based upon their own limited experience with the small group of people they deal with daily and what they read and see in books, TV, and the movies. These sources are useless in providing valid information about the behavior of liars. Even if someone deals with different people every day, it doesn't help. Interactions with strangers don't provide any information because you never get to study them and determine whether your hypotheses are true, as you do with the people you live with and work with. Information from television and movies is totally useless, as the characters are phony and you're either told too much or too little about them to form an opinion about anything except their clothes. Of course, this is all good news to job-seeking liars because these artificial and unrealistic sources are where most people develop their insights into behavior. The successful liars we see in television, movies, and literature (at least until the "good guys" win) are generally portrayed as sweaty, mean, half-shaven, devious con men or as rich, witchy women who dress outrageously and show a lot of cleavage. These successful liars are typically portrayed as so morally reprehensible that they can lie without any trace of guilt or discomfort. This is good news for you, as a fledgling job-search liar, because it encourages the ridiculous myth that only completely devious, evil wretches who dress loudly and show off a lot can lie effectively.

The stereotypes which are used for the losers, the bad people who lie but can't pull it off, are even more fortuitous for job searching liars. The losers shown to the audience are pathetic, weak, mealy-mouthed wretches, and are exposed as liars from the very first frame or page. You can tell by their stubble, their disarrayed hair, their furtive, darting eyes which can never look you in the face, their oily, sweaty sheen, and by their nervous, hesitant voices that they're lying and lying poorly. This, too, is good for you because it leads people to expect that liars can be detected by the way they look, the way they sweat, the way they do their hair, and so on. This is completely false. It's true that a very nervous, poorly prepared liar will demonstrate some of the above stress responses. The same symptoms, however, are displayed by many people who are merely nervous. And none, or few of them, are displayed by well-prepared liars. Since that's what you're going to be when you finish this book, you'll go undetected.

Based upon the stereotypes they learn from movies, television, literature, and from their personal experiences in dealing with a few discovered liars, interviewers expect a fairly consistent and narrow range of behaviors from job-search liars. The signs that people expect from liars are of two types. The first is physical behavior cues and the second, lie content cues. Let's take a quick look at the most common elements of each, interms of behaviors.

1. "They can't look you in the eye." This is the number one expectation about liars. Because liars are expected to be shifty characters, and because the eyes are believed to be the "key to the soul," liars are expected to feel so guilty that they can't look you in the eye and lie. The successful, bigger-than-life villains of the media can do this with ease, but because such characters are seen as symbols, bigger than life, nobody expects to encounter them in job interviews. There's no denying that many poorly prepared and tentative liars do feel guilty and believe that if they look the interviewer in the eye, the lie will be obvious. Not true. Many, many research studies have investigated the ability of people to detect lies on the basis of interpersonal cues. It's never been shown that any observable physical cue is an obvious

indication of lying across all people.

2. "They sweat a lot." People under stress perspire more than at other times. If someone is a poor liar, he'll be feeling a little worried, perhaps guilty, and he'll perspire more than he normally would. If you've got a problem with general interview tension which results in noticeable perspiration, take every chance you can to go to interviews. If you do the interviews, review your performance afterward, and work on your weak points, you'll begin to relax and perspire less whether you're lying or not.

3. "Liars act fidgety and nervous." It's expected that if someone's lying, he can't relax and appear at ease. If you constantly shift your position, fiddle with your hands, play with your jewelry, or otherwise demonstrate that you've got a lot of nervous energy, many people will assume that you're ill at ease and one or two out of a hundred might assume you're lying.

4. "They speak rapidly and in a higher pitch." Again, these are bona fide indications of stress which people associate with liars as well as those simply showing the effects of a stressful situation. It's assumed that liars will talk faster because they're nervous and want to get it over with and/or don't want what they're saying to be closely analyzed. In many people, stress tightens their vocal cords and increases the pitch of their voice. Observers forget that good liars don't hurry and aren't stressed enough to show it.

5. "Liars tend to dress or appear flashy." If the interviewee is dressed in a style that screams "flashy," "show-off," or "unconventional," the inter-

viewer may unconsciously assume that the person also has unconventional morals or is motivated by less-than-pure motives. This is an unfortunate by-product of used car and insurance ads, in which nobody trusts the salesperson who dresses loudly and acts pushy. Of course, this is good news for you, as proper dress (discussed in Chapter Twelve) will help put you in the other group, the polished professionals who dress in an acceptable and reassuring manner.

6. "Liars tell simple, rather transparent lies." Most people don't tell carefully planned lies because they're unwilling to face the guilt which such planning would create. So they lie on the spur of the moment to cover up problems. It's to be expected that such lies will be relatively easy to discover with any type of half-hearted analysis. Employers assume that everyone, even lying job seekers, will do the same. Such extemporaneous lies have no place in job searching. If you carefully plan your lies (and it doesn't take a lot of planning to assure that most job search-lies escape detection), your lies will have the texture and depth that everyone associates with the truth.

7. "They'll tell grandiose lies." The media has convinced everyone that bad people who tell lies are so morally reprehensible that their judgment has been burned off by the sin. In this charred condition, they are thought to be unable to control themselves and they tell totally ridiculous lies that are all out of proportion with what they can substantiate.

As a result, it's expected that a job-search liar will tell outrageous lies that any fool can recognize. If you tell only the lies you need, and don't try to solve all of your job-search problems simply by telling huge lies, you'll have no problems. For example, it's safer to work a phony job at a nondescript company or a phony consulting assignment into your resume than to create a lie that you were the personal assistant to the chairman of IBM. The latter is so absurd that it almost screams, "Hey, I'm lying!"

8. "Liars never admit any flaws." It's job-search suicide to admit any but the most minor flaws in your character. You'd never want to admit that sometimes you're not full of energy to do more work for the company, even though every employee experiences days when he couldn't care less about doing anything except going home. On the other hand, you can't come across as too perfect; to do so indicates that you're afraid to be seen as "one of the guys." Liars are expected to use lies which are too perfect, too all-encompassing because they're hiding something. It's not that the lies are grandiose as in the stereotype discussed above, but that the lies are too flattering in the picture they paint of the liar.

For example, a poor lie for a job which required a lot of public speaking would claim, "Everybody in the organization looked to me when a speech had to be written." It wouldn't be smart to say it that way even if it was the truth. A smarter, less-perfect, and therefore more-believable lie would be, "I did a lot of speaking at seminars and conferences, along with a few others who were comfortable in front of an audience." Even if it's a lie, it's more believable because it isn't quite so flattering and perfect in its reflection on the liar. Liars are believed to be morally degraded to the point where they have no judgment left and use only the most extreme lies to get what they want.

What Employers/Interviewers Expect of Themselves

Despite the above factors, employers, personnel officers and hiring managers all think they're great interviewers. But they're wrong. As we discussed above, research has shown that people in general are terrible at detecting lies (even when they have reason to believe that about half of the time they're being lied to). And the liars used in the research do not typically tell well-prepared, carefully researched and rehearsed lies such as the ones you'll be using.

People think they're good at detecting lies because they engage in a lot of after-the-fact rationalization and fantasizing when they discover they've actually been lied to or when they've made a mistake in personal judgment. If they find out they've made a judgment error about a person, they quickly search for a reason, any reason, to explain why their impeccable insight was foiled this one, rare time. If a new hire doesn't work out, they might think, "I knew it! I should have listened to myself about that creep's silly little mustache! Well, next time I'll know better." Or, if they have had a disappointing romantic experience, they might explain away the judgment error by thinking, "Well, what kind of loyalty can you expect from a guy who wears pajamas with little sheep all over them?"

Our ability to detect liars is notoriously bad for a more fundamental reason: we never detect the majority of lies we're told. There's nobody around who's watching us interact with others, knows the real story, and who can tell us when we're being lied to and about what. Without such feedback, there's no way to determine the accuracy of our detection skills. It's like trying to improve your golf swing without ever using a ball.

As one small, rather enlightening example of the amount of lying which routinely goes undiscovered all about us, consider the typical results of blood tests of newly born children and their parents. Study after study in Europe and the United States has shown that in 10 to 30 percent of the cases studied, the baby's legal father could not possibly have been the biological parent! The mother was sleeping with someone else who fathered the child.

These studies are primarily of typical middle- and working-class people, not welfare families. Since most of the families were still together, we have to assume that the majority of husbands did not know (allowing for the small percentage of "open" marriages and/or cases where the husband had found out and didn't leave). Since it's generally believed that husbands cheat even more than wives, you can only conclude that an awful lot of folks are being deceived. Yet, if you asked most spouses, almost all of them would contend that they would know if their honey was fooling around. Luckily for you, the ability of personnel officers to detect your lying is much more limited than that of spouses.

Analogous cases in the world of job searching periodically make the papers. Most typically, a company finds out that a key employee doesn't have the credentials he claimed. When executives read such stories, they tell themselves, "Well, it's easy to see why that could happen to Acme Gaskets and Pet Supplies -- they're a bunch of idiots. I know my people and they're all legit." Fat chance. In every company I've worked or consulted for I knew of several cases where persons didn't possess advanced degrees which they claimed. And I wasn't looking for or concerned with finding liars. Yet, since they were doing the job, nobody suspected.

Since most of us never find out that we're being lied to, whether it's by a philandering spouse or a crafty job applicant, the very few times when we're correct don't represent anything more than luck or an incredibly bad liar. Yet, since they're the only ones we know about, we blow them all out of proportion and tell ourselves that we've got incredible lie dectection capabilities. And when we're wrong and find out, we come up with a reason that "explains" our failures. Face it and be grateful for it: very few people can accurately detect liars, even those with pedestrian lying abilities.

WHAT YOU SHOULD EXPECT OF EMPLOYERS

The expectations of job seekers also have a profound impact on their ability and willingness to lie. While this entire book is intended to modify and change your expectations as a job seeker, one particular aspect of the job seekers' expectations is particularly important in the context of this chapter. Job seekers have a very much inflated perception of the skills, objectivity, and intelligence of interviewers and the selection process itself. All too often, this distorted and incorrect view leads job seekers to avoid even small, expected lies because they're worried about being caught. Most of the time, such worries (assuming a decent lying performance) are totally unrealistic.

The entire job-selection process, for 99.9 percent of employers, is unscientific, nonobjective, and is subject to extreme personal biases and idiosyncrasies. Most interviewers' judgments about a job candidate's character, interviewing technique, and ability to meet the technical demands of the job are remarkably poor. As difficult as it may be to accept, believe me when I tell you that there is no extensive training program which trains people to be good interviewers. Most management-development training programs spend only a few hours on instruction for interviewers. Even then, most of the training consists of outlining what questions to ask and then having the trainees practice interviewing one another.

Personnel officers rarely get even that much training, as they're expected to know how to do all of the "personnel" things, and they never study these techniques in their college personnel classes. The result is that almost nobody in the business world knows how to properly interview job candidates. Everybody "does their own thing" according to the belief systems we discussed above, and they then make their individual, subjective, biased judgment. That's how the job-selection system works in real life. Those people who are skilled interviewers have developed the skills naturally and are simply better in interpersonal situations.

Keep in mind that the people who are doing the interviewing want you to solve their problem; they want you to be the person they need so they won't have to interview any more candidates. If it's a personnel officer, they'd rather be off at some convention or trying to seduce one of the support staff. They're also probably under some pressure to get the position filled. If you turn out to be what they're looking for, you save them the trouble of further searching. If you're being interviewed by the hiring manager, he needs the slot filled so the work can continue. Hiring managers hate interviewing more than anyone because, unlike personnel interviewers, it's not a primary duty and it takes them away from their own work. So they want you to be the "right" one even more.

Chapter Three

Creating Effective Lie Systems

There's a lot more to effective lying than simply telling the lie itself. If all you had to do to get away with a lie was tell it, just blurt it out, we'd be up to our forked tongues in lies. Successful lying requires a lot more than the lie itself. In order for your lies to work well, they must be part of a complete lie system. The guidelines for establishing and maintaining effective lie systems provide the basic foundation for successful job-search and general lying.

Anyone can tell a lie which, if it was written down and then read from a printed page by a disinterested party, might appear credible. The reader would have no way to evaluate whether the lie was believable or not; on face value, just about anything is possible. The difficulty is that few lies are considered in the abstract; most lies must prove themselves in the continually changing environment of the real world. For example, consider a typical simplistic lie which is common in fleeting social encounters.

A young man is in an airport hotel bar and a woman approaches and tries to pick him up. He's suspicious, as he knows that many married women who travel on business are only interested in one thing from a handsome young man. The woman is attractive, friendly, appears successful, and claims not to be married. The young man decides to give in and he goes to her room, where she uses him shamelessly. When he wakes up the next morning and asks if he can see her again, she admits she's married and was just out for a few laughs. Of course, the businesswoman had lied, they all do. Yet, her lie succeeded with the young man because it was part of a very simple situation, a low-complexity lie system.

If the married woman had picked up the young man in her hometown and he had followed her to her home, the lie probably wouldn't have worked. Once the suspicious young man had seen the swingset in her backyard, the toys and bicycles on the front walk, and, through the kitchen window, the woman's husband slaving away over the stove, the simplistic, "Oh, no, I'm not married" would have been quickly exposed as the bald-faced, insupportable lie it was (unless the woman was a truly great extemporaneous liar as in, "Oh, those toys. I'm staying with my sister and her family for a few days"). The lone simplistic lie fails because it is not part of a sufficiently developed lie system.

THE ELEMENTS OF A LIE SYSTEM

The lie itself is the smallest part of a lie system. Unfortunately, it's the easiest part and, all too often, the only part that's used. If you're going to lie effectively, you'll have to carefully plan and implement not just lies, but compete lie systems. The three elements of a system are the lie itself, the story, and the data.

The Lie Itself

The lie itself is the easiest part of the lie system to create and is the least important in terms of whether the lie will succeed. In the example of the philandering married woman, the lie itself is the statement, "Oh, no, I'm not married." In the job search, the lie might be the statement on the resume which claims "extensive experience in organizing trade shows" or the verbal equivalent made during the interview. Many novice job-search liars assume that the lie itself is all there is to lying. These foolish liars are doomed to discovery and failure. Failure does not result from the discovery of the lie itself, which is a rare occurence; it is more a result of the interviewer's observation of the liar's stress responses.

The most damning errors result from assuming that any situation can be handled by substituting additional lies for the remaining lie-system elements, rather than taking the trouble to design a lie and its supporting lie-system elements in advance. Job-seeking liars make this error because they are lazy; it's easier to forego the hard work and preparation which go into developing a lie system and then hope that they can lie your way out of any situation which occurs. Few can do this well enough under pressure (during interviews) to succeed. The guilt factor which we discussed in Chapter Two also comes into play here.

Many liars who do not carefully plan their lies have not come to terms with the fact that they are lying.

They feel guilty but are having a tough time facing it. Therefore, they avoid planning because it allows them to tell themselves that they didn't plan to lie. This is the same type of psychological self-deceit engaged in by sexually active youngsters who refuse to plan ahead and use contraceptives; the fact that they didn't plan enables them to believe that an unplanned pregnancy "isn't my fault." Of course, such transparent ruses don't deal with the guilt and resultant problems. The job-seeking liar ruins the interview and the teenager becomes/gets his girlfriend pregnant.

The Story

The story is just that; a fictitious chronicle which explains how your lies interface with reality. In the most extreme lies, such as an entirely phony employment record, the story has to be almost a complete alternative reality, which has phony jobs, phony bosses, fake business associates, fake anecdotes about "life on the job," and so on.

In the case of a simple lie, such as claiming a nonexistent degree, the story will be much simpler, consisting perhaps of a major, a location for the school, and an anecdote or two about why you went there and what it was like.

If you're claiming to have worked as a training manager, you'd have to have a wide range of supporting-story elements available for possible use. For example, you'll need to have thought about how many people worked for you, what types of training they did, how much training you developed, who you reported to, what programs you might have purchased, how well the training was received, what the problems were, and so on. You'll need to have thought about the budget of the department. It's impossible to determine ahead of time how much of the above (and much more additional) supporting-story elements will be required to support a particular lie in the interview process. With a typically stupid interviewer, you'll find that most of the story won't be needed. Less frequently, but often enough to be a tangible threat, the interviewer will get off on a line of questioning which draws upon the finest details of your story ("tell me about the product research department's report formats at Ajax Sexual Aids, Inc."). Therefore, you must think out an entire story line, with all supporting data, *before* you attempt to tell the lie. You can't take the chance that you'll be able to come up with something on the spur of the moment. Caught unprepared by a question or a comment, you're apt to display an emotional stress response which will give you away or make the interviewer feel uncomfortable about your self-confidence.

The Data

The supporting data is the "proof" for your lies. Supporting data may be as tangible as phony references to support your claims of a job you never had, or it may be as subtle as the delivery of an amusing anecdote about something that happened on a job you never had. In one sense, the data is any part of the story which is actually delivered. The data that's most critical, once a good story is put together, is hard data such as phony documentation, work samples, and the like. A little supporting data goes a long way toward giving your lies the substance of truth. Good supporting data isn't going to be available unless you've thoroughly prepared ahead of time.

Often, good supporting data isn't required in a specific interview/job-search situation; perhaps they'll never ask. However, you can't afford not to have it ready when they need it.

While it's not a lie-system element itself, there's an additional factor which significantly impacts all aspects of lie systems. This factor concerns the reality in which the lie system must function. Liars are forever making mistakes in terms of what the lies must do. Simply put, the lie system must lead the subject to believe the lie. At each successive stage of the job search, it takes progressively "more" of each lie system element to make a believer out of a listener; the lie system must become more complex.

The lie you're trying to establish with a phony resume functions in the least-demanding reality of job-search lying. The piece of paper says everything you need to say. A resume's missing data elements are deliberately omitted so the reader will be "teased" into wanting to see more, thereby necessitating a phone or in-person interview. If the resume is designed properly, the reader will fill in the gaps with his or her expectations and hopes. The "gaps" are all of the supporting information which would exist if the story were the truth. If improperly designed, the resume will lead them to make unfavorable assumptions about the gaps between the resume's lies and the total picture you want them to perceive.

For example, a sloppily produced resume (even if the content is great) may lead them to believe that you're not a polished professional or that perhaps your claim of "executive skills" is typical resume hype. Once you get a phone interview as a result of a resume, things get more complicated. On the phone, it's a real time challenge, leaving you no time to think about your answers to questions, and no time to pick just the right word. The interviewer will "see" not only the content of your lies, but will also be influenced by the tone of your voice and the level of power and mastery you convey with it. Your lie system must be sophisticated enough to meet the challenges presented by any number of unexpected questions. The face-to-face interview presents your lie system with the most difficult challenge. In person, every nuance of your behavior will be subject to intense scrutiny. Your facial expressions, the movement of your eyes, the way you sit, your clothes, your tone of voice, and so on, will be constantly monitored as you attempt to keep your lie system afloat. Anything can happen, any type of crazy question can be asked, and your lie system must be designed to react just as if the lie were the total and absolute truth.

The important thing to keep in mind is that each of your lie systems must be designed right from the start to function in the most demanding of all job-search environments: the face-to-face interview and all of the surprises and requirements it implies (references, possible checks of education, etc.). Let's say you lie by putting a phony job on a resume to cover a period of unemployment and you only develop the story to the point where the job fits into your overall job history on the resume. What are you going to do when you get a call and the employer asks a detailed question about a technical detail of the work you claim to have done? What are you going to do when, in the face-to-face interview, they ask for references from the firm? What happens when they start asking detailed questions about the company? Is it still in business? Who did they do business with? What was its gross annual sales? You get the point. If you answer one of the above questions in the wrong manner in a moment of confusion, you could lead yourself into a trap or at least a few moments of significant anxiety. Your lies aren't going to work unless every one of them is designed to succeed in a face-to-face interview. Anything less is an invitation to disaster.

THE TEN COMMANDMENTS OF JOB-SEARCH LYING

The ten commandments of job-search lying (don't worry, "Thou shalt not lie" is *not* one of them) provide general guidelines for successful lying in all areas. Keep them in mind as you design and implement your job-search lie systems. If you follow them carefully, you'll avoid most job-search-lying pitfalls.

1. Lie Only When Absolutely Necessary

There's a certain romance in our culture about lying. Although many people would never admit it, they're excited by stories such as the Great Imposter's, where a lying rogue gets away with all sorts of devilish deeds simply because he can lie well (and then perform up to the expectations his lies created). The very same people who fantasize about doing such things themselves would never admit their admiration; they wouldn't want to shock their friends (who feel the same way) or compromise their social position. The type of person who would buy this book is probably not burdened by a similar conflict of morals; you probably want to lie and would enjoy it if you could do it competently. No problem, but don't get carried away by your fantasies of spies and undercover operatives who suavely get away with any deceit they try.

There are many ways to handle job-search problems and lying is only one of them. After reading the prior chapters, you've no doubt seen that effective job-search lying will require more than an imaginative lie or two. It takes a lot of emotional energy to support even the smallest of lie systems. It's hard enough to make the proper impression in a job search when you're telling the truth, so there's no need to place the extra burden of supporting a lie system on yourself if you don't have to. Lie only when it's absolutely necessary.

2. Keep Your Lie Systems as Simple as Possible

The amount of effort required to support a lie system increases geometrically in proportion to the system's complexity. Thus, it'll take much more of your emotional energy and time to design and support a complex lie system compared to a simple one. For example, there are many different lies which can be used to cover a gap in your employment history. In certain situations, the easiest way is simply to lengthen the termination date of the last job prior to the gap and push back the starting date of the first job (if any) after the gap. (Chapter Eight will discuss the detailed techniques, advantages, and risks of these and other techniques). All other things being equal, the crafty and wise job-search liar uses this technique rather than attempting to lie about a completely phony position to fill the gap. Always keep things as simple as the situation allows.

3. Limit the Distribution of Your Lies

While there's much less chance of getting caught than you might imagine or fear with most decently executed job-search lies, every lie is at some risk. Let's face it, the truth is out there somewhere; nobody may know or care where it is, but there's always a chance that someone could stumble into it. The fewer people who are out there looking for it, the less chance of someone falling over it. Increasing the distribution of your lies not only marginally increases the odds of being discovered, it decreases the available pool of people who will be susceptible to a different lie. If you send out a phony resume to a large list of headhunters and then discover that it's not quite the phony resume you need, you're going to have to make a repeat mailing with the revised phony resume and your odds of discovery go up.

For example, one lying job seeker sent out a mailing of more than 1,500 resumes to headhunters all over the country (using the *Directory of Executive Recruiters* mentioned in Chapter One). After two or three interviews, he discovered that the resume was seriously flawed. He had no choice but to fix the error and go out with another mailing three weeks later to the same list. The second resume was much different in job content and even dates of employment. Several headhunters that called mentioned that his materials seemed "familiar." One called to talk about a job but then actually made the connection on the phone and told the liar that he was "disgusting." Perhaps others noticed the discrepancy as well but had no reason to call. It's unusual for anyone to notice but there's no point in jeopardizing any part of your chances.

You've a similar problem when you're aggressively canvasing a particular industry in a single metropolitan area or if you live in a small city and don't want to move. You've got a limited pool of employers to lie to and the more lies you spread, the greater the odds of someone noticing the discrepancies. When weaving your lies in a closed industry or small city, one self-righteous person can spread the word and you're in trouble. The chances of that type of discovery are small, but there's no justification for taking unnecessary chances because of faulty planning or laziness. Limit your lies to as narrow a distribution as you can. If you must go out with large mailings, test the resume's drawing power with a smaller mailing first. Then, if you have to make changes, you'll still have a pool of virgin targets to use for the next mailing.

4. Never Tell a Lie That Doesn't Fit into Your Planned Lie System

As we discussed earlier, the main components of a lie system are the story and data which support the lie. Since you have no control over much of what will happen in an interview, you have no safe choice but to plan for every reasonable eventuality. You can't hope to build an effective lie system on a shoddy foundation. The most difficult lie systems to substantiate are those which start on the spur of the moment and then take on a life of their own. You're having enough trouble running your own life without being dragged along facedown through the cactus by an out-of-control lie. Never tell a job-search lie unless it's part of a planned lie system which you can support.

5. Don't Lie Out of Your League

Many people have been so thoroughly indoctrinated by society, parents, churches, etc., that they cannot hope to succeed in anything but the most pale, tepid lies. When they try anything more substantial, they blush, sweat, look away, and generally appear trapped and furtive. If you've had your natural instincts for lying thoroughly ruined by well-meaning but misguided authority figures, you might as well face facts and forget about using grandiose lie systems. You may be able to condition yourself to get away with little lies, but few people have the time or energy to completely reverse years of extensive conditioning. If you're one of these unfortunates, it doesn't matter that you may be able to design marvelous lie systems on paper; you probably won't be able to sustain them in person. If so, forget the big stuff and stick to the little lies which everyone expects (see Chapter Six).

6. Never Lie for Amusement

Lying can become addictive, used to blunt the pain of a job search. Frustrated with a job search and angry with all of the cretins who must be kissed up to, job seekers often attempt to gain some satisfaction and a measure of revenge by inflicting upon interviewers the biggest lies they can get away with, at every opportunity. The thrill is to "see how much I can get this clown to believe." The payoff, in psychological terms is, "See, here I am out of work and having to kiss up to this idiot, yet he is so stupid he'll lap up the BS faster than I can shovel it." There's also the ego boost of putting down a personnel type (which isn't much of an ego boost at all, considering how stupid most of them are).

Be forewarned! Lying for amusement is a dangerous and risky practice. It starts as a occasional lark to get a quick thrill but soon you're doing it all the time, looking for opportunities in every interview to stick it to them with the really big ones. You tell yourself, "I'm only doing it for laughs when I know the interview is lost anyway, so what's the harm? I don't need to lie for amusement, I can quit anytime I want. I just don't want to quit now." Pretty soon, you're another lie junkie who can't control a habit which has taken control of his job search. I've seen it often and it's not a pretty sight. Once you become a lie junkie, your chances of getting a job are almost zero.

Remember, you're not out there lying for the thrill of it; you're lying to get a job. If you start telling lie simply to slick the interviewers, you'll soon be forced to abandon your planned lie system and you'll eventually end up telling lies that can't be supported. Even worse, you'll stop paying attention to brown-nosing the interviewer and winning the interview in favor of dropping a few big ones for your own amusement. Don't waste your lies or your job search that way. If your lying skills are so extraordinary that they can't be fully utilized in the job search arena, perhaps you should consider a career in public relations or politics where you can earn a handsome living and admiration by lying all the time. While you're searching for a job, stick to serious, get-that-job lying.

7. Never Lie Extemporaneously

Executing a lie system during a job search is much like performing in a live play: you're attempting to create a false reality which the audience accepts as reality for a short time (though it is hoped that your lies will retain their believability for a longer time). The challenge of the playwright is to create a script which appears natural, believable, and spontaneous to the audience but which is, in fact, planned word for word. If the actors in a play were given rough story outlines and character descriptions rather than a script and then told to "wing it," most performances would be disasters. Occasionally, a group of creative actors who know each other well can put together an off-the-cuff masterpiece, but most often, the dialogue would be terrible, the story wouldn't move along smoothly, and the audience wouldn't have a clear idea of the story line. The same is true, but even more so, with job-search lying.

Since you can't outline exactly what will happen in any particular interview in terms of the interviewer's actions, and because you know next to nothing about the interviewer (except the general expectations of most people), it's important for you to maintain as much control as you can by not introducing additional random elements. Your planned lie system must dictate every lie. Never toss in another, "Oh, yes, I had a lot of experience with microcomputer accounting systems when I was with Ajax Peyote Packers of Beverly Hills," unless you know enough about such systems to fake it, can support such claims with your existing lie systems, and can provide references.

8. Minimize the Number of Lie Systems in Use at One Time

It's tempting, if you're desperate for a job, to consider establishing numerous lie systems at the same time, each substantiating a different phony resume. After all, if you can increase your odds by using one pack of lies, several packs should proportionately shorten your search, right? Sadly, no. If only it were so easy.

It's not difficult to put together four or five phony resumes and lie systems. And if you're a practiced liar or a quick study, it's not difficult to play the parts. The problem is that the maintenance of each lie system requires a great deal of psychological energy. Believe me, it's a lot harder than it sounds, especially when you start to get phone interviews.

Consider what happened to me. I lost a horrible (but well-paying) job right at the start of the infamous 1981 recession. Every company in the country was laying people off, shutting down entire divisions, and here I was looking for a job to support a monster house payment, two cars, and so on. Classified ad counts were at their lowest levels since the 1974 oil embargo and I needed a job—fast. I put together eight different resume versions, each in a different field. I had a marketing resume, a sales manager resume, a personnel manager resume, a restaurant manager resume, a data analyst resume, and so on. For anything I had ever done or thought I could do, I put together a lie system. Of course, for each phony resume, I had designed an appropriate employment background and I had arranged for a set of references for each. I shortly found myself in quite a jam.

Right from the start, even when I was clipping ads, it was difficult to keep all of the stories clear. The vast number of options meant that it was hard to focus on any one. When the calls started coming, it was difficult to put on the right face fast enough to give a good interview. Even with excellent record keeping, I always wondered if I was referring to the correct resume and career story in the interview. One time, I answered about 20 minutes of phone interview questions according to my marketing resume, only to discover, after the call, that the employer had been sent the sales manager resume! I was an emotional wreck, trying to balance and anticipate who was calling about what. And it was even worse in the face-to-face interviews. Since I had eight stories on the back burner, it was extremely difficult to "get into the part" of any one. Anecdotes from one resume kept slipping into the others, I'd tend to get the industry jargon mixed up, and so on. And this was despite the fact that I used the same employment dates, the same highly skilled lying friends for phony references, and generally the same fake company names for each version. I was desperate and had to do it, but it was hell. Don't you try such a scheme unless you're equally desperate.

9. Don't Struggle to Save a Flawed Lie System

Nobody likes a quitter. Yet, there are times when

admitting a mistake and giving up is the smartest move. Custer's last stand sounds stirring but I'm sure that many of his men would have preferred to stay at the fort if they knew what kind of a day it was going to be.

It's the same in job searching. Occasionally, you may find that you've created a lie system which just isn't working. Perhaps you don't know enough about the industry to give good interviews; perhaps you find that your fictitious employment history isn't good enough to impress the interviewers. If that's the case, don't be foolish and try to take heroic measures to save your lie system; pull the plug on its life-support systems and let it die in dignity. Then put together a better set of lies. If your lie system isn't working (and you're sure it's not your performance or a bad reference somewhere), dump it and start over. That's why careful planning is critical. You don't have the time to try a lot of false starts. You can't expect every lie system or every element of a lie system to function perfectly. When you've made a mistake, acknowledge it and fix it.

10. Practice as Much as You Can

If you're using a lie system of any complexity, you can't expect to have it work perfectly right from the start. There are bound to be questions, data, technology, jargon, and so forth that will come up which you can't handle because you've never heard of it. That's why you've got to practice your lie system out there in the real world. Take every chance you can to interview. If you can, go to interviews for lower-level positions in the same industry. For example, if you're trying to lie your way into a Vice President of Marketing job (and are not a marketing expert), try to interview for a few marketing analyst jobs in the same industry. You can do this by sending your resume in response to the lower-level jobs. You'll learn a lot about the industry that way.

If you're after a really special job but are worried about your knowledge of the field, you can always do what one of my friends did. She had been a secretary but wanted a job as an office manager/administrator for a large company. She felt that her knowledge of office automation and communications systems wasn't what it should be. So she put a blind ad in the Sunday paper for the same position she was looking for. She got lots of resumes which helped her write hers. She then interviewed about a dozen of the top candidates (she had a friend of hers in another company let her use one of their conference rooms at lunchtime). She pumped the hell out of the interviewees and even tape-recorded the interviews for later analysis (unbeknownst to the candidates). She asked them detailed questions they'd never get on the job itself! If any of the candidates were lying, their lie systems got a real workout. In about four weeks, she knew one hell of a lot about automated filing, billing, communications, computers. Thus equipped, she began her own search and three months later started work in her new job.

Never turn down any interview in the industry you're interested in, even if it's for a rotten job with a company with a terrible reputation. You might not want the job, but you'll learn a lot about the industry. If you're not inclined to do what my friend did, you can still conduct some in-depth research of your own. At one time, I designed a resume showing a completely false employment history as a hospital administrator. I had known a few hospital administrators and they generally impressed me as a bunch of arrogant, slow-witted, pompous asses. I knew nothing about hospitals except that they were supposed to be worried about getting competitive and I assumed that my business background could be put to good use. Besides, none of the administrators seemed to do much except have affairs with their staff members and go to a lot of parties. Not my style but if that's the job, someone's got to do it!

I put together a direct-mail campaign to all of the hospitals in the region, and I answered a lot of ads. The first few interviews were great learning experiences. Whenever they'd mention a jargon item, I'd explain that I wasn't familiar with the term, they'd explain it, and I'd quickly point out that "we" had used another term at "my" hospitals (which I'd make up on the spot). At the same time, I made a lot of visits to hospitals in the area and "just dropped in" and talked to some of the department heads. I explained that I had been out of the country working as a hospital administrator and wanted to chat about how the industry was doing so I'd have a better idea about the job market. After about ten of these visits and seven bona fide interviews, I knew all the jargon and was even using it myself. Once I got past the jargon barrier, I was home free because everything else was the same (nobody did much work, everyone pretended they were being worked to death, and all of the game playing was identical to every other industry

I had worked in). I landed a job and worked two years as the hospital administrator for a 400-plus-bed hospital owned by one of the country's four largest health-care companies.

Chapter Four

Common Job-Search Problems

There is a large number of effective lie systems which can solve any number of job-search problems. Some lie systems are more effective solutions to certain problems than others. For example, you could design a completely phony employment background to conceal one involuntary termination but that would be about as appropriate as using a howitzer to kill a fly. Lies must be carefully matched to job-search problems so that you'll get maximum effect for minimum complexity and effort. This chapter reviews the most common job-search problems so that you can determine which problem(s) you have.

If you're not well-versed in what goes on behind the scenes in the world of personnel selection, you might not realize what constitutes a "problem" for a job seeker. Everyone knows that having a criminal record (which you admit or disclose) is a big obstacle in the job search (unless you lie). But did you know that it's often a considerable problem to have changed jobs too often, even if you were moving up all the time?

The following sections will discuss the significance of each of the most common job-search problems which require lying.

1. Too Many Jobs

If you show more than one job every two years, you've got a serious problem. Employers in most industries don't like to see a lot of job hopping, even if you've been moving up all the time or have been the unfortunate pawn of layoffs, shutdowns, and so forth. And if you show more than five jobs in 15 years, it'll hurt you. Employers are afraid that if you were willing to leave all those other employers in your search for greener paychecks, you won't hesitate to leave them. Then they'll have to go through all the time and expense to find someone else. Don't think that they'll understand if several of the job switches were due to factors out of your control.

You are the one who shows the job hopping, regardless of the reason, and you are therefore viewed as less desirable than someone who never did any work but just stayed in the same job for 10 years. In certain laid-back industries where things hardly ever change, such as insurance, banking, and government work, more than one job every five years is a problem. Employers in smaller cities also tend to be very wary if you have had more than one job every five years. This is because there are fewer job opportunities in smaller cities so the average employee has no choice but to hang onto whatever job he has. People who show a lot of jobs are assumed to have had problems or are seen as dangerously aggressive types who won't stay in a bad job. Both are bad news to hiring managers and personnel officers who take few chances.

2. Involuntary Terminations

There are few people with any enthusiasm for life and a willingness to take chances who haven't been fired. Unfortunately the majority of personnel officers and hiring managers won't hire anyone who admits having been fired. Aside from the reasonable fear that the candidate could be a troublemaker, they're more concerned over what'll happen if they hire the once-fired job seeker and things don't work out great. They're afraid they'll be nailed with a "Good Lord, Fred. You hired that clown knowing that he was fired before?" It won't matter how ridiculous the reason for being fired or how small the griper's complaint, the fear of being held responsible for anything will prevent almost any personnel type from taking a chance on a candidate who's been fired.

This is the reason why you *never* admit on a resume having been fired, and you don't admit it unless forced to do so in an employment interview. Don't believe the nonsense you occasionally see in the press about how "understanding" executives are about people who have been fired. Even though it's happened to all of them (and with good reason, no doubt), they won't think your reason was good. People who have been fired or laid off are considered to be "soiled goods" even if the employer knows that the reason for the termination was purely circumstantial. There's always a large number of applicants available who don't show or admit such a stain. Given the choice, why should they take any chances?

3. Gaps in Employment History

Showing a significant gap between any of your past jobs (or between the last job and the present time) creates an impression that's more subtle but just as damaging as admitting that you were fired or laid off. A "significant" gap is one of two months or more. Gaps further in the past are much less damaging than recent ones. Periods of admitted unemployment are bad news because they create the impression that you were jobless and wandering the streets, unable to convince even one of the millions of employers out there to give you a job. Any idiot knows that it takes six months to a year to find and land a decent job but they quickly forget that fact when they're doing the hiring. Nobody wants to hire a problem and nobody wants to help anyone but themselves when they bring someone on board. If you've been out of work for more than two months when you interview, they're going to think of you as a loser and someone who needs a favor, rather than someone who can help them. Gaps between prior jobs aren't as bad as a recent gap but they still create an unfavorable impression.

4. Bad References

The impact of bad references on a candidate's prospects of being hired gets a lot of press from authority figures and personnel officers. The threat of bad references is often used to scare employees into leaving without a fuss. Thousands have heard the line, "If you'll resign rather than making us have to fire you, we'll give you a good reference." That's hypocrisy for you! They make a deal with an employee who they consider to be bad news and then they're willing to turn around and lie to another company. And they get upset about job seekers who lie? Those bums don't deserve any breaks at all.

Bad references are not the curse they're made out to be. Sure, if a prospective employer actually does get a bad reference from a previous employer, he's probably not going to hire you. Even if you're just what he needs and he's able to get three or four other great references on you, he's most likely not going to take a chance on someone who got one bad reference. There are just too many others out there who have nothing but perfect references. However, the situation isn't as bad as it seems, even if you're not lying. The reality is that very few bad references actually get delivered. There are several reasons for this. First of all, most employers are worried about the possibility of getting sued by a job seeker for whom they might supply a bad reference. If they were to give a bad reference and it was discovered by the job seeker, a court might construe the reference as defamation of character or libel. Even if the prior employer were right about the bad reference, he'd run up a huge legal bill while the job seeker wouldn't be paying a cent (with every other citizen an attorney these days, it's easy to get one to take almost any case on contingency). So the former employer figures, why take the chance? After all, he doesn't owe some other faceless company anything. Besides, he's already willing to lie by commission and give good references to poor employees they want to get rid of, so why not lie by omission and not say anything?

The plain, simple truth is that relatively few employers give any references at all these days, other than a "would or would not rehire" statement. Of course, a "would not rehire" statement doesn't help a job seeker. The up side is that hardly any employers will verify references on the phone. There's no way to tell who's calling and if they give out the information to the wrong person, it could be court time! As a result, most employers will answer reference inquiries only by mail. Many of these aren't answered and those that are generally aren't returned for months (they're the last piece of "put it off until later" work that any personnel office takes care of). As you can see, it's not as easy to get a bad reference as you might have thought. However, it does happen. You're especially at risk if you've worked for a smaller employer who might not realize how risky it is to dump on prior employees. If you do have a significant bad reference lurking in your background, it's better to check it out and then fix it. Chapter Nine will tell you how.

5. Too Little Experience/Technical Expertise in Your Field

There's no denying that the majority of careers are spent marking time while waiting for the right break. Very often, you've stopped learning anything of significance but you don't have the "seasoning" or length of service you need to appear as a credible candidate for the job you want. Don't make the mistake of thinking that wanting a job and being able to do it are enough. Even if you look the part, can talk the part, and can do the part, most employers have a preconceived idea of how much time and/or expertise (acquired through schooling and experience) they want. Even if they have doubts about how accurate they are in determining how much experience a specific position requires, they're not about to take a chance and hire someone who isn't safe. If you want or need to take the next step but your credentials don't show it the way they see it, you've got a big problem.

6. Career Change

Talk of changing careers is as "in" as yogurt, sushi, and tofu. To listen to the media, you'd think every other person was aggressively moving off into a new career, assisted by eager employers who know that job skills are transferable. Fat chance. It's a law of business that every industry thinks it's special and that it's problems and skills are unique. That's one reason why industry after industry keeps making the same stupid mistakes; they've never had any infusion of talent from another industry that's already made the error and learned how to fix it. If you want to change careers, you've got a big problem if you can't show at least something that looks like it's directly transferable. A little "pump job" on your resume can do part of it, but without some lies, you're destined to start much lower on the ladder when you finally talk someone into hiring you.

7. Not Moving Up Fast Enough

If you're intelligent, you probably know you could do a much better job than your boss. You probably also realize that your boss is getting enough money to live on, compared to the starvation-level alms they call your salary. Yet, as in problem number 5, above, you're not going to get a chance to show what you can do in a job like your boss's if you haven't paid your dues.

The situation is even worse if you're a "baby boomer" born in the 1945 to 1955 era. You and millions of other boomers are scrambling for comparatively few spots on the next rung of the corporate ladder. Statistically speaking, you're not going anywhere; the majority of the baby boomers are destined to languish in mediocre positions until they retire. There's just not enough to go around for the fruit of all of all our parents' once-passionate loins. That's a very big problem.

A further difficulty is that the problem of moving up the ladder is time sensitive. If you're not well on your way in your particular field by the time you're 30 years old, you're in big trouble. If, by the time you're 40, you haven't shown that you're on the verge of making it to the big time, you might as well forget it. The emphasis these days is on getting there quick and those who don't are considered losers. Don't think that you've got all the time in the world to move up. The last 20 years of your career are for stabilizing after an earlier meteoric rise; if you haven't had a meteoric rise early, few employers are going to permit you to do it on their time later. If this sounds terribly unfair and like poor business practice to boot, you're right. But that's the only game in town and employers own all the bats, balls, and gloves.

8. Not Making Enough Money

What's the first thing you think of when you think of a new job? Of course, it's bucks, money, dinero, filthy lucre, jack, specie. The first thing you wonder about any new job is, "How much does it pay?" or "How much am I going to make?" That's natural, healthy, greedy human nature and capitalism at its best. Yet, the subject of compensation is treated very strangely by employers. Prior to the actual job offer, you're considered only slightly more attractive than a spore-spewing leper if you even give a hint that you're primarily interested in money. Employers, on the other hand, specify anticipated salary levels as one of the primary characteristics of the job they're trying to fill. They realize full well that what you pay for is what you get. It's all a game of charades; everyone's thinking of money but the job seekers are expected to pretend that all they want is "challenge," "growth opportunities," and the like while employers pretend they want "experience," "seasoning," and so forth. The job seekers want bucks and the employers want a candidate with enough credentials to justify the overpaid salary structure the organization perpetuates. This puts you, the job seeker, in a tight place.

You see, prior compensation levels are themselves a vital qualification. Even if you have the experience and credentials to look like a great candidate for the position, you're not going to get the money unless the amount you're looking for is within reasonable striking range of what you've been making. Let's say you were making 50 thousand dollars per annum in your last job as a marketing director. You'd have comparatively little difficulty getting another job in the 45-to-60-thousand-dollar range. Yet, if you had been making only 30 thousand dollars on your last job but showed more experience and education (either the truth or well-done lies) than someone making 50 thousand dollars, you'd never, ever be considered for a 45-to-60-thousand-dollars-per-year job. Even if you presented exceptionally well in the interview, in the eyes of the prospective employer, you wouldn't be qualified. Each of us is, to a great extent, what we made in the last job. If you're trying to move up in salary to where you deserve or need to be, you're in trouble if you're not close to that salary level already.

9. Inadequate Educational Credentials

This is the saddest of all job-search problems. To any person with a working brain, it's obvious that the only important consideration in selecting employees is whether they can do the job or not. Yet, because it's too much trouble to actually measure job-related skills or knowledge, employers take the shortcut; they specify education instead. The assumption is made that four years of intensified Frisbee, fornication, and alcohol/drug exposure will somehow contribute to increased performance. The result is that almost every job requires outrageously unnecessary educational credentials. The irony is that in the only time this assumed relationship was probably accurate, 30 to 40 years ago, educational credentials weren't the hot item they are now. In the "old days," a college degree was considerable proof of at least having survived a fairly rigorous course of study. These days, college degrees are, in general, a joke in terms of what's required to earn one. But since everyone now has one, employers specify them as a job requirement almost as automatically as they specify a good "attitude." The result: even entry-level clerical jobs now require four-year college degrees, not because the employee needs academic skills, but because there are so many college graduates who are out there looking for work. The result has been degree-requirement inflation at all levels of employment. Almost any job requires a college degree and, if they expect you to use a pencil and paper occasionally, an MBA is mandated. The person who doesn't show the minimum educational credentials for the job doesn't have a chance; there're too many people out there who can show all the paper they need. If you don't have the necessary sheepskins, you've got a big problem.

10. Criminal Record or Other Major Problem

Criminal records and similar major career blemishes aren't the disasters they might appear to be. There's no doubt that if anyone checks on your past and finds out you did a dime of hard time at the penitentiary, you're not going to get anything but the most menial work. It also goes without saying that if you disclose that you were dishonorably discharged from the service, you're not going to be offered a job by most companies.

An employer just isn't going to knowingly invite a potential troublemaker into his fold. Yet, few companies will check on you if you don't tell them. The problem is generally only as big as your disclosure of it. If you don't say anything and can conceal the time period in which the problem occurred, you're in pretty good shape. Few employers, except very large companies, defense contractors, and the federal government will check on you unless they suspect something. If you lie well, they won't bother to check on you.

Chapter Five

Ten Job-Search Lying Strategies

While the number of individual lies which can be told by job seekers is countless, all of them fall into one or more of ten basic categories of lying strategy. These strategies form the foundation upon which specific lie systems are built. Before we get to the mechanics of putting together specific lie systems in later chapters, it's a good idea to review the big picture of what's available to job seekers in the way of general lying strategies. That's the purpose of this chapter.

A few of the strategies listed below involve common, almost mandated lies. Strategy A, which involves shamelessly pumping your existing qualifications and experiences to the point where even you don't recognize jobs which you've actually had, illustrates this. Almost everyone does a little of it and if you don't use it, employers will think you've got a problem (just imagine how bad a completely honest resume would appear). Modifying your compensation history, which is described in strategy C, is common and expected, but frowned upon in polite company.

Most of the strategies here are complex lie systems which require background data, preparation, and planning. Strategy D describes using phony references, and is a complex lie system. You must arrange for people to be your references, supply them with details, and let them know when they can expect a call so they can most effectively slant the reference they give. It's not a big project, but it requires planning and careful attention during the search campaign.

Most of the lie systems, in their fail safe mode, require similar amounts of preparation. Of course, any of them can be executed "on the fly" (you simply lie but have nothing with which to back them up), but there's no sense inviting disaster. A few of the lie systems involve outrageous distortions of reality which should be reserved for only the most serious situations. Strategy I, and especially strategy J, fall into this category. As you might expect, these two, creating a completely phony position and creating a completely phony employment history respectively, require the most planning and preparation time (in order to set up references, provide work samples, etc.). These two also require critical bald-faced lying skills which few untrained liars possess. But you need those skills if you're going to become a success in job-search lying.

THE TEN BASIC STRATEGIES

The ten basic lying strategies are listed below, in approximate ascending order of increased complexity. Let's review each strategy and discuss exactly what it does and how it operates in general. Later chapters will outline aspects of each strategy in detail.

Strategy A: Pumping Up Your Existing Qualifications

As mentioned above, strategy A is the most commonly used lie technique by job seekers. In fact, it's so typical and expected that strategy A has become more of an accepted resume-writing and interviewing tool rather than a lying strategy. It's so routine that stupid (honest) job seekers who are completely candid are placed at a tremendous disadvantage: the plain facts about their most significant achievements and accomplishments pale in comparison to the "pumped-up" hype of the majority of applicants.

Yet, because it's such a commonly used ploy in resume writing and interviewing, there's a danger that you may not use this strategy to its fullest advantage. It is a job-search lying strategy and must be applied in the same manner as a lie -- with careful planning and precise execution. Too many people simply pump up a few of their achievements and think they've done enough. Not so. Random pumping of a few experiences and responsibilities gives your entire presentation a ragged, disorganized look. A perceptive interviewer will notice the contrast between the mundane items you didn't pump up and the ones you lied about or simply embellished upon. Properly executed, pumping provides your entire employment history with a significant increase in stature, achievement, and professional resolve, even if you use all of the jobs you've actually had. Strategy A is so basic and critical that Chapter Six is devoted to it. Regardless of the types of other lies you use, it's essential that you use Strategy A to the fullest extent possible on the truthful aspects (however few they may be) of your experience that remain on your resume.

Strategy B: Altering The Duties, Responsibilities, Achievements, and Titles of Current/Past Positions

This strategy ranges from lie systems which slightly embellish the truth about an actual position to lie systems which use a period of employment with an organization to create an entirely different job (with the only similarities being the dates of employment). This strategy relies upon the fact that few employers respond with detailed information to inquiries about past employees. It's almost laughably easy to claim different job duties and create or inflate achievements to the point of absurdity. You could have been a marketing analyst and you can easily claim to have been directing huge, world-wide marketing programs (if you build your lie system carefully). If the job was more than a few years ago, it's likely that personnel won't even be able to locate your records and that nobody who worked with you will still be around.

With the assistance of strategy D (phony references) or strategy H (consulting or self-employment lies), your lies about your achievements will sail in full wind on clear waters. It's somewhat more difficult to succeed with lies about job titles as they're one of the few things which employers will provide. Yet, there's always the distinction between "official job description titles, which nobody used" and "what we always called the position."

Strategy C: Phony Compensation History

This is one of the easiest of lies. It's so easy to get away with that it's surprising that most job seekers don't use it. I've worked with many underpaid people who could have easily claimed to have been making another five thousand dollars per annum on their prior job. This would have meant that they would have started the new job at least five thousand dollars higher. Yet, they and countless others didn't lie. Why? Aside from serve-no-purpose, outdated morality, they believed that employers always check references and that if they check on past wages, they'll be given the information.

Not true. Lying about past compensation is so easy and necessary to economic health that it should be considered part of your standard job-search resume-writing practice rather than a lie. Lying about compensation, even if you're not seriously underpaid in your present job, is essential because employers always lie about what they can pay for the position.

Employers always try to bring the candidate onboard at the lowest rate they can get away with. Larger organizations attempt to remain below the "midpoint," which is the middle of the established salary range for the position. Often the range between the minimum and maximum salaries for a job is as much as $12,000 to $15,000 per year for jobs paying up to $50,000 per year.

The reason why employers try to bring employees in low is obvious: greed. The reason they give is: "We want to have some room left to give you merit increases." Nonsense. Earning a starting salary of $15,000 to $50,000 per year, it takes two to three years to reach the maximum from the midpoint, given typical three to five percent annual merit increases. The employers know that you're probably going to be stuck with zero career growth if you work for them and they want to be able to keep you in line for at least two years with the hope of more money. You might as well take what you can get up front and then worry about merit increases later. You'll probably end up leaving if there's not enough growth anyway and if you get promoted, you start over in a new position, with a new range. Don't fall for the common tripe you so often hear about "negotiating for salary after the job offer's been made." Believe me, unless they want or need you so bad that their teeth hurt, they've already made up their minds what they're going to give you before they offer you the job. If they need you badly, you're in great shape. If you're just another low-level or middle-management cipher in the organizational hopper, forget about "negotiating." If you try, you'll get them angry. Against all of this, your only recourse is simply to lie.

Strategy D: Phony References

This strategy is the first of the "work" strategies. That is, to make it succeed, you have to do some homework. It consists of using friends or past colleagues as references in place of the people who would be your actual references if you were to make a mistake and tell the truth. There are many variations of this technique, depending upon whether you use existing companies or phony companies and depending upon whether your "reference" actually works there or not.

For example, if you've got friends who you can trust, you can use them as references for jobs you never had in companies for which they and/or you never worked. All of the variations of this strategy will be explained in Chapter Nine. Don't worry if you think that this strategy could be wide open to exposure as it would seem easy to trip up the reference; this is one more instance where you're saved by the incredible stupidity of the folks doing the reference checks. They ask such bland, typical questions (e.g., "Was Harry a good worker?") that anyone who knows your name could give you a good reference. I've had references confuse different lying-resume versions of mine and give a reference on me about jobs that were totally different from the resume in front of the interviewer and I still got the offer! Reference checkers hardly ever ask specific questions and when they do, any reasonably intelligent person can handle them by giving impressive but meaningless general responses ("oh, yes, Harry was one of the most creative, hard-working employees I ever had").

Strategy E: Creating Phony Educational Credentials

We've all seen the stories in the press about people who work their way into incredibly high positions after having lied about their credentials. There have been mayors, state legislators, doctors, teachers members of every profession exposed as having lied about educational credentials. Despite all the hoopla, it remains almost embarrassingly easy to simply lie about education and get away with it if you can play the part and appear to be what you claim in interviews and on resumes.

If you want to do more than simply claim you have the education, there are all sorts of strategies which you can use. There are numerous institutions which masquerade as "alternative approaches" to education which will enable you to "earn" any degree you want for a fee of several thousand dollars or less. Or, if that's too honest for you, you can set up a mail drop as the registrar's office of a phony alma mater and you're home free because you'll be mailing out fake transcripts/verifications to the employers who request them.

Strategy F: Altering Employment Dates

As you might have guessed from above discussions, altering dates of employment is one of the areas where you have to be careful. Dates are one of the few things, along with job titles, which employers will almost always provide in reference checks. Of course, if the employer doesn't check and/or your previous employer doesn't respond -- no problem. You can gamble on either or both of those occurring, but who needs the anxiety attacks in the middle of the night? One way to alter dates is to combine this strategy with Strategy G (eliminating current or past positions from your employment history) and "smooth out" your employment progression.

Strategy G: Eliminating Current or Past Positions From Your Employment History

This strategy consists of dropping one or more of your past jobs and/or your current position from your claimed employment history. This is the strategy of choice if you've got a real disaster with which you don't want to deal and which can't be handled by phony references. Of course, this strategy can't do much by itself, as it's not going to make a great impression if you show huge gaping periods of unemployment; you have to fill the gaps by using other strategies.

This strategy is particularly effective if you've been on a roll of really bad job experiences of short duration. Rather than claiming the embarrassment of five jobs in five years, perhaps you drop four of them, stretch the dates on the one "true" job, and then use strategy H or I to fill the remaining gap. Or you fill in the gap with a single period of employment in which you were self-employed or a consultant. All of a sudden, instead of looking like a fickle job hopper, or a unemployable troublemaker, you look like a stable winner.

Strategy H: Creating a Self-Employment or Consulting Position

There's nothing easier than becoming a consultant. As the old saying goes, "A consultant is someone who is more than 30 miles from home with a briefcase." All you have to do is have some cards printed and claim that you are one. This is one of the all-time great techniques to cover up lengthy periods of unemployment or a succession of bad jobs.

It's not uncommon to be out of work for six months to a year when you're job hunting but that looks real bad to a prospective employer. On the other hand, the same period sounds impressive if you claim to have "been on a short-term consulting assignment for the past six months. It's winding down and now I'm getting serious about looking."

These "consulting" positions are easy to create and substantiate. They cause you to be perceived as a more polished professional than you might already be. You see, everyone who isn't a consultant is impressed with them and wants to be one, so they think it's glamorous. Believe me, it isn't; I've been there and it sucks (unless you're one of the few high rollers who gets paid for your name). Yet, the people who haven't tried it or don't have the guts to risk their homes and careers think it's glamorous. Your "experience" as a consultant will impress them. If you're not in a field that's given to consultants, you can claim to have been self-employed. This strategy is the all-time winner for hiding bad experiences when it's used in conjunction with Strategy G.

Strategy I: Creating a Phony Job

This is the strategy which, after phony educational credentials, is most popular when job-search lying is discussed among the experts in the field of applied lying. It has great appeal as a technique because a phony job can be made to fit the requirements of any job search. You're after a marketing analyst job? Simply create a marketing analyst job as your last position. All of a sudden, you're experienced! Because of its use by non-experts in job-search lying (or those unwilling to learn), this technique gets bad press because there are always a few idiots who try it and get caught. It's usually discovered because it's executed improperly (in lying, as in most other areas of life, failures result more often as a result of poor technique than from conceptual errors).

Strategy J: Creating a Fictitious Job History

This, of course, is the "great impostor" stuff that gets our blood flowing and fires up our enthusiasm for telling really big lies. It's the most exciting strategy because it conjures up visions of spies and daring, of cunning undercover agents who can lie and bluff their way into the most desirable situations. Alas, the truth is somewhat less stimulating. There are few people who can make it work and, fortunately for the job-search liar with a big problem, even fewer people who actually need to go this far. All of the other strategies mentioned above are less trouble to implement and can get generally the same results. The phony career is the last stop on the desperation trail of job seeking. And, like most final desperation ploys, it's usually arrived at only after numerous less-strenuous and desperate alternatives have been overlooked. Don't turn your job search into Custer's Last Stand by making the phony career grandstand play until you've exhausted every other alternative.

MATCHING STRATEGIES AND PROBLEMS

The selection of a particular lie strategy is a very personal endeavor. Your lying skills, temperament, and interests will often have more influence upon your choice of a lying strategy than the specific needs of the job-search situation. Two job seekers who are faced with the same problem may each select a completely different lie strategy as a solution, and the different solutions may be appropriate for their temperaments and skills as liars. There are no absolutely "right" or "wrong" answers. There is only correct or incorrect lying technique. If you have an unsightly gap in your employment history one job ago, you may feel comfortable with creating a short-term consulting assignment to fill the void. Another job-seeker with the same exact problem might prefer to drop the job prior to the gap (assuming it wasn't a "good" job) and fill the entire, bigger gap with a single fictitious job. If both techniques are well executed, both job seekers will do well.

The strategies in this chapter are intended to provide you with a conceptual starting point for selecting your lying strategies. While there are no strategies which are "wrong," there are some that aren't generally effective in certain situations. And there are others which have shown themselves to be extremely effective after years of use by legions of job-seeking liars. While you're on your own (and justifiably so) in your selection of strategies, this section will help to orient your thinking about strategy selection. When we get to the details of designing the actual lie systems themselves, you'll begin to be more comfortable with identifying the elements in a particular situation which might require you to use a lie strategy which differs from the general recommendations made in this chapter. After you've read this section and studied the remaining chapters, you'll have a good idea of which lie strategies will best suit your particular situation.

Figure 10 cross-references each of the lie strategies with the job-search problems which were outlined in Chapter Four. For each problem, a number of lie strategies are ranked in the order in which they should generally be considered for use with that particular problem. The most appropriate or primary strategy for a specific problem is ranked "1," the next most appropriate is ranked "2," and so on. If a strategy is not particularly, or only peripherally, related to a problem, it is not ranked. You'll note that lie strategy A (pumping up your existing qualifications) is denoted with an asterisk. This indicates that this lie strategy is considered routine in all job-search situations. Let's face it, if you're going to try any of the other lies, there's no point in overlooking the easiest ones.

For example, if your problem is too many jobs in a short period of time, lie strategy G, which deals with eliminating positions from your employment history, is the best strategy to focus upon. The second-best strategy for this problem is the strategy H, or creating a consulting position, as it would fill the gap on your resume created by strategy G. If you feel that creating a consulting/self-employment position isn't right for your particular situation, then you might look to lie strategy I, creating a phony job. The lying strategy F, which considers modifying job dates, could be your fourth choice for dealing with the problem of "too many jobs." In effect, this consists of stretching the starting/ending dates of jobs on both sides of the job from which you were fired. Modifying your job dates isn't a very good idea in all cases, but it can be effective. Of course, there might be situations whose particular requirements call for a less-standard approach. You might feel that you can overcome the problem of too many jobs by putting together a couple of knockout phony references (lie strategy D). Normally, this wouldn't be an effective plan for the general problem of having moved around too much. However, if you can bring in the right big guns as references who'll impress a particular employer or type of employer, it might work.

Those strategies denoted by a dash in Figure 10 are not considered to be primary lie systems which are appropriate for dealing with a problem. Thus, strategies C (modifying claimed-compensation levels) and B (altering the job content) are two lie strategies which are not primary options for the problem of "too many jobs," but which are often used as a subsidiary part of the solution.

FIGURE 10. JOB-SEARCH LYING STRATEGIES RANK ORDERED FOR EACH OF THE TEN MOST COMMON JOB-SEARCH PROBLEMS

A	B	C	D	E	F	G	H	I	J
1. Too many jobs									
*	-	-	-	-	4	1	2	3	-
2. Been fired									
*	-	-	1	-	-	2	3	4	-

3. Gaps in history									
*	-	-	-	-	1	2	3	4	-
4. Bad reference(s)									
*	-	-	1	-	-	2	3	4	-
5. Limited experience									
*	1	2	3	-	-	4	5	6	-
6. Need new career									
*	1	-	-	2	-	3	5	4	-
7. Need step up									
*	1	2	3	4	-	-	5	-	-
8. Need more money									
*	2	1	-	3	-	-	-	-	-

9. Poor education									
*	2	3	4	-	1	-	-	-	-
10. Criminal record									
*	-	-	4	-	-	1	3	2	5

Lie strategy key:
A = Pumping up every fact
B = Altering job details
C = Altering compensation
D = Altering references
E = Creating education
F = Altering job dates
G = Dropping job
H = Creating consulting job
I = Creating fictitious job
J = Fictitious background

* = Always used to maximum extent possible

Note that many of the lie strategies in the table assume other strategies. Clearly, if you're going to create a fictitious job to deal with a past firing (strategy I under problem 2), you're also going to have to alter dates (part of strategy B), claimed-compensation levels (C), and so on. Yet, for the problem of the past firing, lie strategies B and C aren't ranked as primary alternatives in Figure 10. The ranked strategies represent the primary strategies with which to approach the problem. Ancillary supporting lies which might be used to support the main lie system but which can't do the whole job themselves, are not ranked.

All other things being equal, you should attempt to use the first-ranked lie strategy to deal with a particular problem if it's at all possible. If there are constraints on your use of the best strategy, utilize the number-two strategy, and so on.

Chapter Six

Pumping Words: Lies Everyone Expects

The "pumping up" of your qualifications, experiences, and credentials is one of the most time-honored of job-search-lying traditions. The difference between "pumping up the old qualifications" and full-blown lying is one of both degree and style. "Pumping" can be characterized as the type of job-search lying which almost every job seeker attempts to practice (although most do it badly), almost every employer expects to encounter, and which wouldn't cause too many raised eyebrows if the actual truth were to be disclosed to the interviewer who reads the resume.

In fact, it's no lie (you can trust *me!*) to state that everyone expects you to "pump up" your qualifications on resumes and cover letters and in interviews. Employers and personnel-office personnel may deny they expect such lies, but they're the ones who have created the practice. Over the years, personnel selection has evolved into a search for defects to be screened out rather than potential to be sought. In such an environment, even one small blemish can ruin your chances. Smart job seekers have responded, even if they didn't understand exactly why, by spreading a thin layer of cosmetic lies over all of their job-search materials.

Pumping is done by first tossing out the small, human foibles from your admitted background; you never admit that occasionally you're late, tired, angry, lazy, bored, etc. Then, you "talk things up" by referring to duties such as having operated the photocopier as "generated all executive-level correspondence," thereby lifting it from the mundane task to the all-important responsibility.

Job searching has gotten to the point where the job seeker who doesn't polish all of his materials with such a coating of lies will never be interviewed. Consider what would happen if a job seeker submitted a resume with the job-experience section shown in Figure 11.

FIGURE 11. EXAMPLE OF A PAINFULLY TRUE JOB-EXPERIENCE SECTION

February 1975 to February 1978
PINKERUP COMMUNITY COLLEGE
Twin Buttes, ID

Computer Programmer I
Responsibilities: Wrote and compiled several low-level programs for assigning classrooms to courses. Mainly did legwork and program cleanup for my direct superior who wrote all of the interesting programs. The equipment was outdated and most of our programs were stand-alone number crunchers. *Achieve-*

ments: I spent most of my time looking for things to do, and attempting to keep busy while I searched for a better job.

The person who uses a resume as candid as that shown in Figure 11 isn't going to be inconvenienced by a lot of interviews. Yet, most of us, if we were to truthfully characterize the majority of what we've done in many jobs, would have resumes that would look much like that in Figure 11. Even though this job seeker displays all sorts of attractive candor and even some initiative ("looking for things to do," "attempting to keep busy"), such candor is completely out of place in the job search. The appearance of candor is commendable but only when it is used to deliver lies. Of course, it's obvious that few job seekers, even the most devoutly religious, would be as candid as the person who wrote the job experience section of Figure 11. Let's take a look at a more typical example of shoddy resume writing. Figure 12 displays a job-experience section which is a more typical example of a non-pumped but not exactly honest job-experience section.

FIGURE 12. A NON-PUMPED RESUME JOB-EXPERIENCE SECTION

February 1975 to February 1978
PINKERUP COMMUNITY COLLEGE
Twin Buttes, ID

Computer Programmer I
Responsibilities: Wrote and compiled programs for assigning

classrooms to courses and performed routine administrative work. *Achievements:* Assisted in reorganization of departmental files and wrote many stand-alone programs.

The resume job-experience section in Figure 12 adroitly avoids most of the painful elements of the truth which were shown in Figure 11. Yet, how many companies would want to interview the resume writer? Not many. It's a pale, tepid presentation of routine duties. Compared to the typical resume pump job, the presentation of Figure 12 doesn't have a chance. Figure 13, however, is the fully pumped job-experience section for the same job shown in the first two illustrations above.

FIGURE 13. EXAMPLE OF FULLY PUMPED JOB-EXPERIENCE SECTION

February 1975 to February 1978
PINKERUP COMMUNITY COLLEGE
Twin Buttes, ID

Computer Programmer I
Responsibilities: Reported directly to the MIS director, for whom I served as troubleshooter and technical advisor. *Achievements:* As a key member of the Data Processing Group, participated in the design, writing, testing, and implementation of programs for numerous functions throughout the institution including scheduling, finance, admissions, and administration.

The job-experience section shown in Figure 13 is resume "pumping" at its best. Gone is candor, gone is the actual truth, gone are admissions of human frailties. In their place are gross distortions of reality. Unlike the first two examples, the author of this resume will have many interviews because he appears to have been at the center of things, someone who got things done and even reported directly to the MIS director. Even if the employer should call to check references, the MIS director (who is actually the Supervisor of Computing Clerks, in a one-room, three-person operation) is going to be so flattered at the title of MIS director, that he will give a great reference. And, face it, the above description is pretty much true, although "troubleshooter" and "technical advisor" are uncommon terms to assign to the coffee gofer. Few people will quibble over things like that when they're giving references, especially if they liked you or your work. And if they don't like you, use the techniques shown in Chapter Ten to set up more enlightened, phony references.

THE TWO FACETS OF RESUME PUMPING

There are two dimensions of resume pumping which are essential for a well-designed, fully pumped resume. The first dimension involves the use of proper wording and phrasing to describe what you did. Some phrases, such as "comprehensive experience as a," lend a more impressive feel to a resume than expressions such as "worked as a." You might as well use the same type of hype to describe what you've done (whether it's the truth or not) as the business world uses to describe its own achievements. This type of pumping is most effective when it is used to enhance the impact of the summary-of-qualifications section which should go on the first page of the resume.

The second facet of pumping is the use of slight, but flattering, lies. This is the essence of resume pumping in which a thin coating of acceptable (to the business world) lies is used to enhance the reality, status, and significance of everything you've done. This type of pumping is most important when used to inflate the significance of the individual job-experience sections which show what you've done for each employer. We'll discuss each of these dimensions separately.

The Use of Effective Verbiage

Don't underestimate the importance of using effectively pumped-up wording in your resume. While everyone tends to scoff at jargon and bemoan its effect on clear communications, the very same people leap at each new word with moist, ready tongues. And, since other smart resume writers are using the most effective wording they can get, yours will read like a fish wrapper if it appears without the expected grandiose phrasing and jargon. Consider the example shown in Figure 14, which is a plainly worded job-experience section from an actual resume (which was submitted to a Fortune 500 employer).

FIGURE 14. EXAMPLE OF A PLAINLY WORDED JOB-EXPERIENCE SECTION

March 1984 to April 1985
HENRY HUCK DAY CARE
Raft, MS

Recreation Aide
I was responsible for participating in various activities with young kids. I had the opportunity to run a clinic for young boys in basketball. I also had responsibilities for purchasing and distributing some materials.

The job-experience section shown in Figure 14 violates so many critical rules of proper resume design that I worry about it falling into the hands of young job seekers who could be damaged by reading it. If you don't think the Figure 14 example is horrendous, please read Chapter Two again.

The entire presentation in Figure 14 is watered down, boring, and not impressive. Phrases such as "participating in various activities" and "opportunity to run a clinic" make it sound like the job was a hit-or-miss affair that the candidate can't even remember very well. A simple change of wording and it's improved 1000 percent. Behold in Figure 15 the results of a proper pump job on this resume.

FIGURE 15. FULLY PUMPED VERSION OF THE JOB-EXPERIENCE SECTION SHOWN IN FIGURE 14

March 1984 to April 1985
HENRY HUCK DAY CARE
Raft, MS

Recreation Aide
Responsibilities: Supervision and administration of daily recreational activities of large numbers of children and adolescents. Design and implementation of teaching clinics in basketball.

Maintenance of complex purchasing and stock-distribution system. *Achievements:* Implemented several new programs and teaching clinics. Improved materials-purchasing and distribution systems.

Now the resume has a touch of power, a feeling that the candidate is a budding young business person who, even while stuck at a day care center in the boondocks of Mississippi, was able to get some important things done. And with no lying at all (at least not anything that I'd like to have called a lie of mine). Who's to say that showing five kids how to field grounders on three successive days wasn't "several teaching clinics"? Only someone who hasn't spent a summer with a bunch of wild animals at camp! Who's going to dispute the fact that putting the receipts for the ice cream cones in a file folder wasn't an "improved materials-purchasing" system? Note the use of the words *supervision* and *administration* instead of the insipid wording used in the Figure 14. The improved effect was created by nothing but clever phrasing which only approaches, but never actually enters, the territory of full-blown lying.

The use of impressive verbiage is even more important when designing effective summary-of-qualifications sections. As shown in the Chapter Two resume example, these summary of qualifications sections are critical for orienting the reader to want to believe to get ready to believe, and to be eager to believe, that you're the person who's going to solve their problems. Therefore, it's essential to describe everything you've done in the most flattering and slightly exaggerated terms. It's always difficult to come up with examples of bad summary-of-qualifications sections because so few people use one! I'll never understand how job seekers can be so stupid.

Not being able to find a bad example from actual resumes, Figure 16 presents something even more outrageous: an example of a summary-of-qualifications section which was shown in a "how to write a resume" book as a good example! It is a terrible summary-of-qualifications section, one that not only hasn't been pumped at all, but hasn't even been slightly polished. It's even more depressing when you consider that the resume was supposedly one that showed 13 years of experience in accounting. That's the best summary of qualifications the job seeker could put together after 13 years on the job? What is the employer supposed to believe that the candidate did the other 12 years?

FIGURE 16. ACTUAL EXAMPLE OF A SUPPOSEDLY GOOD SUMMARY-OF-QUALIFICATIONS SECTION TAKEN FROM A RESUME BOOK

General Accounting
Prepared and supervised all entries in books of original entry and subsidiary ledgers. Prepared tax returns on federal, state, and city levels.

Financial Reports
Prepared monthly and annual financial reports, along with comparative analysis of similar periods.

Auditing
Performed and supervised detailed audits of balance sheet and

income statement accounts.

Cost Accounting
Worked closely with many clients in setting up cost systems for present plus future production plans.

Systems
Helped streamline accounting procedures of clients by use of modern systems (one write systems, IBM inventory controls).

Figure 17 presents the same summary of qualifications material shown in Figure 16 in its final pumped up form.

As you can see, the Figure 17 version appears much more impressive, has a more professional tone, describes a candidate who comes across as more technically skilled, and is more likely to answer the "what's this person going to do for me?" question that most interviewers have on their minds when they're reading resumes. And I didn't add one claim that could be called a lie. It's all verbiage and pumping.

FIGURE 17. FULLY PUMPED VERSION OF THE SUMMARY OF QUALIFICATIONS SECTION SHOW IN FIGURE 16

General Accounting
Comprehensive hands-on and supervisory experience in the preparation of entries in books of original entry and subsidiary ledgers. Wide-ranging and in-depth experience in the preparation of complex federal, state, and city tax returns.

Financial Reports
Extensively versed in the design and preparation of monthly and

annual financial reports, forecasts, and comparative analyses.

Auditing
Successful experience in the performance and supervision of complex, detailed audits of balance sheets and income statement accounts for a variety of clients in many industries.

Cost Accounting
Provided consulting services to a wide array of clients in designing and implementing cost systems for existing and near-horizon production plans.

Systems
Extensive and applied knowledge of computerized accounting procedures (including one write systems, IBM inventory controls).

Of course, the summary-of-qualifications section shown in Figure 17, as improved as it is, still has several basic design flaws. First of all, it doesn't contain any statistics, such as "improved account accuracy by 20 percent," or "contributed to a 27 percent increase in consulting revenues." The use of such numbers is critical if you want to give your resume a hard-hitting and "can get results" feel. Needless to say, if you don't have any exact figures handy, you make them up. If you claim to have reduced turn-around time on processed claims by 17 percent, who's going to dispute that? Chances are that your old boss didn't even know what you were doing most of the time, much less how well you did it.

One additional major design flaw in the summary-of-qualifications sections shown in Figures 16 and 17 is the lack of a qualifications statement that pumps up the personal character, integrity, and outstanding work habits of the candidate. Figure 18 presents a sample of three personal-character statements, any one of which could have been used in the summary-of-qualifications section shown in Figure 17.

FIGURE 18. SAMPLE PERSONAL-CHARACTER STATEMENTS

Dynamic, resourceful accounting professional. Conscientious, analytical and well-organizated accounting professional with in-depth and wide-ranging experience in all facets of accounting science.

Industrious and disciplined accounting systems expert. A patient, methodical, yet highly productive individual who excels in high-pressure, time-sensitive situations.

Detail-minded, imaginative financial analyst. Aggressive yet diplomatic finance professional with exceptional abilities for follow through and planning.

As Figure 18 clearly demonstrates, the personal-character statement is out-and-out pumping. After all, who's to be the judge of "exceptional abilities," "analytical," and "excels in high-pressure, time-sensitive situations"? They know that the board of Certified Public Accountants didn't write the resume after years of careful observation of your work habits, but that doesn't matter. The content of the personal-character statement will influence the reader's mind-set in a way that will lead them to more favorably interpret the information presented in the remainder of the resume.

Those who don't pump with a personal-character

statement in the summary-of-qualifications section are missing a big chance to make themselves look a lot better with little or no effort. When you use a personal-character statement, be sure to use terms that are flattering for the types of jobs you're after. Not all words describe characteristics that are universally valued in every profession. For example, qualities such as "methodical" and "modest" might not make the most effective impression if you're going after a sales job, but would be excellent for a researcher.

Of course, the key to successful verbiage pumping is in the words themselves. Figures 19 through 22 present a variety of words which can be used to upgrade the pump quotient of your resume's summary-of-qualifications and job experience sections. Figure 19 presents a list of action words which should be used to characterize all of your past activities. For example, you didn't "hire two people to work for you." Rather, you "recruited and supervised the day-to-day activities of several line personnel." You didn't "come up with new ways of doing the work"; you "conceived, designed, implemented, and administered several productivity-enhancement programs."

FIGURE 19. RECOMMENDED ACTION WORDS FOR PUMPING

Accelerated	Administered	Arbitrated
Accomplished	Advised	Arranged
Achieved	Alerted	Assembled
Activated	Analyzed	Assisted
Actuated	Anticipated	Attracted
Adapted	Appraised	Audited
Addressed	Approved	Authored

Built
Calculated
Catalogued
Charted
Checked
Closed up
Collected
Compiled
Completed
Composed
Compounded
Conceived
Concluded
Conducted
Conferred
Confined
Conserved
Consolidated
Constructed
Consulted
Contracted
Contributed
Controlled
Cooperated
Coordinated
Corrected
Corresponded
Counseled
Created
Criticized
Decreased
Delegated
Delivered
Detected
Determined
Developed
Devised
Diagnosed
Diagrammed
Directed
Disapproved
Disciplined
Discovered
Dispensed
Disproved
Disseminated
Distributed
Documented
Doubled
Edited
Effected
Eliminated
Enhanced
Enlarged
Established
Evaluated
Examined
Exceeded
Executed
Expanded
Expedited
Facilitated
Fashioned
Forecasted
Formulated
Founded
Funneled
Gathered
Generated
Governed
Grouped
Guided
Harmonized
Headed
Identified
Illuminated
Illustrated
Implemented
Improved
Increased
Indexed
Influenced
Informed
Initiated
Innovated
Installed
Instituted
Instructed
Interpreted
Interviewed
Introduced
Invented
Investigated
Issued
Launched
Lectured
Led
Logged
Made
Maintained
Managed
Maximized
Minimized
Moderated
Modernized
Modified
Motivated
Navigated
Negotiated
Obtained
Operated
Optimized
Ordered
Organized
Originated
Overhauled
Oversaw
Participated
Performed
Pinpointed

Planned
Positioned
Prepared
Prescribed
Presented
Presided
Processed
Procured
Produced
Programmed
Promoted
Proposed
Protected
Provided
Realized
Received
Recommended
Reconciled
Recorded
Recruited
Rectified
Reduced
Refined
Removed
Rendered
Reorganized
Replaced
Reported
Represented
Researched
Reshaped
Restored
Routed
Revamped
Reviewed
Revised
Revitalized
Safeguarded
Saved
Scheduled
Secured
Selected
Served
Serviced
Set up
Shaped
Shut down
Simplified
Slashed
Sold
Solved
Sorted
Sparked
Speeded up
Staffed
Started
Stimulated
Straightened
Streamlined
Strengthened
Structured
Studied
Suggested
Terminated
Tested
Tied together
Took charge
Trained
Transacted
Translated
Triggered
Upgraded
Used
Verified
Wrote

Figure 20 presents a list of words which are helpful in putting together effective personal-character statements in your summary-of-qualifications section. Use at least three or four of the adjectives in each personal-character statement.

FIGURE 20. USEFUL ADJECTIVES FOR PUMPING PERSONAL-CHARACTER STATEMENTS

Accurate
Active
Adaptable
Adept
Aggressive
Alert

Ambitious	Eloquent	Orderly
Analytical	Energetic	Organized
Articulate	Enterprising	Patient
Artistic	Enthusiastic	Perceptive
Assertive	Exacting	Persevering
Astute	Executive	Personable
Attentive	Extroverted	Poised
Capable	Fair	Positive
Cheerful	Follow-through	Practical
Competitive	Forceful	Precise
Composed	Forward-thinking	Productive
Confident	Frank	Professional
Congenial	Friendly	Proficient
Conscientious	Generous	Purposeful
Considerate	Genuine	Qualified
Consistent	Good-natured	Realistic
Contributor	High energy	Reliable
Cooperative	Honest	Resourceful
Courteous	Imaginative	Self-controlled
Creative	Independent	Self-reliant
Democratic	Industrious	Sincere
Dependable	Inspiring	Sociable
Detailed	Intuitive	Stable
Detail-minded	Kind	Stamina
Determined	Knowledgeable	Systematic
Dignified	Logical	Tactful
Diplomatic	Loyal	Thoughtful
Discerning	Mature	Tolerant
Disciplined	Methodical	Truthful
Discrete	Modest	Understanding
Economical	Objective	Versatile
Effective	Observant	Vigorous
Efficient	Optimistic	Well-educated

Figure 21 presents a list of words which are useful in pumping up your claims of experience. Many poor resume writers simply say that they have "experience in this" and "experience in that" and expect the reader to be impressed.

No way. If you simply claim "experience," you're leaving it up to the reader to determine what type of experience it was. If he just interviewed a real loser who had years of experience but was basically a clown, "experience" isn't going to help. Yet, if you claim "successful experience" or "first-hand, applied experience," you're setting up an expectation that your experience is valid and significant.

Better, if your entire resume is sprinkled with flattering characterizations of your experience, the overall expectation you'll establish will be very positive. Whenever you use the word "experience," or a substitute, use one of the words from Figure 21 to precede it.

FIGURE 21. EFFECTIVE ADJECTIVES FOR THE WORD "EXPERIENCE"

Administrative	Intensive	Significant
Applied	Major	Sound
Comprehensive	Management	Structured
Executive	Outstanding	Substantial
Extensive	Performance-oriented	Successful
First-hand	Positive	Technical
Ground-floor	Practical	Thorough
Hands-on	Profitable	Versatile
In-depth	Proven	Well-rounded

Of course, if you're doing a good pump job on your resume, you'll be filling it with your industry's counterparts of "successful experience in accounting systems," "extensive experience in retail sales," and "comprehensive experience in all facets of manufacturing operations." It doesn't take very long for the reader to get tired of the word "experience" itself. If you don't vary it a little, it begins to sound like a litany of "experience, experience, experience."

Figure 20 can come to your aid again by providing a helpful list of words which you can substitute for the word *experience*. So, instead of "successful experience in retail sales," you state, "proficient in all facets of retail sales" or "adept in one-to-one retail sales." I recommend that you use one of these substitutes for every third reference to your "experience."

The Use of Slight But Flattering Lies

There's a fine distinction between the aggressive use of effective verbiage and the use of actual, but small, lies. Both are expected on resumes but it's a good idea to keep what you're doing straight in your mind. It's easy to get carried away and begin to use medium to big lies as part of the pumping process (after all, if a little lying works, why not use a lot?).

While there's certainly nothing wrong with wholesale lying, the danger is that you'll end up putting together lie systems without the planning and attention to detail that's essential to success in interviews. The lies we're talking about in this section are lies which don't require a formal lie system (the lie, the story, and the supporting data) to back them up. You should be able to support pumping related lies with a simple explanation or two without having to worry about complicating another part of your story. Let's look at an example.

Figure 22 presents a job-experience section taken word-for-word from an actual resume. As an interesting sidelight on job-search lying, the resume from which this was taken claimed an M.A. degree from the institution at which I earned my Ph.D. The only problem is that the school doesn't have an M.A. program in the area the applicant was claiming (the degree was supposedly "earned" at the same time I was there, and in my major). Worse yet, the applicant claimed to have obtained the degree while working 40 hours per week during the day for the U.S. government. The school did not have an evening program in my area! This just goes to show how carefully you have to put your story together to make it foolproof (although the odds are that nobody would stumble onto the actual truth as I did; in this case, it was a one-in-a-million shot).

Given the above comments, I hesitate to call the job-experience section in Figure 22 a non-lying version. Let's just say that it's poorly-written, non-pumped, and badly lied version (what a mess!).

FIGURE 22. INEFFECTIVE LYING IN A JOB-EXPERIENCE SECTION FROM AN ACTUAL RESUME

May 1982 to September 1985
U.S. CIVIL SERVICE
Washington, D.C.

Employee Training Specialist
I developed and conducted training programs designed to alleviate problems. I worked with the Managers of the Forms and Regulations Division, in designing effective training programs for its staffs. I developed and conducted in-house supervisory, secretarial, and instructor training programs and new employee orientations which involved supervision of 30 union supervisors

bimonthly. I consulted with managers, section heads, and supervisors on training needs.

Figure 23 presents a fully pumped and lie-covered version of the same job-experience version. In terms of resume style, note the dropping of the use of "I," the separate "Responsibilities" and "Achievements" sections, and the use of several "small" lies which nobody could easily expose.

FIGURE 23. FULLY PUMPED AND LIE-SATURATED VERSION OF THE JOB-EXPERIENCE SECTION SHOWN IN FIGURE 22

May 1982 to September 1985
U.S. CIVIL SERVICE
Washington, D.C.

Employee Training Specialist
Responsibilities: Complete divisional responsibility for the development and delivery of productivity enhancement and management-development training programs. Provided consulting resource directly to division heads in areas of training, productivity, and employee relations. Supervision of 30 personnel. *Achievements:* Developed numerous new training and organizational-development programs and interventions which contributed to lower supervisory turnover and decreased absenteeism. Implemented division-wide secretarial skills program which increased clerical and secretarial efficiency by 11 percent. Administered the delivery of 11,200 person-hours of training, a 22 percent increase over previous years with an 8 percent decrease in staff.

The lying pump job shown in Figure 23 is one that any job-seeking liar would be proud to call his own. Note the use of many statistics, such as "11,200 person-hours" (always use "person" instead of "man"; too many people in personnel work are women and minorities and they're pathologically sensitive to even the most innocent of unintended slurs -- there's no sense taking a chance), "22 percent increase," and "8 percent decrease in staff." All of these statistics make the resume writer not only look like he can get results, but also make it appear as if they really kept track of what was going on. The best part is that nobody could ever check the numbers, especially if the checking was done a year or two later. If you tell little lies that flatter the entire operation as well as yourself, nobody who's giving a reference would have any reason to say anything negative, even if they weren't sure of the numbers. Note also the "supervised 30 personnel." There's no sense in wasting valuable resume space by mentioning that it was only for a few hours every other month. If questioned, you'd simply say something to this effect: "The supervisors reported to me on a dotted line in terms of their responsibilities for implementing the training programs. I worked closely with them as needed and participated in their annual reviews to the extent that their sections were implementing organizational-change programs." Say what? You get the point.

As long as you act sincere and don't try to hide the actual truth if they go looking for it, the pumping actually looks even better; they'll see that you're being honest (fat chance of that!) at the same time that you can write a very professional and businesslike resume.

Figures 24 and 25 present another example of before and after job-experience sections. Figure 24 was presented as part of an example of a good resume in the latest edition of a very famous job-search book by a well-known headhunter who uses his name to peddle watered-down advice. The job-experience section shown in Figure 24 isn't particularly bad, but it's not going to impress many resume screeners. It sounds like it was written by a sixth grader, it's too wordy, not hard-hitting enough, and obviously not filled with the little lies upon which interview invitations are made. The fully pumped and lie-injected version presented in Figure 25 will be much more effective.

FIGURE 24. NON-PUMPED JOB-EXPERIENCE SECTION FROM A FAMOUS JOB-SEARCH BOOK

March 1981 to Present
ACME BIRTH CONTROL DEVICES, INC.
Sweet Slue, GA

Controller
Responsibilities include financial reporting, reviewing applicable accounting standards to insure maximum internal control. Prepare capital expenditure reports for parent company. Supervise internal auditing, cost and tax departments. Conduct special analyses of acquisitions. In complete charge of budgets and cash flow. Liaison with computer department. Understand Systems 34. The finance department has been operating at the same cost as it did four years ago even though sales have increased by 50 percent. This has been mentioned at every

executive committee meeting as an example of good management.

The fully pumped version in Figure 25 is a work of lying art and skill which will live through the ages. The beauty of lying "just a little" is that few of the people who worked (or work) with you, in any job, will know enough about what you do to enable them to question your claims. Even more incredible (and we'll discuss it at length in Chapter Ten) is the fact that such claims are hardly ever mentioned if the interviewer actually talks to a reference (if you elect to provide an actual reference rather than a phony one).

Note the "semantic lie" in Figure 25, "Direct majority of computer enhancements for division." It sounds great, but of course it's not true; the applicant merely worked with the people in the data processing department on finance-related projects. Yet, it could be true because many finance people are involved extensively in computers these days. If anyone should ask, the candidate would simply state something like, "Well, we were doing an awful lot of enhancements for finance and budgets, billing, and so forth. I handled all of the project-management duties associated with the enhancements. Of course, I didn't have extensive (meaning anything at all) involvement with all (any) enhancements in production." Sounds reasonable to me and I'm always sensitive to lies. If an employer didn't expect a lie, he wouldn't ask or worry, he'd simply read the resume, be impressed, and forget about it. Most interviewers will do the same.

FIGURE 25. FULLY PUMPED AND LIE-INJECTED VERSION OF THE JOB-EXPERIENCE SECTION PRESENTED IN FIGURE 24

March 1981 to Present
ACME BIRTH CONTROL DEVICES, INC.
Sweet Slue, GA

Controller
Responsibilities: Total accountability for all financial reporting and controls. Direct 22 finance professionals in all aspects of reporting, account management, forecasts, and planning. Conduct capital expenditure analyses for parent company. Supervise internal auditing, cost and tax departments. Conduct special analyses of acquisitions. Direct majority of computer enhancements for division. In complete charge of budgets and cash flow. *Achievements:* Improved efficiency of department over 50 percent. Implemented numerous new computerized financial reports using Systems 34. Improved forecasting accuracy by 27 percent. Reduced accounts receivable by 17 percent, resulting in average annual interest savings of $275,000. Implemented more accurate capital budgeting procedure which reduced capital expenditure reserves by 18 percent.

DON'T OVERPUMP

Everything in this chapter is pretty tame stuff in the world of job-search lying -- types of lies I expect you to be able to implement without reading any further. If you have no serious job-history problems, proper verbiage and pumping, exceptional materials, and good search strategies, this will be all you'll need to dramatically improve your odds of finding a job quickly.

But don't try to make the gentle art of resume

pumping do the job of full-blown, gut-busting lying. If you have problems of the types mentioned in Chapter Five, don't try to fix them by more aggressively applying the techniques of this chapter alone. Overpumping is much more dangerous than not pumping at all. If you neglect to pump your resume, it'll look standard, boring, and unexciting. That's bad, but somehow, even pedestrian, boring clods always manage to finally get a job somewhere.

With a serious problem, you need to bring in the serious lies. Pumping can't take care of serious problems on its own because it's not a lie system; pumping is the frosting on the cake. If you try to overpump rather than use lie systems, you'll end up looking ridiculous because you're putting too much frosting on a weak foundation; this is like putting six pounds of frosting on a cupcake. Don't try to make pumping do more than it's designed to do: enhance the overall effect of whatever your basic story is going to be. Lie all you want (or need) on your resume (using the techniques of the following chapters) and then apply the techniques of this chapter to your resume. That type of pumping will enhance your lies so they'll appear natural, sound outstanding, and look impressive.

Chapter Seven

The All-Purpose Lie

This chapter presents one of the most generally useful and easiest-to-apply lie strategies: claiming that you are (in your "present" job) or were (in a "prior" job) a consultant or self-employed. This lie is extremely handy because it is easy to set up and substantiate. More importantly, it sounds very impressive. This chapter will show you how to establish a phony period of consultancy or self-employment in your job history.

WHY CONSULTANCY AND SELF-EMPLOYMENT LIES WORK

There are two principal reasons why claiming to have been a consultant or self-employed works so well. The first reason derives from the ease of using this lie. The second reason is based upon employers' perceptions of what it's like to be a consultant and/or self-employed. You must have a clear understanding of these reasons so that you can play up to them in your lying.

The reason why the self-employment or consultancy lies are so easy to tell is that you're in total control of almost all of the data elements. If you're a finance type and you say that you were self-employed as a tax preparer/consultant, you're in total command of the lie system you'll be using. You don't have to worry about meshing your story with an actual company as you would if you were setting up a phony job. And you'd be in complete control of phony references because you could use all sorts of friends as "past customers."

If you were claiming to have been a financial consultant to businesses, all you'd need would be a few friends who could say that you consulted with their "privately owned investment company." Who's to dispute it?

The self-employment lie is easy for any category of employee. Suppose you're a factory worker and you want to step up or don't want to admit having been out of work for ten months. You can claim to have operated your own business for the last two years in which you supervised 15 people in all aspects of home repair, cleaning services, landscaping, construction, and so on. All of a sudden, you're not "only" a factory worker, but you're a seasoned supervisor and businessperson! A few phony references, a few business cards, and you're in business.

The second reason why this type of lie is so useful is that there's an intense fascination with consultants and self-employed businesspeople in this country (and over much of the world) which is all out of proportion with reality.

Most people who work for large companies feel stifled and trapped. They think they're being held back by the system and treated like third-class employees. In most companies, of course, they're correct in their perceptions (most of them deserve such treatment but that's another story). At the same time, they're fascinated and jealous of people who work for themselves. They've all read the stories of self-made millionaires and high-level consultants who fly from job to job in their personal Lear jets and they fantasize about themselves being in the same situation. As a result, they respect and envy consultants and self-employed people.

Most typical employees, particularly people in personnel who deal with many different consultants, believe that being a consultant would solve all of their problems. They therefore view anyone who is or has been a consultant with special respect and a little awe. This becomes a great advantage when you're trying to get them to hire you.

Of course, the reality of consulting or running your own business is much different. It's important for you to understand why it's different so you can explain why you want to give up the golden spoon to work for them. The truth is that most consultants are scratching along, barely making it from one house payment to the next, and most self-employed people are even worse off. Thousands of self-employed people lose their shirts every year as a result of economic variations in the economy, a bigger competitor moving in down the street and taking all the business, and/or simple mismanagement.

And then there's the work load. If you're in business for yourself, you work one hell of a lot more than 40 hours per week. It's more like 60, with no one to take up the slack if you're having a bad day or you're sick (most self-employed people claim 80 to 120-hour workweeks but this is usually poorly executed lying). You don't want to tell them you have it bad, as it'll make you appear to be a complainer or a loser but you do want them to know it's rough and not as much fun. They'll then like you even more for easing their jealousy.

THE WORLD OF CONSULTANTS

A consultant is one who provides a service to a client company for a fee. The consultant may be self-employed (an independent consultant), may work as part of a consulting firm (as a regular employee of the consulting firm which consults with other companies), or may be an employee of an organization who consults at large within it (an in-house consultant).

I advise you to claim that you were (or are) a self-employed consultant if you decide to use this lie. If you claim to have worked with a firm of consultants, or as an in-house consultant, you complicate your lie system by having to provide phony references for the job. In effect, you're using the fictitious job strategy rather than the consultant strategy. That's okay if that's what you need, but why make it hard on yourself? Unless you perceive that you need the increased prestige and image for your consulting "reputation" which association with a large consulting company can bring, you might as well claim to have gone it alone.

Consultants who work for consulting companies are much like employees of any company who work for a salary and an occasional bonus. Self-employed consultants work under all sorts of arrangements, depending upon the nature of the service, the industry they're working in, and complexity of the work.

How a Consultant Operates

Consultants work for a fee that's negotiated in advance. Some of the fee-arrangement terms which are handy to toss around when you're sounding like a consultant are:

Fixed Fee (FF)

This means that the negotiated or proposed work will be done for an agreed-upon set price. If the project runs over estimated costs, the consultant takes it up the shorts.

Cost Plus Fixed Fee (CPFF)

This is the fee arrangement most common in work done for the government. The consultant is guaranteed a fixed fee (usually 8 to 12 percent) in addition to reimbursement for all costs. The proposal (more on this in a minute) usually estimates the costs but, once the contract is signed, costs have a convenient way of getting out of control (meaning that the consultant gets to work more hours which include a lot of money for overhead expenses). The costs include all labor hours, materials, travel, and so on.

Time and Materials (T&M)

This is the fee arrangement most typical of technical consulting services in private industry. A set rate is agreed upon for the cost of an hour's worth of work and the consultant simply bills the client for the cost of each hour spent on the project. There's typically an agreement as to how much work will be done in an hour (such as checking one ledger book in eight hours or interviewing six job candidates in eight hours). The materials are costs for travel, lunches, and other non-labor expenses. There are many other variants of fee arrangements, but most consultants work those given above.

A consultant's service is usually technical advice of some sort or the provision of a service that involves professional skills. Companies call in a consultant when they don't have the available skills or time to look into a problem themselves. Often, they're looking for a different viewpoint. If you're in a professional or technical area such as medicine, law, finance of almost any kind, engineering, human resources, data processing, and the like, you can very easily claim to have been a consultant, as these are the areas in which they're most often used. If you're working in an area such as traffic routing of shipments, or claims processing in an insurance company, it's going to be a little more difficult to set up a credible consulting lie which relates directly to your past jobs; there would be few opportunities for consultants to work for a company in these areas. There are consultants in every conceivable area, but most are not widely known or seen.

You should avoid lying about things that are way out of the ordinary businessperson's realm of experience. For example, there are probably consultants who specialize in secretarial shorthand work. If you've been a secretary and want to claim a consulting gig, it would not be smart to claim to have been a shorthand-consulting specialist (even if you are expert in it) as it would appear strange and possibly raise attention. Better in that case to claim to have been an office-efficiency consultant specializing in secretarial and support functions. You'd get the same result but the lie would work more comfortably and be accepted more often without notice.

Consultants get business by several means. Almost all consultants claim to get most of their business from satisfied clients who refer friends and business associates. This is generally a lie. Most consultants to private industry spend 50 to 90 percent of their time hustling up business by telephone solicitations, rubbing elbows at social functions, and mailing brochures and letters to executives. Since few non-consultants know or want to believe this truth (it dashes their fantasies of how "great" it would be to be a consultant), it's better to claim to have obtained all of your business through contacts (you might as well lie just like a consultant). The interviewers will be impressed at your connections and they won't be so apt to ask to see copies of brochures and mailers.

Most consulting business from the federal government is obtained by reading the *Commerce Business Daily* (called the *CBD*) which is published weekdays by the Commerce Department of the U.S. government. The *CBD* lists all of the RFPs (Requests for Proposals) and RFQs (Requests for Qualifications) from all branches of the U.S. government and military which are seeking to purchase goods or services for which there are no existing agreements. The RFPs are solicitations for proposals and the RFQs are requests for outlines of firms' capabilities for specific projects which will supposedly be used to design future RFPs (RFQs are actually used to see what problems the agency will encounter when it attempts to "throw" an upcoming project to a favored consultant; see unsolicited proposals below). Each entry in the *CBD* runs from two lines to half a column and describes what the government wants in general terms. Most people who are not consultants have never seen a copy of the *CBD* because it costs quite a bit. So don't worry about lying about having received it.

If a consultant is interested in the RFP, he sends away for the "proposal packet" which describes in detail what the government wants and how the proposal must be organized. The proposal packets are anywhere from 20 to 100 pages long for typical technical consulting and can run into thousands of pages for complex engineering jobs. Nobody will admit it but it's generally believed that most agencies have already made up their minds who they're going to award the contracts to before the RFPs are posted. That's why many sage old consultants claim that it's a waste of time to bid (prepare a proposal) in response to an RFP.

Much work is obtained through "unsolicited proposals" in which the consultant sees a need (or dreams one up) and sends in a proposal which isn't expected. Typically, the consultant and the agency work together in secret on unsolicited proposals for whatever the agency wants done. A good unsolicited proposal eliminates, in many cases, the need to open the bidding up to all comers. This is done all the time when some government bureaucrat doesn't want to have a bunch of idiots getting involved in making suggestions on his project. That's why so many retired government personnel work for consulting firms; their old buddies still on the job will arrange to throw them business via unsolicited proposals. As you can see, the entire morass of government consulting is a moral cesspool which makes job-search lying look like a solemn novena to the patron saint of honesty.

The major problem with lying about having been a consultant to the federal government, aside from the minor one of references, is what you're going to do if someone asks to see a proposal that you've worked on. You can always say you don't have any copies left but it sounds bad even if it's the truth. I've done a lot of consulting with the government myself as an employee of a consulting company and I don't have any copies of my work done. Since everyone is so jealous of consultants, they expect you to have a whole library of proposals, RFP, and so on, just like they imagine they'd have if they were a consultant. If you're not trying to get a job with a federal contractor, a good way to handle the rare request for work samples is to claim that everything you worked on was classified top secret. In many cases of consultants, that's true. If they're not in the business, they won't know. You simply claim to have done your work with a government agency like the CIA or the Joint Chiefs of Staff and nobody is going to wonder why you don't have work samples.

In private industry, most business is obtained by sales techniques and the proposals tend to be a lot more informal. Some big companies will post RFP in the major papers but usually they simply notify a few consultants/consulting companies of their needs and then review the proposals. If you're going to claim that you did a lot of consulting work with private companies, it's better to claim that you worked on very informal hand-shake agreements on a Time and Materials basis. This eliminates the need to come up with examples of proposals. Being asked for sample proposals is a very low-probability event, but it could happen. I've used the independent-consultant lie many, many times and I've only had one person ask me in detail how I got my business and ask to see a sample proposal. The guy worked for one of the large aerospace contractors and I think he wanted to steal some of my proposal-formatting ideas. You can't expect to always be lucky enough not to be asked for samples, so be sure to discourage them early in the interview process with either the top-secret or informal lie.

THE WORLD OF SELF-EMPLOYMENT

As mentioned above, many consultants are independent, self-employed businesspeople whose business happens to be consulting. Many occupations don't readily facilitate the use of the "I was a consultant" lie. If you're seeking work as an electrician, production supervisor, secretary, and so on, it's difficult to claim that you were a consultant in that field. Of course, if you're trying to lie your way into another field, you can always claim to have been a consultant in the new area, giving you instant experience.

If claiming to have been a consultant doesn't fit

your job specialty or your inclinations, you can claim self-employment. Anyone in any type of endeavor can claim to have been self-employed. The only exceptions are for types of work that only large corporations do for themselves, such as compensation and benefits specialists. But in those cases, you can claim to have consulted! It's up to you.

Be careful of occupations where you need to have a license to operate as a self-employed business. It's one thing to claim to have been a consultant, which requires no license; it's quite another to claim to have been a building contractor, which requires a license. If they ask what your license number is, you're in trouble.

Another type of self-employment lie that must be avoided is the one which claims possession of a professional license to practice. The danger isn't so much in your potential employer asking to see the license, as few will, but in liability risks if something goes wrong. For example, if you were to claim that you're a Certified Public Accountant and get a job on the basis of the lie, you could be liable for damages if the firm sues you for making an error when they found out that you don't have a license. They probably wouldn't sue anyone for a normal error if the employee had a license, but your lack of one would provide them with a convenient scapegoat upon which they could vent their frustration and anger. Areas such as social work, psychology, and the like are similarly dangerous if you're caught in a lie about licenses, especially since there may be criminal charges filed.

As you can imagine, it's far safer and easier to

substantiate less complex self-employment lies. Claims of having run a small business with five to ten employees are always good, particularly if you're merely trying to establish a history of general business and supervisory experience. You'll look like you've had exposure to all of the nuts and bolts of business such as hiring, firing, supervision, budgets, planning, marketing, and so on. At the same time, you'll have the "aura" of one who has competed in the great capitalistic struggle on your own and lived to tell. This looks very good to employers. What's more, such experience looks even better when you're attempting to get back into the comfortable folds of a big company; it makes all the losers who would never try it on their own feel as if they're not quite the failures they know they really are. See, your lying is actually helping people feel better about themselves!

SELF-EMPLOYMENT AND CONSULTING LIE SYSTEMS

Unlike the small, simple "pumping up your qualifications" lies presented in Chapter Six, lies about consulting and self-employment require full-blown lie systems.

If you want to make these strategies work dependably, you'll have to develop all of the elements of the lie system before you venture forth to lie your way into a new job. As you'll recall from Chapter Three, a lie system requires several elements: the lie itself, the "story," and the supporting data. Let's take a look at how a lie system is put together for one situation which requires a consulting lie and another situation which requires a self-employment lie. In the appropriate story and supporting-data sections, we'll discuss the typical concerns and data elements that you'll have to deal with in building your own lie systems.

Consulting Lies: The Situation

Jack Stoutheart is looking for a job in personnel administration. For the past three years, he's had a series of five really bad job experiences. He had two jobs that lasted less than six months, one of which he was fired from, and none of the jobs has been anything more than a clerical personnel job. Prior to the string of bad jobs, he had been working as a compensation analyst for the reputable, well-known firm of Ajax Chemicals, Ltd. His salary there had been $24,000 per annum. He left that job to take a chance on a unknown company which looked like it was growing fast. The new job turned out to be a loser and the company went out of business in nine months, forcing Jack to take whatever he could get in a hurry. The result: one bad job after another, none of which paid more than $16,000 a year.

He knows that he's in trouble if he tells the truth, as he looks like a hyperactive job hopper with serious adjustment and judgment problems. Worse yet, he's lost three years and he's in a low-level position. Even if he could get a decent job, he'd have to start right back at the bottom. In terms of the job-search problems outlined in Chapter Five, Jack faces problems one (too many jobs), two (been fired), and seven (needs step up). Jack decides to employ the "I've been a consultant lie" as a primary lie system (strategy H from Chapter Five) which will require using strategies G (dropping a job), D (altering references), and C (altering compensation) as secondary lie systems.

Consulting Lies: The Lie System

"I have been working for the past three years as an industrial-relations consultant in the areas of compensation and benefits." Jack's resume shows the following job-experience section for the past three years.

Jack's job-experience section for the above lie is shown in Figure 26.

FIGURE 26. JOB-EXPERIENCE SECTION FOR PHONY CONSULTING JOB

June 1983 to Present
STOUTHEART ASSOCIATES
New York, NY

President, Owner
Responsibilities: Market and conduct/direct consulting support to small- to medium-sized firms in the areas of compensations and benefit analyses and evaluations. Direct from 2 to 7 support staff and consultants. *Achievements:* Marketed and conducted numerous wage and salary surveys, reviews of wage scales/job grading systems, and personnel research. Provided services to over 53 client firms in 7 different industries.

Consulting Lies: The Story

The story is the logic behind the lie, the pack of small lies that smoothly joins the major lie to whatever portions of reality you happen to be using. The story is what makes the bald-faced lie live, breathe, and be believed. I'll present the story in the words of Jack, so that you'll have some feel for the types of comments you'll have to make when putting together your own consulting lie system. Most of what Jack will say is generic consulting lie material; that is, you can use it almost word for word. Where comments by me are essential, I'll present them in parentheses. Following the section on supporting data, I'll present a final-discussion section which will discuss the advantages, dangers, and variants of "I was a consultant" lie systems.

"I was working at Ajax Chemicals, Ltd., and enjoying the job and learning a lot. The people there were outstanding and I believe that I would be with them today if the consulting opportunity hadn't come along." (Always pour on the praise for former employers, as this will put the interviewer at ease, make you seem like a winner and someone who's easy to work with, and will decrease the odds that they'll check references. Of course, since Jack can get a good reference from Ajax, the last decent job he had, he wants them to check, as the good reference will provide a smooth and believable point from which the consulting began.)

"One day, one of my friends, who was then president of a small manufacturing company with about 75 employees, asked me if I might be interested in performing a little consulting work on the side. I always wanted to try my hand at consulting, so I said okay. I did that first job at nights and on weekends while I was still at Ajax. It was very stimulating and I learned a lot. (It's important to provide a believable transition from full-time work to consulting, as few intelligent people are going to accept that you would simply quit a good job and dive right into consulting).

"From then on, things sort of took off on their own. One of my friend's suppliers needed some work done and I got that one by referral. The word spread that I did a good job, probably at too low a fee, and subsequently I had more than I could handle on a part-time basis. I knew that I'd probably never again have the opportunity to try it on my own if I didn't take advantage of the circumstances, so I quit my job at Ajax and went into consulting full-time.

"It's been fun and stimulating but the hours are a burden, sometimes 80 to 90 per week, and the money is fine but it doesn't always come in when you need it. And then there's the problem with getting good help when you need it. I've got some great people, including a couple of personnel-manager types, who work for me part-time away from their regular jobs, but they can't always hop right onto a project when I'm buried with two or three jobs at once. So, while I've learned more in the last three years than I would have learned in ten years on a regular job, I think I'd like to return to a more stable work environment and learn more about one organization than a little about many different ones."

This is all great stuff. Note the humble tack of having learned a lot but it's just too much work and too hard. This makes it believable that Jack would want to leave the "glamorous" world of consulting which the interviewer is jealous of. Better yet, it brings Jack down to the interviewer's level, as Jack is tacitly admitting he couldn't stand the heat in the kitchen.

Note also the "learned more in three years than I would have learned in ten years on a regular job." This makes Jack seem like more of a heavyweight and will help him substantiate a move to a position that's higher up the ladder than the job he had at Ajax. Also important is that Jack claims to have supervised several fairly high-level people. This will overcome any doubts about Jack's supervisory skills, should the job in question require previous supervisory experience.

Consulting Lies: Support Data

If everything goes as planned and you lie expertly, this lie can be pulled off with no more equipment than a three-piece suit and an attache case (the old joke is that a consultant is "anyone who's more than 40 miles from home and carrying an attache case"). Of course, few things work out as planned so you're going to need some supporting-data elements. As you'll recall, supporting data is the tangible evidence that you present to back up your lies. There's only one element in the consulting lie that's absolutely necessary. It is the reference.

1. References from Former Clients

One or two of these will put the seal of believability on your story. Best bets are friends who work for large companies who are willing to say that you did consulting work for them, either when they "recently had their own business" or at the firm where they work now. If you've got any highly placed friends, use them. Don't use anyone who has a low-level job that's readily apparent to the reference checker.

Out-of-town friends are great for this use, as you'll appear to have been a consultant who traveled around the country. People who don't do a lot of traveling think that it's exciting. It sucks, but claiming to have traveled a lot will make you look like you were a more prestigious consultant. There's also less chance that the reference checker will know anything about any actual out-of-town companies at which your friends might work. When you use in-town references, there's always a remote possibility that the reference checker may "know someone who knows someone" at the firm where you claimed to have been a consultant. Instead of calling your reference, they might call their own contact, who would say, "I never heard of this Jack Stoutheart. Besides, we don't use consultants, *ever*." This is a remote probability but it's lowered by using out-of-towners for phony references (if you have them). The reference should be told what the story is, as well as the general nature of the work you did for them. Don't make your claims too grandiose (or someone may ask to see a report or two).

2. Business Cards and Stationery

You should have a set of 500 business cards made for your consulting firm, showing you as the owner or president. They'll cost less than $25 (unless you get fancy). The cards are extremely effective since they are tangible proof that you are what you say you are. You should present them to each of the people who interviews you. The little pieces of cardboard will go far in building your credibility.

Business stationery is even more impressive, if you use it to answer the classified ads. It will not only make you appear more professional compared to all of the "plain employees" who are seeking the job, it will also validate your consulting claims right from the instant they open your envelope. This is the one instance when it's permissible to respond to an ad using an employer's stationery: when it's your own company. You can get 100 to 200 sheets of business stationery, patterned after the cards, of course, printed up for $25 to $50. Matching envelopes are essential. Go to a few printers and take a look at their sample books. You'll see many examples which are attractive and convincing.

3. Work Samples

You may run into an employer who wants to play hardball and wants to see a work sample. If you haven't been a consultant in the area you're lying about, you have a problem. Aside from the top-secret and informal ploys, the best solution is to try to find one ahead of time, from friends or a library, and then have it retyped after you edit it into shorter form.

A good source of many impressive-looking research reports can be the Ph.D. dissertation or M.A. (or M.B.A.) thesis shelves of a local university. If you were Jack Stoutheart, claiming to be compensations specialist, you could always go to the M.B.A. section and poke around until you found a thesis or dissertation on some aspect of the local area's compensation practices. If it was recent (last year or two) or current with the dates of the consulting work you were claiming, you could edit it down, get it retyped, and you're in business, probably for about $100.

This situation demonstrates the necessity of

always taking copies of anything that looks remotely useful with you when you leave a job. If someone does a market study, get a copy. If someone has a proposal for anything, get a copy. You can never tell when you'll need them. In every industry, there are many special studies and surveys which are prepared regularly. If you get one of them retyped, and change the wording a little, you'll have an acceptable work sample. An alternative route is to simply state that you "don't share clients' work with anyone, as a matter of policy." If you can come across cool enough, this works fine. It's my chosen approach, as it eliminates the need for a lot of messy secretarial work and expense. Another alternative is to say that you've been on so many interviews lately that you've used them all up and don't have any more copies. Use the statement, "After all, I tried to keep secretarial costs down so I only kept a copy or two. Everyone I gave them to promised they'd return them but little by little they're all gone. I'm sure that my references can provide you with detailed information about my work." Nobody ever asks references detailed questions so you're home free.

4. Answering Machine or Service

It's pretty hard to convince anyone with a brain that you're working as a consultant and you don't at least have an answering machine to record calls that come in. Many personnel people don't have brains but a rare few do. Those who do have more than four neurons might doubt your story if they call and your phone rings and rings. If you're job searching, an answering machine is essential, even if you're not lying, as employers will give up if they call twice (or even once) and you're not there. If you don't have one, buy one. You can get a decent one for less than $100. If you do use an answering machine, use a serious, non-flaky message, such as: "Hello, you have reached (area code and number). No one is available to take your call right now. Please leave your name and number and I'll get back to you as soon as possible. Thank you for calling." A good alternative is to hire an answering service but, for more than a few months, it begins to run into high expense.

Consulting Lies: The Advantages

As mentioned earlier, the primary advantage of this strategy is the fact that you're in complete control if you set it up right. You can specify the type of work you did, the type of industries you worked in, the number and type of personnel you supervised, and how much you made. A major advantage is that so few people, even those quite successful in business, have any idea of how consultants actually operate. Their ignorance works in your favor.

This strategy is particularly effective if you're looking for a substantial pay boost. Jack was making only $25,000 per year in his last real job. He can easily claim to have made $50,000 per year in his last year of consulting if he's looking for a job in that range.

Be sure, however, not to price yourself out of the market. Nobody wants to hire someone who will have to take a pay cut; they assume the new employee will be unhappy and will leave at the first opportunity.

Also, be sure to have thought about the consultancy's gross income (total billings before taxes and expenses) and how much it netted (the money that was left over). If you can't answer a question about that sort of thing when they start to discuss salary, you're in trouble. For example, if they ask how much you made, and you say $30,000 but allude to gross income, they'll come back and offer you $25,000 with the comment, "Well, twenty-five thousand dollars should be a real pay boost for you since you'll have no marketing expenses or insurance costs." Then you're in trouble.

A good rule of thumb is to multiply the salary you're after by 1.5 and claim the total as your gross, explaining that you had a lot of expenses. Get this into the discussion as soon as they start talking money.

Consulting Lies: The Disadvantages

If you're fairly well versed in your area of expertise, you won't have any problems with handling content questions about your consulting assignments and how much you supposedly know about your field. If you're reasonably intelligent and have been doing a good job in your area, you know enough to be a consultant.

But problems arise if you haven't been doing very high-level work and you're trying to fake it. You might not sound like an expert in your field and this will set off alarm bells in the interviewer. If you can't sound like you know what you're supposed to have been doing working as a consultant in the field you've selected, try the self-employed gambit or fictitious-job lie (Chapter Eleven) instead.

Self-Employment Lies: The Situation

Ann Ruskin has been working as a secretary for five years in two different jobs since she graduated from business college. In both jobs, she was trying to work her way into a more responsible position but just couldn't make the jump from being a secretary to the lower rungs of management. She believes, probably correctly, that she's been typecast as a secretary and that few organizations would give her a chance at anything more. She decides to lie about what she has been doing rather than admit her current position, and attempt to get a new job as a supervisor.

Self-Employment Lies: The Lie System

"I've been operating my own secretarial-services company for the past three years."

Ann's job-experience section for her secretarial services company is shown in Figure 27.

FIGURE 27. JOB-EXPERIENCE SECTION FOR PHONY SELF-EMPLOYMENT JOB

December 1984 to Present
RUSKIN SECRETARIAL SERVICES, INC.
Los Angeles, CA

President, Owner
Responsibilities: Market and conduct/direct office-support and secretarial-services contracting to small businesses and professionals. Supervise 2 to 5 full and part-time employees. *Achievements:* Built business to annual gross of $80,000 in 15

months. Expanded to provide word-processing and transcription services.

Self-Employment Lies: The Story

"I started the company three years ago, after having worked as a secretary for two years. I took the first secretarial job because I wanted to get some experience in handling the real problems of not only secretaries and other support services but in what businesses need in terms of support personnel." (This shows good planning and foresight.)

"When I felt I had learned enough and done enough marketing to locate potential clients, I quit my job and started the company. At first, I had to be the manager and the employee, going out to be the fill-in secretary." (Note the use of the word "manager" so they'll start to think of Ann in that way). "But that was good experience (nothing is ever a problem for this comer!) and pretty soon I could begin to send other people out on jobs. I've tried to keep things small (which explains why they might not have heard of the "company") and get employees from personal contacts, retired office workers and the like. I mainly supply secretaries but we also do a little technical support work as well, although it's difficult to always have someone available." (The modesty is appropriate and shows a real businesslike sense of reality).

"I'm seeking an entry-level management position because I find that I really enjoy the complex challenges of juggling personnel and administrative problems. I know that I'd enjoy working for a much larger company than mine (flatter the interviewer's company and reinforce the "I ran my own company" lie) which would present me with opportunities to do more over the years and really grow as a business-person. Besides, to tell you the truth, (oh, the honesty of this person!) it's getting to be a strain, being the only one who's responsible for the entire operation. I'd like to operate with the safety net that larger companies have; there's someone else to worry about whether the light bill gets paid, and so on."

A good variation is to claim that you've already sold the business because the personal time demands became too large. This helps explain why you have the time to look for a job and also why you don't have to be at "work" (home) answering the phone and handling problems. You can then make the statement, "I recently sold the business and made enough to be able to take my time looking for a job." This enhances your aura of success.

This variant helps in another way. If you claim to currently be in a business, there's always the chance someone will want to use one of your "services." This is a problem if you don't have any. I had a friend who was using a "self-employed" air conditioning service company lie and, in the midst of the job search, got a call from the personnel manager of one of the companies he was interviewing with. The lady had remembered that he was in the business and needed to get her air conditioner fixed! He told her he was overloaded that day (luckily, it was a hot summer night so he had an excuse not to come right over) but told her he'd try to handle it. He called around, found somebody to fix it, had them bill him, and he billed her (plus five percent more which he gave to the repairman to help with the charade). Her firm hired him a week later as its director of maintenance. A happy ending but much too nerve-wracking for my tastes.

Self-Employment Lies: Support Data

The supporting-data elements here are much the same as they were in the consulting lie system. The one essential element is the set of references who can verify that they did, indeed, use your services. Interviewers will request these references less often than in the case of the consulting lie, because a consultant is attempting to obtain a position as a technical expert in his or field. The reference checkers want to be sure that the consultant knows his or her "stuff."

In the case of the self-employed "run the business" person, you're selling not technical expertise in a given area but a general mix of business skills. The mere fact that you ran a business for several years serves as "evidence" that you have these general skills. Nevertheless, you'll be wise to create several references. A good ploy is to create a reference that will claim to be buying you out as soon as you get a new job. This person can state that he is running a similar small business and wants to expand. This makes your business seem even more legitimate and valued. Almost any friend of yours can help by contending that he operates a small business and that he uses your services and/or wants to buy you out.

If you're claiming that you're still operating the business, an answering machine or service is critical to provide a good front. The business cards and stationery are also good convincers. Keep in mind that someone may ask how profitable you were (or are) and about how much the business is making. You can't afford to give them the answer which they deserve (which is "That's none of your business!"), so have some answers ready.

Remember, you want to position your income so that your earnings in the job you're after will be a small increase for you compared to the net income of the self-employment. That means that if you're after a $30,000 per year job, your after-expenses and -taxes net income from self-employment would have had to work out to about $25,000 to $28,000 per year. If you had employees in your business, remember to keep your story straight. It wouldn't sound good to claim that you had five full-time employees but only grossed $60,000; that wouldn't leave any money for expenses or your salary (not to mention that the employees would be starving on such low wages). That's why it's critical to think out the whole story ahead of time.

Self-Employment Lies: The Advantages

The primary advantage of claiming to have been self-employed is that you'll be automatically setting yourself up with supervisory skills (if there were employees; why not?) and general management background. If you claim three to five employees, you'll be seen as someone who had to do all of the unpleasant and challenging things that supervisors and managers are supposed to do, such as being tough and firing people.

It's also useful from the viewpoint of the technical skills qualifications of the job if the self-employment was in the technical area the prospective employer is after. So, if you're trying to get a job as supervisor of mechanics at an automotive dealership, it's smart to claim that your business was a custom automotive repair shop. If you're simply trying to get into general business areas, it's better if your phony business has an office "feel" to it, possibly secretarial services, productivity consulting, or the like. There will be many people who will believe that a person who has managed 20 mechanics isn't sufficiently sophisticated to manage 15 clerical staff. It's ridiculous but that's the business world. Fit your lies to their expectations.

Self-Employment Lies: The Disadvantages

There are few, if you can handle the technical content. As long as you keep your lies in line with your abilities, you'll have no problem with this type of lie.

One minor issue that will have to be dealt with in many interviews is the question of how you'll "fit in" after having been running your own show for so long. I always have to laugh when they ask this one. Usually when I'm asked that question, I'm stuck in some boring job, working my guts out for an idiot just like the interviewer, and he thinks I'm flying all over the country being a hot-shot consultant! And he wants to know if I can put up with all the frustration and regimentation of the typical office!

I say, "Of course, it's no problem. I find that having to deal with the myriad personalities of many customers and their demands is much more trying than learning to get along with a smaller group of people whom you come to know much better. Believe me, running my own business has taught me more than I ever wanted to know about putting up with frustration and making sacrifices for long-term gains." When asked this type of question, use the above answer almost word for word (do not take along the book and read it to them) and you'll have no problem.

SUMMARY

Aside from pumping up your credentials and qualifications as described in the last chapter, this consultant/self-employment technique is the most generally useful of the "replacement" job-search lies. If you've got to replace one or more bad jobs, or fill large, unsightly gaps in your employment record, try to find a way to apply a self-employment or consulting lie before you turn to any others. It's a classic because it's extremely believable and easily executed.

Chapter Eight

Altering the Facts

In Chapter Six, we discussed techniques for pumping up your existing qualifications and experiences in order to give your resume (and any resultant interviews) an enhanced aura of accomplishment and success. The techniques discussed in Chapter Six were not full-blown lies; if questioned, there was always some tentative link with reality which you could employ to explain the discrepancy. ("Well, the 'official' title of the job was 'Administrative Assistant' but I actually functioned as 'Assistant to the Chairman.' The Chairman had never had an assistant before and had said that there would be no new jobs created, so when he needed an assistant, I was hired in but a vacant and existing job slot was used.") That's not the case with the lies discussed in this chapter. The lies presented in this chapter expand the principles of pumping to the status of complete and total lies. If you get caught using the methods presented in this chapter, you'll be exposed as a liar. Of course, if you lie effectively, your odds of being exposed or suspected are low.

WHY TO USE LIES

Lies about job titles, responsibilities, achievements, and compensation are a very special category of job search lies. Unlike the consulting and self-employment lies, these lie about existing positions, not positions that are fictitious. As mentioned above, this entails a certain amount of additional risk, which can be reduced but never totally eliminated by proper technique. In the final analysis, there's always a real, live employer out there who could theoretically provide information that could refute your story. These lies aren't like the innocent pumping lies which enable you to walk a fine line between semantics and lying. So why would you use these types of lies when you could merely pump aggressively or more safely create a phony consulting position or a fictitious job?

The primary reason to consider these lies is that they're so easy to get away with that the small added risk is usually worth the returns. Depending upon what you're lying about, the manner in which the past employer verifies employment, and how you set up phony references (Chapter Nine), the ability of employers to catch you varies. Given proper technique on your part, and astute observations as to how the employer verifies references, you can always assure that your risk is very small before you try anything. If your risk appears greater than your need to use these particular lies, use another strategy.

Another reason why lies about aspects of actual jobs are popular and often attractive is that they're easy to tell from a stress viewpoint. It's hard work for a novice or fairly inexperienced liar to set up and maintain a fictitious job (at least the first few times, anyway). It's much easier, in terms of stress and the psychological burden, to lie about one or two aspects of an actual job while telling something that looks like the truth about the rest of it.

If you're not a practiced liar, you'll find that it's easier to lie about something if the lie is embedded in and delivered with the truth. If you actually had the job, most of what you say about it will be not lies but only job-search exaggerations. The few actual lies won't worry you as much because you'll be more relaxed. Simply because you'll be telling the truth most of the time, you'll feel less guilt, you'll demonstrate fewer stress responses, and everything you say, mundane truth and bold lies, will have the ring of candor and sincerity (it's almost enough to make you tell the truth more often).

In fact, most exceptional job-search liars (including me) started their lying careers by using the types of lies described in this chapter mixed with some elements of the truth. Once they find lying at a certain level comfortable and successful, they begin to lie more aggressively and completely, building up these skills to their full potential.

WHEN TO USE LIES

Lies about job credentials, dates, compensation, and so on are particularly effective in certain situations aside from the inherent advantages discussed. If you're facing one of these situations, you may have to consider these lies even if the risk is somewhat higher than you'd like (although it's never acceptable to take anything more than a low risk; see Chapter Thirteen for a discussion of the risks presented by various types of lies). These situations are:

1. You need the name or prestige of the company on your resume. If the company has a big name or great reputation in your field or industry, it may be almost essential that you include it on your resume. The names of well-known companies, particularly very large companies, are almost magic on a resume. The company's impact is fully out of proportion with anything additional you could have learned there, compared to what you would have learned at any respectable firm. If you can safely cover most of the reference-checking pitfalls, you may find that you want to try to keep even a bad job experience on your resume, in the hopes that the added impact of it will balance the added risk. In a sense, if you're looking for positions in a large industry with a great many potential employers, you probably can afford to take the risk.

The lie works in this way: if you're right about the prestige of the company's name in your industry/field, you'll probably find that the mere name of the past employer will get you into a lot more interviews than would the name of a fake, and therefore unknown company (or a real, but unknown company). Many of these interviewers won't bother to check any references, some will check them poorly, many reference checks will never be answered, and most will swallow your fake references hook, line, and sinker. In effect, a significant proportion of the interviews will be relatively safe. If you conduct a large search and have a great many interviews, there's always a very real (but small) chance that you could be exposed. At the same time, you'll almost certainly land a better job faster. You have to evaluate the risk and make a determination of how much risk you're willing to take (and how badly you need a job).

2. If the job was more than five years ago. If it's been more than five years since you worked for the company, it's probably safe to wildly distort many aspects of the job. The reason for this is that many companies don't have computerized personnel records and they don't keep all of their past files in an easily available location. For example, I work in the personnel department for one of the country's 50 largest companies. In our office, the only computers are PCs that are used by individuals for memos, spreadsheets, and so on. All personnel records for persons who left the company more than three years ago are shipped to corporate headquarters in New York, which sends them to a warehouse in yet another state, New Jersey. Good luck on trying to find out about someone who worked here six years ago! If you have a job that you'd like to lie about which you left more than five years ago, you can probably lie with impunity about it if you set up alternative personal references. We'll be looking at an example of this type of lie system later in this chapter.

3. If the company is now out of business. If you are lucky enough to have worked for a company that's gone out of business, you're in great shape for lying about it. The chances are almost 100 percent that nobody can find anything about what you did there. Coupled with a phony reference from a "past supervisor" you could lie with abandon about every aspect of the job. Of course, there are few out-of-business companies with reputations that smack of solid busi-

ness, but that consideration is irrelevant for your purposes, unless you're in the area that's viewed as the cause of the problem. This is only a problem for widely known company failures. For lesser-known outfits, nobody knows what happened and you can easily lie about how you saw the trouble coming, and so forth.

THE LIE SYSTEMS

There will be few instances in which you'll lie only about the dates, titles, compensation, or the responsibilities of a job. Most of the time, you'll want to lie about many aspects of the job, as proper lie technique and story line will require many small changes. You might as well lie about as many dimensions as your situation requires because the risk of exposure from multiple lies isn't much greater than lying about only one (with certain exceptions, which will be noted).

Therefore, while I'll individually present the lie systems for dates, compensation, and responsibilities and achievements separately, I'll use examples which will be realistic. This will clearly demonstrate the underlying principles of each type of lie system while also demonstrating proper, applied lie technique.

Job Dates: The Situation

Joan Blosh is an engineer whose actual employment history is shown in Figure 28 (Figure 28 shows salary and reason for leaving in the job history for your information; such data must *NEVER* go on a resume).

FIGURE 28. ACTUAL JOB-HISTORY DATA PRIOR TO APPLICATION OF JOB-DATE LIES

January 1986 to Present
SLIP SHOD MANUFACTURING

Salary: 22K
Reason for wanting to leave: Bad job

May 1984 to December 1985
TRIGGLES ENGINEERING, INC.

Salary: 32K
Reason for leaving: Husband relocated

November 1982 to April 1984
Out of work

June 1978 to October 1983
BLEBBINS DESIGNS COMPANY

Salary: 27K
Reason for leaving: Laid off

Joan is now attempting to leave a terrible job at Slip Shod Manufacturing. In terms of job-search challenges, she faces four significant problems:

1. Very short time on the present job.
2. Horribly long period of unemployment (19 months in 1982 to 1984.
3. Relatively short time on job at Triggles.
4. Leaving for reasons that have a bad "taste"

(husband relocating, laid off). She wouldn't mention these on the resume but you can be sure they'd be asked in the very few interviews she'll get if she told the truth.

Job Dates: The Lie System

There are numerous lie systems which could be employed here. We'll look at the best example which incorporates date lies.

Job Dates: The Lie Itself

Joan decides to employ a combination lie which changes some of the dates and also uses a phony consulting job. She puts together a resume with the job history shown in Figure 28.

FIGURE 29. JOB HISTORY OF FIGURE 28 WITH JOB-DATE LIES

January 1985 to Present
SLIP SHOD MANUFACTURING

Salary: 38K
Reason for wanting to leave: Bad job

November 1982 to December 1984
SELF-EMPLOYED (CONSULTANT)

Salary: 35K
Reason for leaving: Long hours, unpredictability of income

June 1978 to October 1982
BLEBBINS DESIGNS COMPANY

Salary: 27K
Reason for leaving: Laid off

Job Dates: The Story

The job history shown in Figure 29 is a major improvement over the Figure 28 original. Instead of one decent job, a bunch of losing causes, and a period of unemployment, Joan can now show three fairly stable job situations. The lies which she employed, and the important points about each, are:

1. Moved the date of her present job back one year. If you're currently employed, there's a good chance they won't make a formal check of references as they won't want to jeopardize your current job. If they ask, on an interview form or in person, for permission to contact your present employer, refuse. Regretfully mention that the employer is paranoid about people looking for jobs and fires anyone he catches. Notice that the Slip Shod job now shows some staying power. Coupled with the earlier job at Blebbins, Joan looks like Ms. Stability.

Of course, she still has to deal with the inevitable interview question of, "Why do you want to leave Slip Shod?" This question is easily handled by such expressions as, "Look, let me be honest with you (this always works best when you're lying), the folks at Slip Shod are a great bunch but the company just isn't state-of-the-art like yours. I want to grow as a professional and the only way I can do it is by working for the best." They'll love it.

2. Dropped reference to the job at Triggles Engineering and substituted a period of consultancy

for Triggles and the period of unemployment. This example is an outstanding demonstration of the necessity to combine lies for maximum effectiveness. Two smoothly crafted, simultaneously applied lies can do far more than the same lies applied individually. An interesting additional lie can help make Joan look like even more of a comer. Now, she can mention that her husband had to relocate for another job at just about the same time as she got laid off at Blebbins (if the subject of why she left comes up at all) and, rather than look for another job, she started a consulting business. It's a natural. It makes her look like a tiger, having taken advantage of a bad situation to start her own business.

Yet, she's not showing that she's so much of a tiger that she doesn't want to retreat back into regular work to be with all the losers who are interviewing her (and who resent consultants).

3. Lies about her compensation. As long as you're telling lies, you might as well throw in the easiest and most rewarding lie of all. We'll discuss compensation lies later in this chapter, but notice how Joan's current compensation went from the slave wages 22K per year at Slip Shod to 38K per year. The hope is that they won't check the present employer, who probably wouldn't give out salary information anyway. At the same time, the current claimed compensation of 38K seems reasonable for someone who was making 35K per year as a consultant. Of course, the 38K at Slip Shod isn't going to seem reasonable unless the resume is shamelessly pumped up to show commensurate responsibilities which would justify such a salary.

Job Dates: The Data

One of the most important bits of support for the above lies is going to be the impression which having been a consultant will make on interviewers. Outstanding will be a few letters of reference from "satisfied" customers (which Joan would get from friends or make herself on cheap stationery) who could serve as great phony references.

It's also a good idea to drop a few business cards on them, with comments such as, "I don't do any consulting these days but perhaps you might have seen the name in a trade journal or at a trade show; I always promoted a lot" (I guarantee that at least five out of ten people will say that they think they remember it. They hate to say no and appear stupid). A fake reference posing as the past supervisor from Blebbins couldn't hurt, especially if the real reference might not be outstanding. If the real reference would be great, it should be used. Otherwise, forget it and lie.

JOB-TITLES LIE SYSTEMS

Lies about job titles are somewhat risky because a fair percentage of companies will confirm job titles along with dates of employment in response to reference checks. Clearly, if you state that you were the Vice President of Marketing and the reference check turns up the bad news that you were a Marketing Analyst I, you have a problem. However, there's a fair amount of latitude for lying about job titles in some specific areas and situations.

This area of lying is difficult to present in terms of

exact technique. The situation, the industry, and the job seeker/liar's skills interact to present a unique set of circumstances. I don't want to lead you to believe that there are any hard and fast guidelines about title lies; there are only general recommendations.

Basically, you're always safe in lying about titles if you can come up with a reasonable explanation of the difference between what you claimed and what the reference turns up. Since no employer with any brains is going to check out references before he interviews you, you'll have a chance to make a good impression on him and look like what you've claimed to be on the resume. So there's a chance that he won't bother to check. If he does check, there's a chance he won't get an answer. If he does check and gets an answer, there's an equally good chance that he'll only get information on the dates. And there's the added chance that the person checking won't notice any discrepancy; the dates and name of the past employer will check out and he'll probably not worry about it. Don't forget that most of the reference checking will carry on long after you start work and that most of the checking is done by low-level clerical personnel who don't know what they're doing most of the time.

Certain types of jobs practically beg for lies about job titles. Secretarial and clerical jobs are a safe area. For example, why claim to have been a "secretary" when you could have been an "executive secretary" or at least an "administrative secretary"? There's no set definition that's hard and fast between companies as to the responsibilities, pay, or skill levels of the various secretarial titles. If they should check and find out that you were a "Secretary I," you could claim that you were performing the duties of an executive secretary but there weren't any job slots for an executive secretary in the department due to budget problems. If they like you and think you can do their job, they'll swallow it application, resume, and thank-you note (especially if you line up great phony-references).

Other areas that practically scream out for job-title lies are those in which many different jobs are being done simultaneously, such as in data-processing analysts and research. Regardless of what you happen to be called officially, it's always handy to add some additional label to the title such as "Programmer Task Manager" (everybody manages tasks) or "lead" (as in "Lead Researcher," "Lead Analyst"). If they do check references and get an answer, chances are that no one will say anything if the dates are confirmed. Needless to say, don't lie about dates and job titles for real companies because the odds of getting caught are too great if they check and get an answer.

RESPONSIBILITIES AND ACHIEVEMENTS LIE SYSTEMS

As you'll recall from Chapter One, the recommended resume format requires that you present each job-experience section in two parts: responsibilities and achievements. Even if you're thinking of foolishly disregarding the suggested format, you're going to have to present an outline of your duties and achievements in some manner. I'm not even going to consider the possibility that any would-be liar could be so stupid as to simply list jobs without taking the opportunity to pack in flattering details about each of them. Responsibilities are those things that you're claiming were/are a normal and expected part of a position's duties. Achievements are those extraordinary things that you accomplished while on the job.

Lying about responsibilities and achievements is one of the great, untapped, and under-used areas of job-search lying. Even if the interviewer will be talking with your actual past supervisor the minute you leave the employment interview, the overwhelming majority of job-earch lies about responsibilities and achievements will not only not be discovered, they won't even be explored! It's hard to believe but true. Chapter Nine will explore the subject of reference checking in detail but a brief explanation here will demonstrate why this type of lie works so well.

Most reference checks will be done by disinterested personnel who merely want to be assured that you are telling the truth about when and where you worked. They'll also want to get some assurance that you are of sound moral character. Most reference checkers don't know anything about the job itself, so they'll ask little or nothing about the specifics of what you did, such as systems knowledge for programmers, etc.

Similarly, the hiring technical manager (your prospective new boss) will concentrate mostly on character issues, under the usually mistaken impression that he or she was able, in a brief interview, to determine if you know what you're talking about. As a result, even if you use a real job and actually put down real, live, past supervisors as references, the chances are 95 to 1 that you can get away with shameful lies about the nature and significance of the work you did. Let's look at an example.

Responsibilities and Achievements: The Lie

Beulah Issel is seeking a job as an economist. Figure 30 presents the job-experience section for her most recent job as it actually appeared in my mailbox without pumping, without proper resume format, and without outright lies about her duties and responsibilities (at least no well-done, outright lies).

FIGURE 30. ACTUAL EXAMPLE OF A JOB-EXPERIENCE SECTION WHICH ACHES FOR PROPER APPLICATION OF LIES ABOUT RESPONSIBILITIES AND ACHIEVEMENTS

Dorkmeister Development Company
10 West Dorkmeister Way
Dorkburg, TX 90667

TITLE: Economic Planner

DATES: September 10, 1981 to July 7, 1986

DESCRIPTION: Area of responsibility involved analysis and decision making on existing and proposed industrial and commercial land uses. This included, for example, a technique to analyze shopping center proposals; analysis of demand for future commercial and industrial land use; housing market analyses; revisions of the current corporate plan; and any other forecasting such as employment and tax statistics that fell within the purview of the planning department.

Whew, can you believe how bad Figure 30 is?

There ought to be an obscenity law that prohibits consenting adults to view or design such materials, even resumes, in the privacy of their own homes. I don't know if Beulah ever found a job or not but she probably should apply for a job with a religious order; she's honest enough (although they'd probably hire a candidate with a more impressive, fully pumped, and lie-covered resume). Let's suppose, for the sake of charity, that Beulah got smart, bought this book and put together the job-experience section shown in Figure 31.

FIGURE 31. JOB-EXPERIENCE SECTION SHOWING PROPER APPLICATION OF RESPONSIBILITIES AND ACHIEVEMENTS LIES

September 1981 to July 1986
DORKMEISTER DEVELOPMENT, INC.

Economic Planner
Responsibilities: Analyze feasibility of proposed development projects and forecast profitability, tax implications, and cash-flow impacts. Propose and conduct market-demand research and surveys. Provide fiscal and research consultation support to executives as required. *Achievements:* Designed new technique for evaluating impact and profitability projection on proposed shopping centers. Revised the long-range corporate plan to include impact of changes in the federal and state tax laws. Developed procedures to quickly analyze impact of proposed land uses on future usage requirements. Completed many special studies for executive and board use.

Who can deny that the new, improved, and lie-riddled job-experience section of Figure 31 sounds and looks like a properly lie-filled job-experience section which any liar would be proud to have in his resume?

Responsibilities and Achievements: The Story

The story illustrated by Figure 31 more or less speaks for itself. Some of the points which require explanation are:

1. Remember that lying about responsiblities and achievements is different than pumping them up. If you're only going to be pumping, you don't have to worry about reference checks, as the contrast between the stark truth and the pump job will be seen as typical resume hype and summarily excused. If you're lying, as Beulah is in the above example, the reference checks must be taken into account as a remote possibility. While they probably won't expose you, be careful not to make any outrageous claims if you're going to risk using real references. For example, if Beulah were to claim in her achievements section that she "developed a completely new corporate planning system," she'd be taking a chance; a reference checker might be compelled to ask, "How's the new planning system of Beulah's working?" Of course, phony references would have no trouble with this line of questioning.

2. Notice the use of "revised the long-range corporate plan," "developed procedures," and "designed new technique." They're lies but they're hard to actually disprove without firsthand knowledge. They sound believable if Beulah can handle the heat

in the interview.

3. The expression, "completed many special studies for executive and board use," is particularly good for general use. Always refer to anything you do for management as "for executives."

4. If you wish to lie even more aggressively, simply move a few of the more impressive achievements to the responsibilities section. For example, if the "for executives" lie was placed in the responsibilities section as "perform confidential research for executive and board use," it sounds even better. The achievement section could then contain a lie such as "performed confidential analyses of potential impact of several key acquisitions."

5. If you're going to be using phony references for your past superiors (but the actual job dates and titles), you can lie outrageously and without fear. Believe me, nobody who's calling or writing for a reference check to the personnel office is going to ask about or be given answers to questions about the content of the work you did. It just isn't done. If you supply a phony reference who poses as a past supervisor, and that person substantiates your claims, you're in like a porch climber. The only chance of exposure would be if someone suspected your reference and called the company and tried to track down the supervisor of the department where you worked. The odds of that happening are 10,000 to 1; you could conduct lying job searches for 500 years before that happened once. And even then, chances are, for jobs more than five years past, that your previous supervisor has moved on, died, is out of the office, the department reorganized, or all of the above.

Responsibilities and Achievements: The Data

The only key data element to the above type of lies is a phony reference who will take the place of the actual supervisor. In reality, you don't even need a phony reference if you're willing to take a minor chance at being caught (maybe 2-3 percent) by using the actual supervisor. Just to point out how superficial the questioning of references is, consider my experience in a past search when I was posing as a controller. I used several out-of-town friends as phony references who were represented to have been chief financial officers who had been past supervisors of mine. Not one of them had ever worked in the financial arena in any way. One of them was a personnel manager in a steel factory and the other was an operations manager for a transportation company. Neither of them knew anything more than general knowledge about finance. Yet, they handled numerous and often lengthy phone references with a number of high-level finance types with no problems. In fact, after I was hired as a controller by a large manufacturer in New York, my new boss asked me if I thought one of my past bosses would "be interested in interviewing with us to head up finance in the company we're acquiring next year. I liked his style on the phone."

COMPENSATION LIE SYSTEMS

Compensation lies are a strange breed of job-search lie. Most other job-search lies are used to hide or grossly distort the truth which, if it were known, would compromise the applicant's chances of being interviewed and/or hired. In effect, there's a problem which must be hidden from the employer. Compensation lies deal with a "problem" that's not usually one that needs to be hidden. In most cases, admitting the actual compensation level of a past job isn't something that will kill a candidate's chances. The only time when this isn't true is when the amount of past compensation is so low that it makes the candidate appear to be lying about what he did (giving rise to the observation, "No company would pay someone so little to do that unless the job was very low level or the candidate is a loser!").

If you're trying for jobs that pay 20 percent or more over your actual current or last salary, you're at tremendous risk to be viewed as a poor candidate simply because you're not making enough. The second reason to lie about compensation, even if you're not trying to make a large jump in job types and salaries, is because you can get more money for doing nothing but lying.

A brief explanation of how compensation levels are determined and how job offers are made will provide you with some insights which may enhance your technique in regard to compensation lies. Most sizable companies (over 100 people), and many smaller ones, have job descriptions for each of the positions in the company. These job descriptions outline the duties of the job, the acceptable qualifications, educational requirements, the type of personnel which report to the position, and to whom the position reports.

For each job description, the personnel department usually maintains some sort of rating or grade system which assigns a grade level to each job. Thus, the president of the company may be a grade 15, a secretary a 4, and a marketing manager an 11. As you might expect, the higher the grade, the higher the salary. Each grade has a salary range assigned to it. Thus, the range for a grade 4 might be $10,000 to $17,000. Compensation people go to great lengths to keep the midpoint of each range near the average salary for people in similar jobs in similar industries in the area. Thus, if someone is hired from the outside with some experience, they try to keep the initial salary offer at about the midpoint. If they can bring people in at or near the midpoint, the pay structure can be maintained in a statistically attractive form. As people are given increases and move up the range within their grade, senior people quit, die, or retire.

New, younger, and more inexperienced people are then hired or promoted and are typically paid at or near the bottom of the pay range for their grades. For the secretarial grade 4, the midpoint in our example would be $13,500. A new hire with some experience would, all other things being equal, be offered about $13,500.

It's the "about" and "all other things being equal" considerations which make compensation lies profitable and almost irresistible for the job-search liar who desires more disposable income. If the secretary claimed to have made $12,500 at her last job, the prospective employer would eagerly offer a starting salary at the midpoint, thus providing the new hire with a decent increase (in his eyes, anyway). This salary would maintain the salary and grade structure. Yet, if the secretary claimed to have made $14,500 in her last job, and appeared to be an excellent candidate, the employer would probably give in and offer $15,000 to $15,500. He would believe that he'd be getting a top-notch secretary (after all, someone else thought she was worth $14,500) and he'd think it was worth it to pay more than the midpoint. The key is to realize two points:

1. Each grade level has a pretty wide range. The approximate ranges are shown in Figure 32.

FIGURE 32. APPROXIMATE SALARY RANGES AND MIDPOINTS

Midpoint salary	Salary range	Range size
$10,000	$8,750 to $11,250	$2,500
$20,000	$17,500 to $22,500	$5,000
$30,000	$26,000 to $34,000	$8,000
$40,000	$34,000 to $46,000	$12,000
$50,000	$42,000 to $58,000	$16,000
$60,000	$50,000 to $70,000	$20,000

As Figure 32 clearly demonstrates, there's much leeway within each salary range for putting together an offer. When they come back with an offer, they're trying to get you for the cheapest price they can get away with, given what they know about your past history, and the availability of other candidates. Unless there are special circumstances, such as a high unemployment rate in your profession, they won't ever offer you less than you were making (unless you'd be moving from a very expensive area such as New York City or Los Angeles to a small town in the Midwest).

If you claim to have been making $27,000 and they're using the salary structure shown above, they'd try to offer you $29,000 to $30,000 so they could stay near the midpoint. But, with no other changes or additional lies, if you claimed to have been making $29,000, they'll come back with an offer of $31,000 to $32,000 and you'll get another $40 a week for no effort. Of course, the big payoff comes when you're in the upper salary ranges, because you can add another five thousand a year to past jobs and there's room in the salary range to handle it.

2. Compensation lies aren't just for the here and now. Compensation lies are an investment in your future. Your starting salary is going to affect a lot more than your first paycheck. If you go in at $28,000 instead of $30,000, after three annual 6 percent merit increases, you'd be making almost $2,400 per year less than the liar who went in at $30,000. Personnel departments will explain (when they encounter a candidate who knows the ropes and wants a bigger initial starting salary) that they want to "leave room for future pay increases." How nice of them. Any finance type will tell you to take present dollars over future ones anytime; take yours up front by lying. Even if you were to be at the very top of your grade going in,

chances are there'll be across-the-board increases for cost of living, grade "adjustments to realign the structure" when other businesses begin to steal talent, and/or you'll get promoted. When I've supervised good people who worked hard who were at the top of their grade, I merely rewrote their job descriptions; this is common practice. There's always a way for a manager to get more money for good workers.

MONEY IS POWER

Even if your presented (true or not) qualifications look great, to a very large extent, your perceived value is going to be significantly influenced by your past earnings. Let's face it, we live in a society in which the value of a person is most often measured in money. How much you make determines where you live, what you eat, what type of education you can get, what social groups will accept you, what type of car you can drive, and how intelligent everyone thinks you are (which is why we have to listen to rich movie stars tell us about politics and the environment while nobody listens to the lower-paid and therefore less respected scientists).

Money, in most cultures, and especially ours, is power. When you interview, you want to be coming from a position of power. You must give the impression that, if they hire you, they'll be gaining by the addition of your power; that they're the ones getting the best deal. How much money you claim to have made in your last few jobs will have a great impact on their perceptions of your success and value. As long as you don't lie yourself out of the price range for the job, you'll look like a better candidate if you're making more than the other candidates.

Given the above, you should always lie about compensation unless there are strong contraindications. If you know that one of your past employers always provides compensation in references, don't lie about the compensation from that job. If you work for some sort of governmental or pseudo-governmental agency (such as a utility), don't risk this lie (or job-title lies) because government-type outfits don't blink an eye at violating employees' privacy (they know they probably won't get caught). In most other applications, there's little reason not to lie and many reasons to lie.

WHY COMPENSATION LIES WORK

As briefly mentioned earlier in this chapter, lies about compensation are among the easiest to perform. There are two primary reasons why lying job seekers can get away with claims of inflated compensation.

1. More and more often, companies are refusing to provide any salary information at all when they verify employment. As a result, many other companies don't even ask for it. If you're using phony references for past supervisors, there's a good chance, when the prospective employer is small, that he won't make a formal reference check with the personnel department of past employers. No reference check means that your inflated compensation claims are accepted.

2. There's no widely accepted methodology which employers use to evaluate compensation versus job titles and responsibilities. Despite detailed

compensation studies, there's as much as a 20 percent difference between what companies will pay for similar jobs. Generally, the different pay reflects different technical levels or added responsibilities, but this is immaterial for the job-search liar. You're always going to be lying yourself in as one of the top talents in your area, so the upper possible salary limits for your job are appropriate (if you can give a great interview).

As a result, claimed-compensation levels, if they're not too far out of line, will be accepted and believed. For example, there's no hard-and-fast rule as to how much computer programmers make. The pay depends upon a host of factors such as the industry, the types of systems, the level of responsibility of the position, the hiring company's traditions, the current demand for programmers with the specific skills needed, and so on. One company may pay $25,000 per year for that which another company pays $30,000. In the absence of any rigid compensation guidelines, almost anything reasonable is believed because so much variation is encountered even when the truth is told.

Let's look at an example of compensation lying applied to a series of jobs.

Compensation Lies: The Situation

John Frobish is compensation manager for a mid-sized manufacturer. He is switching jobs, would like to make more money than his compensation to this point would allow, and is attempting to move up to a position as director of human resources. We'll assume that the truth or the lies about his experiences are appropriate for these goals. His actual compensation history is presented in Figure 33.

FIGURE 33. ACTUAL COMPENSATION HISTORY BEFORE APPLICATION OF COMPENSATION LIES

Past job titles	Actual compensation
Personnel Specialist	$12,000
Technical Recruiter	$17,500
Compensation Analyst	$22,000
Assistant Compensation Manager	$28,500
Compensation Manager	$33,000

Given the industry John works in and the level of the position he's after, he knows that the approximate midpoint of the range for a human resources director is about $60,000. There's no way anyone who admits to making $33,000 is going to be considered for a job that pays anywhere from $50,000 to $70,000. Even if he had all of the experience, was expert in the field, and met all of the educational and experiential requirements, not one employer in one thousand would offer him the job; they just wouldn't believe he could do it if he hadn't been making even remotely similar money on his last job. Faced with this problem,

Frobish decides to lie.

Compensation Lies: The Lie Itself

John puts together a job history which contains the same jobs (don't forget, he could use completely phony jobs or consulting positions as well) but inflates the salaries (and will also have to lie aggressively about the job responsibilities and achievements). The actual old and the attractive new salaries are shown in Figure 34.

FIGURE 34. COMPARISON OF COMPENSATION HISTORY BEFORE AND AFTER APPLICATION OF COMPENSATION LIES

Past job titles	Actual compensation	Lies
Personnel Specialist	$12,000	$18,000
Technical Recruiter	$17,500	$28,750
Compensation Analyst	$22,000	$34,500
Assistant Compensation Manager	$28,500	$41,000
Compensation Manager	$33,000	$52,500

Target Job	Target job midpoint salary
Director, Human Resources	$60,000

Compensation Lies: The Story

As you can see, the pack of compensation lies shown in Figure 34 results in a compensation history which leaves Frobish at $52,500 going into the interviews. His inflated salary makes him an ideal candidate as he'd be going in right at the bottom of the $50,000 to $70,000 range for the position, leaving plenty of room for growth and leading the employer to think he'll be happy for several years. Also note that the progression of salaries shows rapid and dynamic growth; John looks like a real all-star.

There's more to the above lies than meets the eye. You have to be careful of some tricky areas. They include:

1. Be sure to take into account the amount of time you're claiming for each job. If you're showing a job with a longer tenure, be sure to proportionately incorporate into the compensation the types of salary increases which would have been given to a real winner. Don't forget to consider what the starting and ending salaries were for each job. It's helpful to lay out a time line and work out your compensation lies by year, factoring in annual increases of 5 to 10 percent and substantial increases when you switched jobs. Hardly anyone looks that closely, but there's no need to take any chances.

2. Be careful of the change in dollar values over longer periods. Remember, $10,000 per year in 1970 wasn't a bad starting salary for a management trainee, but would be horrible for anyone now.

3. Don't get greedy and price yourself out of the market. John Frobish is just about at the limit of credibility in his claims for jobs in those areas over the

last 10 to 12 years. It's a good idea to review wage and salary data for your industry (or the one you're lying about) before you put your lie system together. You can check federal and state wage survey data at libraries or can check back issues of publications such as the *National Business Employment Weekly* (of *The Wall Street Journal*) which publishes periodic salary surveys of various professions.

4. Don't get careless and reckless. Since it's so easy to lie about compensation, it's easy to simply go nuts and tell lies which you can't support in person. Remember, the employers are paying for image, power, and perceived value. If you stammer, sweat, and twitch like a $20,000 per year rookie, nobody is going to pay you $35,000. On the other hand, if you're a hard-working, competent, but underpaid $30,000-per-year person who can do the job of a $50,000 winner *and* play the part, you can get away with compensation lies easily.

Compensation Lies: The Data

Aside from any necessary corroboration from references to substantiate the lies, there's nothing else you need in order to support compensation lies. However, as mentioned above, if a past employer is known to provide compensation data on reference checks, don't try it. Rather, use a phony job (Chapter Eleven) or set up a phony consulting position (Chapter Seven). Of course, if the uncooperative employer is very far in the past (six years or more), you might want to try it, anyway. And if a job was early in your career, you can still use it and its real compensation if you've had enough succeeding jobs to "run up the salaries" to the level you need. The actual job would add a refreshing touch of truth to your lies about later jobs.

GET IN THERE AND MIX IT UP

The techniques in this chapter are a mixed bag. That's exactly how you should be applying them -- in combination and simultaneously. By applying several lies at once in artful combination, you create a rich, contextual fabric that feels real and looks like it's the truth. It's more work to put together complex, elegant lies, but it's worth the effort. They raise fewer questions and generate less doubt in your targets. Take the effort to carefully design the lies you'll take from this chapter and your lies will be works of art.

Chapter Nine

Modifying and Creating References

References are people or institutions who vouch for a job seeker's character, corroborate his claims of experience, and, if the job seeker has properly organized the job search, wax poetic about the candidate's virtues. The topic of references is sure to come up at some point in 99 out of 100 interviews. References aren't the problem that most job seekers think they are.

While a bad reference can kill you, almost every aspect of the reference-checking procedure operates in favor of a lying job seeker. Even if you're not lying and your references aren't great, there's generally not as much of a danger as you think. On the other hand, good references will enhance your position and serve to put the employer at ease. If you're lying, good references are essential, as they provide tangible, real-world tie-ins to your claims. In this chapter, we'll look at how references should be used (in any job search), how they're checked, and a variety of effective ways to lie about them.

TWO TYPES OF REFERENCE CHECKS

There are two types of reference checks. Each involves different types of verification processes by the prospective employer and each requires a completely different approach to lying about it.

Formal Reference Verification (FRV)

The first type of reference verification, the FRV, consists of written or telephone inquiries made by prospective employers of the formal records of the job seeker's past employers. This type of reference check is usually conducted by someone in the personnel office of larger employers. FRV is almost always conducted by mail because most employers will not give out employee information without written authorization from the employee. They're afraid that if they give out information about an employee without that employee's permission and the employee suffers some damage, the employee might sue them. Many prospective employers will attempt FRV by phone anyway, in the hopes that the person who takes the call will help them out and/or not know the rules. And, of course, not all personnel offices and small employers understand the risks involved in giving out personnel information without permission.

So it is possible for a prospective employer to check out an applicant by phone, although more and more employers are deciding to verify employment only in response to written requests. When you're interviewing, many employers will have you fill out and sign releases (see examples later in this chapter and in Chapter Ten) in which a job candidate requests that prior employers and schools provide information to the prospective employer by return mail. If a prospective employer doesn't have you sign releases, chances are he won't be conducting an FRV. If he tries to do an FRV without signed releases, chances are he'll be turned down, particularly if the past employer is a large company. If you're wondering whether a prior employer gives out references on the phone, use the Reference Checking Test outlined at the end of this chapter.

The fear of litigation and almost every other random factor of the reference process operates in favor of the job-seeking liar in terms of the FRV process. FRVs are often conducted by the recruiter or the clerical staff in the personnel department. These people phone and/or mail requests for information to prior employers and schools (Chapter Ten discusses the particulars of the educational reference situation in detail). In many cases, information takes months to get back and, in 10 to 60 percent of the requests, isn't ever received. Other employers are having crises, cut-backs, recruiting problems, and so forth, so they're not too concerned with responding quickly (or at all) to requests from other companies. Larger companies and government bureaucracies (they're much alike) are more likely to respond (in their own sweet time) as they can afford to keep all sorts of people on the payroll just to take care of these requests. When the information is received back at the prospective employer's personnel office, it's filed away by low-level clerical help. This is a great advantage for liars, as people in personnel aren't usually smart enough to recognize phony job verifications, fake transcripts, and so on. The only hazard with FRVs is the situation in which a prospective employer gets a negative answer from a past employer, such as, "we never heard of this guy." If you carefully design your materials and lie systems, this won't happen.

Personal Reference Verification (PRV)

The second type of reference verification, and the one which is most important in making a positive impression on prospective employers, is the personal reference verification (PRV). While many employers conduct both FRV and PRV, many settle solely for PRV, in the belief that testimony from a live person who breathes into the other end of the phone is superior to the information collected via mail from an FRV. It's also more immediate and therefore more convincing. The person-to-person contact of a PRV is valued much more than time-delayed correspondence of an FRV. Middle-sized and smaller companies will generally rely solely on PRVs as it's too expensive and time-consuming to conduct FRVs on all prospects or new hires.

The PRV process itself generally consists of short (5- to 15-minute), one-to-one discussions of the candidate between your reference and the potential employer. The reference is most often a prior supervisor and is almost always a person who is identified by the job applicant either on the application form or his reference sheet (explained later in this chapter). PRV is most often conducted by the hiring manager (the candidate's future boss) but this practice is also changing as a result of litigation fears. Increasingly,

PRV is being conducted by personnel types because of the fear that uninformed hiring managers will ask incorrect or illegal questions. When you're asked for two or three "references," the employer wants people who can be contacted for PRV.

PRV outcomes are second only to the applicant's interview presentation in determining whether a job offer is forthcoming. A good PRV or two always tips the scales in your favor. Employers put a lot of faith in PRVs and this faith (however misplaced) demands that you give your PRV lies careful attention. The mistaken belief that PRVs are "eyes into the applicant's soul" stems from all personnel officers' and most hiring managers' faith in their incredible powers of interrogation and character analysis. They think they'll be able to "get all the answers" about a candidate because of their ability to "grill" the reference. This faith is sadly misplaced. Most of the questions are so general and standard that they're worthless ("Tell me, is Sal a good worker?") for determining anything other than the fact that the applicant can breathe and can walk. Yet, the very nature of these general questions makes it easy for a lying (or truthful) reference to make you look great. A friend who can give a great PRV is a valuable job-seeking asset; treat him well.

THE PROPER USE OF REFERENCES

In this section, we'll review how references should be used in order to maximize their effectiveness and to follow the expected conventions of the business world. The principles we'll outline in this section must be followed whether you're telling the truth or lying.

What are "References?"

When employers ask for "references," they want to talk to people who are familiar with your work, such as former supervisors; they're looking for people to call for PRV. They'll never ask you directly for information for FRV as they'll get it from your application or information release forms. If you can't give them the names of at least two former supervisors for PRV, it's going to look a little strange, unless you're just out of school or have had only one prior job. In that case, the names of one or two former professors, teachers, and/or community leaders will have to be used. Unless you've absolutely no other choice, don't use clergymen, friends, and/or relatives as references. Friends and relatives (if their last names are different from yours) can participate as phony references in some very effective lies, but they're worthless as straight references; everybody knows they'll lie and, even if they told the truth, they don't know anything about your work.

The optimum approach, often only possible through lying (or if your record is so good you don't have to lie), is to provide a supervisor's name as a reference for each of your last three positions on your resume, not counting any job that you're still working. Never use your current supervisor as a reference unless he knows you're looking and is helping you out, as when there's a plant closing or your spouse is moving. If a current employer is helping you find another job, he'll lie even better than a phony reference (when it's in their interests, meaning anything they want to do, businessmen lie with great skill, as long as everyone pretends they're not lying). When an employer has the opportunity to contact a former supervisor for each of a candidate's past jobs, the prospective employer feels secure, even if he doesn't call them all. You don't want to give more than five references; three is all you need -- use only your best ones. If there's any doubt about a reference's reliability, check him out and don't use him if there's any hint that he might be less than great.

When References Should Be Provided

References should never be provided before a face-to-face or phone interview has taken place. Even if you're telling the truth, you can't afford the risk of having an employer call one of your references before you find out what the job is like; the reference won't have enough data as to what he should say until you've filled him in. After you've talked with the prospective employer, you'll know what his main interests are, what skills are most important to the job, and sensitive areas which the reference should avoid. If an ad requests that references be sent with the resume, don't send them. Anyone who asks for references at that point is either a rookie to the recruiting game or an idiot. An alternative or simultaneous explanation involves academic positions where it's traditional to provide three references with the application. If you don't send the references, the application probably won't be considered. You can also assume the prospective employer will contact the references in advance of talking with you. Whenever you're applying for an academic position, be sure to notify your references that they might get a call as soon as you submit the application or resume.

Most typically, an employer will ask for the names of three references at the first in-person interview. This is the appropriate time to provide them. If the job is out of town, the employer may request references during the first phone interview so he can check you out before paying for the trip. Over the phone, you'll have to give them verbally or offer to send a reference sheet (see the next section). If you don't have a reference sheet with you, or if you do but sense that the employer may call the references before you can contact them, tell the employer that you don't have the phone numbers handy and you'll send them along or call them in the next day. That gives you time to brief your references.

One good way to provide the references and demonstrate an effective touch of courtesy is to include your reference sheet along with the mandatory interview follow-up thank-you letter (see Chapter One).

Many job application forms ask for the references on the form itself. Since a completed job application is required by many companies before an applicant will be interviewed, you don't have much choice. In some cases, for low-level jobs and with bureaucracies, you'll have to fill out an application, leave it, and then wait to see if they'll call you in for an interview. Don't worry about providing references on the application in advance of an interview in these cases. Employers generally won't waste time calling references before they interview you in person or on the phone; the provision of references on the application in these cases is usually only a formality.

How to Provide References

References should be submitted on a sheet similar to the one shown in Figure 35, which maintains the style of the resume format shown in Figures 1 and 2. The example shown is for Jack Stoutheart, whose resume was shown in Figures 1 and 2. Note that there's a former teacher or supervisor provided for each job-experience section which was shown in the original resume. It's not necessary to number them but it gives the reference sheet an organized appearance.

Note also that the first reference is not a current supervisor. There's no surer way to end up out of work than to let a current employer know you're looking. Never give prospective employers permission to check with your current employer. Since Mr. Stoutheart couldn't safely provide a current supervisor, he did the next best thing and used the name of a customer and professional colleague. If Mr. Stoutheart was not claiming to be currently employed by World Beater Extruders, Inc., it would be acceptable for him to provide Mr. Ricardo Flexibillo as a former supervisor reference for the position (assuming, of course, that he would give a good reference). It's not essential to provide a substitute reference for a present employer but it's a nice touch.

REFERENCE LIES: PRV LIES

The universe of PRV lie systems is shown in Figure 36. All possible situations involving PRV lying fall somewhere in the structure of Figure 36. The various combinations of circumstances are described in the body of the figure and the resulting types of reference lies are shown at the bottom. "Status of the organization," "it exists," and "it's phony" refer to whether the job you're lying about is with an organization that's real or fictitious. If you're lying about an organization that doesn't exist, it's not so much a reference lie situation as it's a fictitious job lie. We'll briefly discuss the reference lying implications of fictitious job creation in this chapter, but don't believe that the creation of a fictitious job can be accomplished solely by the development of a phony reference or two. Refer to Chapter Eleven before you try to create any phony positions.

FIGURE 35. RECOMMENDED FORMAT FOR REFERENCE SHEET

126 Forsythia Drive
Glenside, CA 91307

(818) 555-5555

REFERENCES
of
JACK STOUTHEART

1. Mr. Harvey Hawker
   Vice President
   Megabreath Manufacturing Company
   22334 Production Way
   City of Industry, CA 93444

   Current client and fellow officer of L.A. Industrial Sales Council

2. Ms. Cora Gated
   Sales Manager
   Densepack Packaging, Inc.

   Former supervisor

4534 Box Road
Orange, CA 99832
(213) 888-0000

3. Dr. Billy Joe Hustle — Former professor
   Professor
   Glenside University
   1122 Academic Place
   Glenside, CA 91327

4. Ms. Fonem Todeath — Former supervisor
   President
   Boileroom Sales, Inc.
   123 Tuxedo Place
   City of Commerce, CA 94555

Note: The following would be used in addition to or instead of reference number one if Mr. Stoutheart was not currently employed or felt that Mr. Hawker might give a bad reference.

1. Mr. Ricardo Flexibillo — Former supervisor
   Vice President, Sales
   World Beaters Extruders, Inc.
   22111 Mallable Street
   Los Angeles, CA 91221
   (213) 545-2222

FIGURE 36. THE UNIVERSE OF REFERENCE LIE SYSTEMS

<table>
<tr><td colspan="5">STATUS OF THE ORGANIZATION</td></tr>
<tr><td colspan="4">EXISTS</td><td>IS PHONY</td></tr>
<tr><td colspan="2">YOU WORKED THERE</td><td colspan="2">YOU NEVER WORKED THERE</td><td rowspan="2"></td></tr>
<tr><td>REFER-ENCE WORKS</td><td>REFER-ENCE DOESN'T WORK</td><td>REFER-ENCE WORKS</td><td>REFER-ENCE DOESN'T WORK</td></tr>
<tr><td>TYPE A</td><td>TYPE B</td><td>TYPE C</td><td colspan="2">CREATION OF PHONY JOB</td></tr>
</table>

If the organization exists, the reference lying situation can be further defined by whether or not you work there or have worked there in the past. And, regardless of whether or not your employment history involves a job in the organization, the lie system can be further characterized by whether or not your phony reference works at the organization. For example, if you're lying about an organization that really exists, and if you actually work there (or have worked there), and your reference is also someone who works there (but who's not your past supervisor; that's why it's called reference lying), you're using reference lie type A. As Figure 36 shows, reference lie types B and C occur when different sets of circumstances apply. You'll note that if the organization exists but neither you nor your reference have ever worked there, you're once again talking more about the creation of a phony job than about a straightforward reference lie.

All of the reference lies shown in Figure 36 involve PRV. That is, they're lies in which a confederate of yours provides a warm body via telephone, who plays the part of one of your former supervisors. Techniques for dealing with any concurrent FRV attempts by prospective employers are discussed later in this chapter. The following sections will discuss each of the reference lies outlined in Figure 36.

Type A: Reference Transfer

Reference transfer is an extremely effective technique. As shown in Figure 36, this lie involves an existing organization in which you once worked (or in which you're currently employed). It consists of using a confederate who works in the organization in place of the actual reference you'd use if you were telling the truth. If you've got the right friends (or favors owed), reference transfer can actually be used to create a phony job in some situations. Reference transfer can be used to best effect if you're still working in an organization (and trying to get another job) because you'll be around to coach your reference and maintain some degree of "guilt pressure." This guilt is often helpful because once you're not working there anymore, it may be difficult to get one of your past "friends" to help you out.

Advantages

The primary advantage of this technique is that it provides a reference who is located within the company and who can be reached by phone at the company. If a potential employer calls Fred's Aerospace Corporation and talks to a phony reference who claims to be a past or present supervisor, whatever you've told the employer in the interview will have the ring and heft of the truth if the reference does a good job. Who would doubt it? After all, the call went through a switchboard or a secretary, or was actually answered by the reference himself.

If you're still working at the company, there's another significant advantage to this technique: the ease and detail with which you can brief your reference. I once used this lie while working in the office next to my phony reference. We were providing each other with reciprocal reference transfer lie support as we struggled to escape from bondage. Since we were both still employed there, it was necessary to develop a story line which could, if needed, explain the fact that each of us was looking, still employed there, and was able to use someone who was a "former supervisor" for a reference. This was necessary because the rules of business make it anathema for an employee of an organization to "bad mouth" it to an outside organization, especially in behalf of someone who's trying to get another job.

The story we prepared stated that our reference

had been a prior supervisor of ours who was now in charge of special projects, was also looking around, and who wanted to see us get something more challenging. The story was ready but never had to be used by either of us. Nobody thought to ask how an employee could get a reference from a current high-level employee of his current employer without getting into trouble for looking for a job. Even though it might not always be asked, people will wonder about it, so make sure you've got a similar story to tell if you sense some anxiety on the part of the interviewer. The above story always works fine.

There were many times when one of us was actually present while our "reference" was handling the phone interview with the employer. Simply by repeating the employer's questions out loud ("Well now, let me think. 'What were Garth's biggest assets?'"), my reference provided me with an opportunity to supply quickly written notes about what to emphasize. Of course, this coaching wasn't essential as we always carefully briefed each other (and all of our other lying references) immediately after either of us had a telephone or face-to-face interview. But it does demonstrate the benefits of working closely with your references.

If you're not currently employed in the company, you sacrifice the ease of coaching but don't have to worry about explaining how you can get a reference from a current employer. You can also more easily claim that the reference was your past supervisor for the entire tenure of your position. If the reference isn't working in the department in which you claimed to work, no problem. All you (or the reference) have to do is mention that he has been assigned to "fix up some problems" in another department. That will make the reference seem even more of a hard-nosed winner and will make his opinion of you even more impressive. Most often, nobody will even ask or wonder about the reference's current job title or circumstances.

Limitations

The primary limitation is being able to find someone who's willing to help you. Once that's taken care of, the only other problem with this technique is the remote possibility that someone else may answer the phone and give the deception away. For example, you may be using a friend who's a data analyst to pose as a personnel manager who had been your supervisor. Suppose he is out of the office and a secretary or a passerby in data processing (DP) picks up the phone. If the person who answers says something like, "Good morning, data processing," or, "Sal is down in the computer room running a program," the caller might get a little suspicious, as few personnel managers or ex-personnel managers would have offices in DP or have occasion to run programs.

Equally dangerous would be the caller who asks for the department first, in this case the personnel department, and then attempts to locate your reference. If the prospective employer is told by some troublemaker that your reference isn't in the personnel department, you've got a problem. This is one reason why it's best if you can get a reference from someone who's in the department in which you're claiming to have worked (unless you're using the "taking care of a problem" ruse or a different lie technique altogether). This isn't really much of a danger if the reference is clever, but it is a consideration if you're using less-than-gifted liars.

The main requirement is to have a friend who works for the organization and who is willing to lie for you. Such a person is often harder to find than you may think. The same person who gleefully reports in detail about his extramarital sexual escapades conducted on business trips often turns surprisingly moral when asked to help out on a job-hunting lie. There's no charitable explanation for this type of hypocritical behavior.

The best person to use is someone who's in the management ranks and who is in a position of some authority. Clearly, if you were or are a stock clerk, you're going to have trouble getting a vice president to lie for you. However, if you're in middle management, one of your past or present colleagues should work fine.

How To Effect a Reference Transfer

The actual execution of the lie is simple. Simply identify your confederate as a reference on your reference sheet or on the application and then brief him as to your story when you think he might get a call. It's important to provide him with a copy of the resume you're using, so he can keep the dates, job titles, and so forth straight. Whenever I'm conducting a lying job search, particularly one which involves multiple phony resumes, I provide my references with a report cover in which all of the resumes are bound and labeled. This prevents the various versions from being misplaced and/or confused. It's a simple matter to tell him that he's going to get a call on resume version Number Five and then give him a few pointers as to what the interviewer may be most interested in. After you've used someone as a reference a few times, or if he knows you very well, it isn't absolutely necessary to brief him in detail each time (although it's always the safest bet) as he'll become familiar with the type of questions which will be asked and will be able to handle the typical questions with ease. The questions are usually so general that you don't have to worry about minor details which could expose the fraud.

The most critical point in making this lie strategy work is to have a good, enthusiastic liar as a reference. Don't try to talk reluctant, so-called "friends" into it if they're not willing. They'll make a mess out of the whole situation. And if they've got cold feet, they'll back out on you after their first baptism of fire and you'll be stuck with a lie system and reference sheet that's worthless.

If you can't find anyone in the organization itself who'll lie for you in place of the real reference, you have several choices. You can switch to the reference lie Type B (reference substitution as explained below) and use someone completely outside of the company. The slight danger here is that the prospective employer may be more inclined to conduct an FRV if the "past supervisor" isn't there at present. This is a very small risk if the reference makes you look good but it's a factor to be taken into account.

If lie Type B isn't possible, you'll have to consider more drastic measures, such as dropping the job altogether and substituting a self-employment or consulting situation or a phony job. If you need the credential or name of the company on your resume and thus can't drop it, you'll just have to find someone to help you with reference substitution.

Type B: Reference Substitution

Reference substitution is similar to reference transfer. You want or need to take credit for working for a specific organization but you can't use a current employee of the firm as a phony reference. As a result, you must substitute the real reference with a lying confederate who doesn't work for the organization.

Advantages

The most attractive advantage of this technique is the ease with which friends and relatives (with different last names) can be used to great advantage. Of course, you can use relatives with the same name if you establish a phony name for them and only give out home phone numbers. If everyone in the family is in on the lie, no problem. *Do not* try this with families with young children; they lie about everything they do but they'll blow your cover in an instant if they get to the phone first.

Reference substitution avoids the main difficulty with reference transfer: finding someone who works for the organization who will lie for you and who can lie well. This type of uniquely skilled and willing individual isn't always available when you need him. With reference substitution, your pool of available liars is much greater. Almost anyone can be used as a former supervisor, as long as he can be reached by phone and can lie well. This type of reference is a great help if you had to leave the organization under unfavorable circumstances which can't be well hidden because you need the company name on the resume and/or you're afraid the prospective employer will conduct an FRV as well as a PRV.

For example, suppose you were fired and you believe that the company might answer the FRV with a "would not rehire" comment. That's bad news (a section near the end of this chapter tells you how to test to see if this will happen). In most situations, you'd simply drop such a job and create a phony job or consulting position. Yet, if the prospective employer knew that you had been employed there (as might occur if you were referred by a contact who mentioned it) or if you needed to claim the company because of its reputation, you might be forced to work with the problem. Reference substitution presents an effective way to handle this type of situation.

If you've got a known or potentially discoverable problem (from the perspective of the employer), the only way to make yourself look like a good candidate is to discredit the prior employer and explain away the problem as having been his or someone else's fault. The problem with this is that it's never a good idea for a candidate to dump on any employer, past or present, in an interview, as the potential employer will be inclined to think you may bad mouth him as well once you're on board. You've got to have someone else do the dumping. You can't use reference transfer, as it might seem strange to the prospective employer that the reference would stand up for you rather than his current employer. Reference substitution deals with this problem as well as it can be handled. If you're using a reference who doesn't work there "anymore" (which might mean never), he can paint a very positive picture of you while engaging in some subdued negative comments about the employer.

Your reference might explain the situation by telling the employer, "Look, this must be completely confidential between us. Bob was one of the best Account Representatives I ever supervised. Hell of a worker and smart, too. Unfortunately, one of the executives was involved in a little hanky-panky with Bob's secretary and Bob wouldn't go along with an illegal plan to fire the playmate before things got out of hand. There was a blowup and Bob wouldn't fire the young woman, and quit in disgust when it became apparent that they were going to do it anyway. I'll always admire him for the integrity he showed. My financial position forced me to hang on until I could move. I wouldn't be surprised if they gave Bob a bad reference just to get even." The reference would seem credible because of the plea for confidentiality, the subdued tone of the criticism, and the mature attitude. Even if the FRV came back as a "would not rehire," a personal reference such as the above would probably carry the day.

This type of reference substitution lie can be used to handle almost any type of problem. Of course, most of the time when you've had a firing, it won't be necessary to keep the job in your resume; you'll be free (and better off) to design a phony job to use in its place. Unless the job is critical to your marketability, never attempt to stay with a problem and try to explain it. It's always better to move on to new territory and start with a clean lie over which you have complete control.

Limitations

The only potential problem with this technique is that the reference has never worked for the organization and wouldn't be able to handle company-specific questions. This is a very minor hazard due to the sloppy nature of reference questioning but it could be a problem for highly technical positions. During one of my successful campaigns to obtain a job as a hospital administrator, I used several non-medical industry friends as references who I claimed had been past hospital administrators for whom I had worked. None of them ever had any trouble handling references interviews with the Senior Vice President of Human Resources from some of the nation's biggest hospital chains because the questions were so mundane.

An additional minor point revolves around the present employment situation of your reference. It's not too impressive if someone calls your friend Bob Jones who is supposed to be a big-shot former supervisor of yours and the phone is answered with, "Mr. Jones? Hey, Jones, some guy on the phone wants you. Have you got that Chevy's oil changed yet?"

It's best if your phony references are at least middle managers or people who can sound like them and the reference they're supposed to be. It's also essential that they have working arrangements which are conducive to taking reference calls. Of course, you can simply give home phone numbers for your references and let them return the calls at their leisure. In this situation, a mention by the reference that he's now "in consulting" or "retired from the company to run my own company" is a good way to put the interviewer at ease (he might wonder why the reference wasn't called at a regular office). Again, it might not ever be a problem but it never hurts to prepare for all contingencies.

How To Effect A Reference Substitution

The technique of reference substitution is identical, aside from the identity of the phony reference, to that of reference transfer. Simply identify your friend or relative as the reference, brief him when you think he might get a call, and send him copies of all of your relevant resumes.

Type C: Reference Creation

Reference creation subsumes quite a few attractive reference lies. While it might appear to be the most drastic reference-lying technique, it's actually the easiest reference-lie technique to execute. In its classic form, reference creation uses an employee of an organization to provide a glowing PRV about a job which you never actually had. There's a fine but essential point of difference between this technique and creation of a totally fictitious job.

The distinction is this: in reference creation, the reference and the job actually exist but you never worked there; in a fictitious job situation, nothing exists, nothing is real. In reference creation, your lie system is inextricably bound up in the existing company. In a fictitious job situation, you're completely free to design the lie system from the ground up.

Advantages

The primary advantage of this situation is being able to use an existing business and an existing reference who works there. The reference is merely vouching for the fact that you once worked for him. This ploy is particularly effective if you've got any highly placed friends. If a high-level official of a company, such as a vice president or higher, serves as your reference, few people are going to have doubts (larger companies may still conduct FRV, but that's always a danger). The reference can simply claim that you were employed in any job you need, as long as it's one that the company has and the reference can make a believable case for you having worked for him or her.

Limitations

The only limitations of this technique are those that are typical of reference lying: the danger of an FRV being conducted and uncovering the fact that you never worked there. With small businesses where the owner/boss is on your side, this is not a problem as your confederate can intercept any FRV materials and handle them. If it's a big company, almost nobody is going to be able to quietly adjust the system to catch any FRV; somebody in personnel would realize what was going on and your reference would look real bad. Don't ever ask lying references to risk their own welfare and careers; you owe it to them to come up with better, safer lies.

How To Effect a Reference Creation

As you might expect, the execution of this lie is easy. For example, a friend of mine, who we shall call Gort, was interested in acquiring a particularly choice hotel-management position. Unfortunately, his background did not include any job experiences in the hospitality industry. However, Gort had a friend who had a part interest in a ski lodge and who was willing to vouch for Gort's claim that he had managed the place for five years. Gort outlined what kind of reference he needed, sent the friend a copy of the resume, and put him down as a reference. Gort is now working for a major chain as manager of a 500-plus-room three-star hotel.

There are some types of businesses which aren't useful in reference-creation schemes. I had a relative who owned a small bar and who would have been willing to lie for me when I needed it. But how many bars have Human Resource Managers? If you don't have any connections with people who have appropriate businesses, use the second variant of this technique which involves wholesale lying on everyone's part. In this variant, the reference claims that you worked for him in an existing business for which neither of you is or ever was an employee. This borders on fictitious job creation but is more dangerous as there's always a danger of an FRV, which can be handled in fictitious job creation. Only use this variant if you absolutely must have the specific job and company on your resume.

Let's say that you need to claim that you've got experience as a manufacturing engineer. You know that if you could put three years experience with Ajax

Engineers, Ltd., on your resume, you'd look great. Unfortunately, if you don't know anyone at Ajax, regular reference creation is out. However, if you have someone who can lie well, you can set him up as a past supervisor at Ajax. You simply pump him up as now owning his own consulting outfit or company and then claim him as a past supervisor. If your prospective employer gets a great PRV, he may not conduct an FRV, unless he has a very large company or is government related.

Creation of References for Fictitious Jobs

Chapter Eleven presents the techniques of developing completely fictitious jobs in detail. While references are an important part of the lie systems of phony jobs, there's a lot more involved than simply setting up a lying reference. We'll discuss briefly the reference aspects of fictitious jobs in this section, but be sure to read Chapter Eleven before you try to develop a phony job.

Advantages

The beauty of these techniques is that neither you nor your reference is bound by the sometimes mundane limitations of reality. As long as both of you keep your stories straight, the sky is the limit. An added plus is that you can handle FRVs by using the reference's home address as a business address and having the reference send out employment verifications if an employer checks. This is explained later in this chapter.

Limitations

Like all other PRV lies, the primary limitations revolve around the quality of the liars you use for phony references, and the way that you handle the problem of FRVs.

How To Create References

This scheme is handled just like all the others. Put together your story, brief your references, provide them with your resume(s), and let them know when the calls might come in. If the company is "still in business," all you have to do is use the reference's home address as the company address and the reference can even handle an FRV by sending out a letter on company stationery. This hardly ever happens. If the company is "out of business," everyone can claim ignorance of how to get any data and the employer will have to settle for the interpersonal reference. In almost all cases, this will be enough.

Formal Reference Verification (FRV) Lies

The only strategy for executing FRV lies is to set up a process which permits a prospective employer to actually conduct an FRV on your claimed past employers and get back the favorable response you need. That is, you have to arrange for phony companies to answer FRV correspondence just as if they were your actual past employers. The only alternative to this strategy is to simply hope that prospective employers will not conduct an FRV if the PRV works out okay. This is a risk, especially with larger organizations, as their procedures may mandate an FRV regardless of how much the recruiter and the hiring manager love you after the PRV.

Advantages

As there's only one way to provide for phony FRVs, there's no differential levels of effectiveness to discuss. If you're establishing a lie system which allows you to use an FRV, you're a fool if you don't set it up. Once established, this provides the basis for a completely safe reference lie system which few employers could break even if they suspected something.

Limitations

As you may be realizing, many of the PRV lies set up situations in which there's not any provision for handling FRVs. The PRV lies involving existing companies in which you haven't worked are the ones that put you at great risk. It's often much safer to go with a completely fictitious job or consulting lie rather than risk an FRV.

How To Execute FRV Lies

There are two ways to set up phony FRVs. One involves using companies that can't be checked because they're not in business anymore. You can use the name of an actual company that's gone out of business or you can claim that you used to work for a company that's since gone out of business (but never existed). These techniques are most useful when the job you're trying to create is a few years back (which would explain why the company's not in any directory).

An alternative method is to set up a confederate's

home address as the address of the company for whom you're claiming to have worked. If the confederate notifies the mailperson that letters addressed to Ajax Dog Deodorants, Inc., will be coming to his address, they'll be delivered with no problem. Then the friend can respond by sending out a verification letter which states that you worked there. Of course, you must supply the stationery and the typing, but that's a small price to pay for absolute assurance of surviving an FRV. The letter is merely a typical business letter which verifies the information claimed on the release form you will have filled out for the prospective employer (see the next section). Figure 37 presents an example. Note that the letter is signed by a personnel employee; it helps the facade to make the phony employer appear to have a personnel department.

All things considered, the out-of-business ruse consists of the least work. However, it's risky if you're using it more than once in a job history, as many employers won't hire anyone on whom they can't get at least two decent FRVs. And it does look a little suspicious if everyone you've worked for is out of business.

REFERENCE CHECKING TEST

Unfortunately, we live in a society where not all people can be trusted. Sad, but true. Many times, your noble sense of honesty and fair play will encourage you to use actual references. You may believe the reference likes you or your work. You may trust him. You may even feel a little guilty about lying (I hope that doesn't last long!). Many former supervisors tell departing employees not to hesitate to use them for a reference. Yet, what happens in many of these cases? You guessed it -- horrible references. There's no need to put up with the risk of an unfavorable reference. If you know they're going to be bad, you lie instead. You find out if they're going to be bad by testing your actual references.

FIGURE 37. EXAMPLE OF EMPLOYMENT-VERIFICATION LETTER SENT IN RESPONSE TO AN FRV REQUEST

Name of company
Street Address of company
City, State, Zip
Reference's phone number

Date

Name of Person Requesting FRV
Title
Company Name (Prospective employer)
Street Address
City, State, Zip

Dear Name of Person Requesting FRV:

In response to your inquiry concerning the employment record of [employee's name], we are pleased to provide the following data:

Dates of Employment: ______________ to ______________

Job Title: ____

Final Monthly Compensation: __________________________

Final Status: This employee is eligible for rehire.

Respectfully,

Mr. John Frombaggen
Senior Employment Specialist

Conducting Tests of Formal Reference Verifications

You can personally call the personnel department of a past employer and test your own formal references. If department employees will give information on the phone, you'll save a lot of time. Ask about salaries, dates, job titles, compensation, and rehire status. If they give out any bad news on the phone, it's time to start putting together a phony job. If the personnel employeees won't talk on the phone, you've got to test the FRV by mail. You'll have to have the prospective employer send your former company a signed (by you) release authorization in which you give your permission for the past employer to release his information on you to a prospective employer. The prospective employer is, of course, a confederate of yours. Use the form shown in Figure 38 and simply use the address of the confederate (or your own post office box if it's different than your last address with the past employer to whom you're writing).

Photocopy the filled-in form like that of Figure 38 and send one to each of the past employers you're testing. They'll respond with a letter similar to the example shown in Figure 37.

PERSONAL REFERENCE VERIFICATION (PRV)

All you've got to do is have a friend, relative, or colleague pose as an employer and call one of your references for a PRV. Give the reference tester a copy of your resume and tell him to really dig for the dirt. Have him ask leading questions such as, "What did Garth have the most problems with?" and "If Garth has one weak area, what would it be?" Bad references will leap at these types of questions and destroy you.

FIGURE 38. SAMPLE PRIOR-EMPLOYMENT-VERIFICATION RELEASE FORM

PRIOR-EMPLOYMENT-VERIFICATION RELEASE

I,[your name printed], Social Security Number: [the number], authorize [name of phony company] to contact the following employer(s) for the purpose of verifying the information I provided on my application, including dates of employment, the position I held, the reason for my termination, my compensation, and my eligibility for rehire.

I understand that this release will be used solely by (name of phony company) and not to provide information to any other sources.

Prior Employment Data

Company Name: ________________ Dates of Employment:

Address: ________________________ From: _____ to: _____

____

Supervisor: ______________________

Company Name: _______________ Dates of Employment:

Address: ______________________ From: _____ to: _____

____

Supervisor: ______________________

Company Name: _______________ Dates of Employment:

Address: ______________________ From: _____ to: _____

____

Supervisor: ______________________

Signature: ______________________ Date: ______________

Please send information to: (Name and address of phony employer).

Have the reference tester call from his office so he can give a number if the reference wants to return the call at a later date. The reference will be less apt to suspect anything if your confederate can be reached at a real office. Of course, if he can do a smooth job, he can always call from home under the ruse of having his own business and thinking of adding you to the firm. If you detect the slightest bit of trouble, don't use the reference; lie instead.

SUMMARY

My continuous cautions about possible dangers and discovery should be heeded, but don't let them hamper your lying about references. The risks do exist, but they are small. I've lied about references and phony jobs for years and have never had anyone catch on to anything. Many of the employers I fooled were sharp people and many even conducted background investigations (see Chapter Thirteen) which failed to turn up anything. You can get away with almost any reference lie you try. However, the reckless liar is walking a hazardous path. Be careful and you'll get away with even the boldest reference lies.

Chapter Ten

Obtaining Educational Credentials

If this is the first chapter you turned to when you picked up this book, that's understandable, as educational credentials have become one of the most critical qualifiers which employers use to determine who will or won't be called in for an interview. If an employer specifies that only candidates with M.B.A.s will be considered for a position, hundreds of resumes showing M.B.A.s will be received. Any that don't show an M.B.A. will be quickly consigned to the send-'em-a-rejection-letter pile. If advanced degrees and even basic college bachelor's degrees meant anything, this preoccupation with educational credentials might make sense.

Unfortunately for everyone, most of this obsession with degrees and credentials is nothing but the corporate business world's version of keeping up with the Joneses. Since every business is staffing even the most menial of its office positions with college graduates, few employers are willing to settle for less because they don't want to appear unsophisticated and less state-of-the-art than their competitors. As a result, specification of educational credentials has become more important than worrying about which candidate has the best experience or skills regardless of whether he or she has a degree. Companies are requiring education simply because everyone else does.

An even more depressing perspective on this emphasis on education is the fact that there are no reasonably convenient, reliable ways to actually determine who is the best candidate for a job among a number of similarly qualified candidates. Worse yet, there isn't even a reliable methodology for determining what general characteristics are best for a particular position. Few employers would admit it but aside from prior experience performing the job, there are no statistically reliable predictors of better performance for 95 percent of all general office positions. And for technical jobs, prior experience is much more of a predictor than education. From your perspective as a job candidate looking in at the system from the outside, it may seem almost unbelievable that employers don't have any idea of the exact qualifications which will best meet their needs. But it's true, they don't.

The employment ads all look as if a personnel computer analyzed the job in detail and then spit out a list of required qualifications -- but it's all a mirage. The ads are written by middle managers and/or personnel people who only use their individual, best judgment as to what qualifications they should require. Since they have no objective, research-based method for determining what they need, and because they're afraid of being second-guessed if something goes wrong, they load in all of the qualifications they can think of or which they've seen in other ads placed by competitors. That's where the "five years of experience in red-widget design, knowledge of electronic spread sheets, bachelor's degree required, master's preferred" and so on come from. Most of the qualifications may have nothing to do with whether a candidate can or can't do the job, but they're specified simply because everyone else requires them.

There are some incredibly detailed and scientific means available to measure the personality and aptitude factors which relate to success in specific jobs in specific companies. Yet, only five to ten employers in the entire world use them to any extent because they're complex and costly. Almost all of the remaining employment testing that's done is totally worthless for predicting a candidate's success on a job, is generally interpreted incorrectly, and is scientifically meaningless. In the complete absence of any objective way to determine what qualifications to require, employers believe they're being objective by asking for all of the standard items that come to their pointy little heads. Unfortunately for job seekers who haven't had the luxury of four years of comprehensive, hands-on experience in fornicating, drinking, and drugs at State U., the mentality which specifies "bachelor's required, master's preferred," eliminates them unless they lie.

Aside from the issue of possessing the educational credentials themselves, there's an important implication which you must understand. Because education is a qualifications hurdle that must be passed to obtain entry into the interview itself, it's of little importance from that point on. Hardly anyone is really concerned, for most general business jobs, about what you actually learned or the types of classes that were taken to earn a degree. In some research and highly technical fields, this may not be true, but in general, possession of required educational credentials is merely a checklist item. Once met, it is no longer an issue. This is markedly different from lies involving job responsibilities and achievements which must become part of the fictional fabric of your entire presentation and life history. If you claim to have been a high-level executive and/or a consultant, you're always going to have to behave as if you've had those experiences. You'll be expected to talk like an executive or consultant and work as if you've had the experience; people are going to expect you to behave in a different manner than if you didn't have such experience.

With education, nobody is going to expect much of anything. Everyone has met Harvard M.B.A.s who can't operate the towel machines in the rest rooms, Ph.D.s who can't remember to put their shirts/blouses on right side out, and employees with B.A.s who can't read or write. Therefore, most employers don't have any particular expectations about how people with degrees should act when compared to people without them. Once you've lied about education to get into the interview, if you can give a good performance face-to-face, you'll do fine (if you cover the reference check).

TYPES OF DEGREES

There is almost an infinite number of degrees. I'm going to concentrate only on those types that have the most applicability for job-search liars; that is, credentials which are devoid of any relationship with practical on-the-job skills. Therefore, I'm not going to discuss the M.D. (medical doctor), D.D.S. (doctor of dental surgery), and similar degrees which require extensive specialized skills. This book is intended for use by liars who can do the job but who can't, without lying, present a set of credentials that will get them hired. If you're trying to get a job that you can't do, you don't deserve to count yourself among the fraternity of clever rascals who have lied their way into great careers; if you don't have the skills for the job you're trying to get, you're making a big mistake.

The following are sketches of what the various types of degrees signify. If the following descriptions aren't meaningful to you, you're going to have a lot of trouble maintaining the lie properly unless you do more reading and studying. In this country, the degrees which are typically required of job seekers for no sensible reason are the bachelor's degree and the master's degree.

The bachelor's degree is the basic college degree which is earned after four years of full-time study. There are many varieties of bachelor's degrees, with the most commonly required being the B.A. (Bachelor of Arts), the B.S. (Bachelor of Science), and the B.B.A. or B.A.B.A. (Bachelor of Business Administration or Bachelor of Arts in Business Administration, respectively). A Bachelor of Arts is typically granted for study in the social sciences or humanities such as psychology, art, sociology, English, literature, history, and so on. A Bachelor of Science is typically awarded for concentrating on subjects such as physics, chemistry, and engineering. There are other varieties of related bachelor's degrees such as B.S.E.E. (Bachelor of Science in Electrical Engineering) and B.Mus. (Bachelor of Music).

The area of concentration in a course of study (as when someone gets a Bachelor of Arts in sociology) is called a major. In terms of the examples and advice given in this book, I'm going to assume that you do not need to have detailed technical knowledge in the field of study to do the job. This means that employers in the industry or specialty area of your job search are requiring a degree simply because they want it for the prestige, not because of the subject content of the studies. Therefore, it will make little or no difference to the employer as to which major you say you studied. If you're going to claim a B.A., you can select a major as it suits you. It's currently valuable to have a bachelor's degree in business so you might want to lie about a B.A. with a business major or a B.B.A. On the other hand, if a research institution is looking for a history major to do some historical-research work, they're probably looking for a B.A. (major in history) who has had fairly intensive preparation in history. You'd either have to be well prepared or a fool to try to fake a degree in history for this type of job.

The next most common degree is the master's degree. They typically require one to two years of full-time work after the bachelor's degree (10 to 14 more classes). Typically shown as M.A. (Master of Arts) and M.S. (Master of Science), they represent the advanced versions of B.A.s and B.S.s. Traditionally, schools require master's candidates to complete an original research paper as a master's thesis. In the last 15 years or so, there's been a movement afoot to allow candidates to take an additional two classes (six semester hours) instead of completing the thesis. This is due to the poor writing and research skills of the people in the programs, students' complaints about the difficulty of doing any real work, and the school's fear of losing students to easier programs (particularly when many of the students are adults who are working full-time during the day and are working on degrees only so that their employers will pay them more). It's also far easier on the faculty to teach two more classes of 20 people each than provide thesis reading and support time for 40 people who can't read or write. And to think the system calls job-search lying immoral!

There are two additional degrees that are common. The first is the associate degree which is awarded by community colleges for two years of study. These are worthless in terms of job-search lying as there's no point in lying about an associate degree; if you're going to lie, lie about a B.A. or B.S. The other degree is the Ph.D., or Doctorate, which stands for Doctor of Philosophy.

To earn a Ph.D. typically takes from two to five years of full-time study beyond the master's degree. It always requires an original research project of some type which is called the dissertation. The Ph.D. may be awarded in almost any major, such as history, physics, psychology, art, chemistry, philosophy, and so on. It's generally not a good idea to try to fake a Ph.D. in order to simply impress an employer (that is, when they don't specify the Ph.D. as a job requirement). The reason for this is that Ph.D. holders, outside of their technical areas, are viewed as "academics" who can't function effectively in the "real world," meaning business. By faking a Ph.D. you don't need, you're often ruining your businesslike image. Far better to lie about an M.B.A. Another type of doctorate which you'll occasionally see is the D.B.A., which stands for Doctor of Business Administration. Unless you know the specific tastes of a particular employer, don't try to lie about a D.B.A. in order to appear more qualified than folks who have M.B.A.s; you'll tend to look too academic.

WHICH DEGREES TO LIE ABOUT

Given all of the above, the most useful degrees to lie about, for general job-search use in typical business environments, are the bachelor's and master's degrees, with particular emphasis on concentrations in business studies, such as B.B.A., B.A.B.A., and M.B.A. I recommend that if you have a bona fide bachelor's degree, that you lie about having a master's. If you don't have a degree at all, lie about a bachelor's in business. The reason for this is that if you haven't been to college at all, you won't understand enough of the jargon and procedures to hold your own in even a general conversation about what goes on in graduate school. If you doubt this, see if you understand and can answer all of the questions given in the next section; any college graduate could make up stories for them with no trouble. If you haven't been to college at all and you try to lie about a master's degree, you're going to be at a severe disadvantage if anything specific comes up for discussion. You may be able to handle it, but why take the chance unless it's desperation time?

OBTAINING THE EDUCATION YOU NEED

There are four basic techniques for coming up with the educational credentials you need. They are:

1. The straight lie: an outright lie supported by no documentation.
2. The straight lie and fake documentation: an outright lie supported by fake diplomas and transcripts.
3. The straight lie supported by phony registrar's office: an outright lie backed up by documentation sent by a phony registrar's office.
4. "Earning" (purchasing) the degree from an alternative college: involves enrolling in an institution that awards degrees based on "life experience" and some correspondence work. It's not really a lie but it's not a real degree, either.

STRAIGHT LIES: THE LIE, THE SITUATION, THE STORY

This is the most common and abused type of educational lie. It's the easiest to perform but is accompanied by the most risk in some situations. A job seeker simply claims that he has the required educational credentials on his resume and hopes that no one will check with the school.

There's not a lot of story required to give validity to the claim that you earned a bachelor's or master's degree. If you can act like a hard-working, responsible business person, you can play the part of a college graduate with ease. However, you should be prepared to answer a number of questions about your education which may pop up during the interview. Examine each of the following questions and develop an answer which supports your particular lie (type of degree, major, etc.).

1. What was your grade point (or favorite/most difficult subject) in school?
2. How did you get along in school?
3. Tell me about your extracurricular activities in school.
4. What honors, offices, and awards did you hold in school?
5. What proportion of your education did you pay for?
6. What were your SAT (GRE) scores?
7. What was your social life like in school?
8. Why did you go to college?
9. What was you major, and why did you pick that subject?
10. Did you do as well in school as you could?
11. Why didn't you do better in college?
12. How many times did you change your major?

You'll generally find that the above questions will be more often asked of recent graduates. If you're lying about education which took place many years ago (more than ten years ago), they'll ask few questions about it as they'll be focusing more on recent job experiences. Nevertheless, you've got to have an answer to each of them, just in case. Having answers to the above questions is much more important for those claiming recently completed education. These "graduates" are probably being hired more on the basis of their education than on their job experience.

Therefore, they'll be asked more questions about it.

In the three other types of education lies that follow, it's important that your answers to the above questions be consistent with any phony documentation. That is, you wouldn't want to claim that chemistry was your most difficult subject if your phony transcript didn't show a chemistry class. Odds are that nobody would notice, but skilled liars take no chances. I won't repeat the above questions in each section but they're an important part of the other educational lie systems as well.

Straight Lies: The Advantages

The primary advantage of this technique is that it requires absolutely no effort other than typing the degree on your resume and mentioning an anecdote about college now and again during the interview. If you know for a fact that the employer doesn't check educational references, you can use this strategy with impunity (if you appear convincing). Most small employers probably won't check with schools. Most large employers always check because they can afford the clerical expense. If you have to fill out release forms (shown later in this chapter) when you start work or in the interview, they're going to check. In that case, if you've lied, the best thing to do is call them the next day and tell them that you've accepted another job. They'll move your file to the not-hired section and won't bother to check references. There's no sense in letting anyone know that you're lying, particularly in a smaller community or a closed industry where the word might get around.

Straight Lies: The Disadvantages

The danger, of course, is that the employer will check educational claims with the institution. If he does, there's a good chance you'll be exposed. This doesn't happen as often as the occasional newspaper stories might lead you to believe, but it does happen. If an employer checks with the school from which you claimed to have earned the degree, he'll get an answer within two to four weeks. Then, in most companies, you're fired.

Straight Lies: The Variants

A useful variant is to claim a degree from a defunct school. There are all sorts of small liberal arts colleges that have gone out of business in the last 20 years. Pick one that's out of your area and simply claim that you got your degree there. If they ask you to fill out a release form, write "It's closed down now and I don't know what their address is or if they even exist anymore." If you can then supply a former professor as a personal reference verification of your education, you're in luck ("Well, darn it, the school's closed but I have kept in touch with my faculty advisor, Dr. Jones. I could give you his name"). Simply use a confederate as the "professor."

STRAIGHT LIES AND FAKE DOCUMENTATION

This technique would be used in essentially the same situation as the preceding lie except that the liar is concerned about providing fake documentation in the hopes that the employer will be dissuaded from checking directly with the claimed institution.

A little story is required beyond a decent performance in the interview. In order to present the fake documentation in a believable light, it's a good idea, during the first interview, to present the phony diploma or transcript with a comment such as, "I was preparing for the interview this morning and I happened to come across my diploma. So I brought it along in case you wanted to verify my education." Use the same type of line if you're bringing along a fake transcript. If they say something like, "Oh, that's not necessary. We check directly with the school," you'll have to terminate that job effort as mentioned in the preceding lie. If they say something like, "Well, just let me get a copy of that for your file," you're probably home free. Most small employers will fall for it. With larger ones, their system will probably check on it anyway.

The data for this lie is a fake transcript or diploma. Coming up with a fake diploma was relatively easy at one time, but it has become a real problem in the last few years as diploma mills have become the whipping boy for society's guardians. Instead of worrying about small concerns such as organized crime, illegal drugs, murders, and so forth, the FBI and many state governments have been aggressively going after what they consider to be the major legal problem of the 1980s: fake diplomas. As a result, many fine sources of inexpensive phony diplomas and transcripts have been driven out of business. In a later section of this chapter, I mention two reference books which list diploma mills and alternative degree sources. The persecution of diploma mills has gotten so vigorous that not one of the diploma mills listed in the latest edition of each book could be reached by phone. Telephone information in each city didn't have a number for any of the named companies or institutions.

Given this sad situation, it's unlikely that I can provide names of diploma mills which will be in business by the time you read this text. In order to escape prosecution, diploma mills are moving fast. Your strategy, should you decide to purchase your diploma, must be to peruse the classified ads in the backs of magazines. Men's magazines and sports and gun magazines seem to be the best places to look. Another alternative involving so-called "Bible colleges" is outlined later in this chapter.

You've got to be careful when purchasing phony diplomas. There's no reason to pay many hundreds of dollars for a fake piece of paper when you can get the same thing for anywhere from $5 to $100. Some degree mills charge up to $1,000 for fake diplomas. This is a patent rip-off. If you're going to pay $1,000 for a phony degree, you might as well pony up another $500 to $1,000, do a little correspondence work, and obtain an "alternative education" degree from a school that sends a transcript to employers upon request.

The primary advantage of obtaining a diploma is that you've got something tangible to show the employer. Even if the employer generally checks on education by mail, a phony transcript or diploma, accompanied by an impressive interview style, may just dissuade them.

The major problem with this technique is the same as that of all techniques in which there's no independent source of verification to support your claims (as there is when a real school certifies your claims). If the employer checks, you're caught.

STRAIGHT LIES SUPPORTED BY THE PHONY REGISTRAR'S OFFICE

This is the same basic situation as in the two previous strategies, except that the liar wishes to arrange for an address from which phony supporting documentation can be sent to employers when they request it.

The story is the same as in the previous two techniques except that the applicant will be able to provide an address for the "school" from which the prospective employer will receive verification of earned education. Confederates working or living at that address (friends or relatives) will respond to requests for information by sending forms which you've provided. This method is almost foolproof as it enables the employer to verify your educational claims by means of his own systems.

The primary element in this system is the verification letter or transcript. A transcript is a listing of all of the work done by a student at the school, as well as some background data. You'll either buy or design a phony transcript and then set up a "registrar's office" from which the transcript may be ordered or verified. When requested by the employer to fill out the release form they'll send to the school, you simply put in the address of your confederate, such as "Mr. Fred Jones, Registrar, Phony University, 12 Main Street, New York, NY 10034." If they don't ask for educational information on the release form, simply put the address on the employment application next to the school name and the claimed degree.

Most large schools now have transcripts that are sophisticated computer printouts. If you're going to fake a transcript, it's a better idea to claim that your alma mater is a small school and use an early model transcript, shown as in Illustration 2 as they're easier to fake. Small schools which can't afford large computer departments still complete transcripts by typing on them with typewriters, sometimes different ones every semester, depending upon which clerk's typewriter was in use. Almost all transcripts earlier than 1965 were of the typewriter variety. If you're claiming a degree earned before 1970, you can use the older variety without risk. If you're claiming a recent degree, the newer variety is a little safer but the risk still isn't great if you use an older model. The people filing the transcripts in personnel just aren't smart enough to catch on. Your only risk is if the transcript is sent directly to the manager or a sharp personnel type. It's a small risk but it's there.

If you're going to assemble your own fake transcript, you need to be very careful of format. Almost all transcripts have the following characteristics:

1. A basic printed format onto which all information is typed.

2. Shown are classes, class hours, grades, and grade points by semesters, quarters, or trimesters.

3. An official seal, usually in blue or red, is stamped right over the middle. In addition to the colored seal, or in place of it, they may have an embossed seal. Somewhere on the transcript is a statement which refers to the seal and/or embossing

such as, "This transcript not official unless stamped." The stamp content may be either the school seal or the words "Official transcript."

4. The transcript is usually folded into a separate envelope which is sealed with a paper seal across which is stamped something like, "This transcript not official unless this stamp is red and envelope is sealed."

5. The transcript will also show any previous education, the high school the student went to, grades on entrance qualifying exams, dates of graduation, and degree awarded.

As you can see, it's not easy to design all of these things yourself. If you have a personal computer that creates a decent-looking form, you can put together a basic transcript blank that has professionally appearing headings. If it doesn't look exactly like a printed transcript, don't use your own equipment.

An alternative to producing it yourself, if you live in a larger city, is to approach a few printers with a rough idea of what you want. If you're making up the name of the school, there's no legal problem. All you have to do is find a printer who wants the business. You can then have a few printed and then type in your own data. A good source of content is to ask a friend or relative with a degree to let you have a copy of their transcript. If they're in a field that you don't mind claiming as your degree major, you can copy their courses and entrance test scores (make sure you give yourself good grades). You can have an embossing stamp made for $50 to $100 and a rubber stamp (for a colored "official transcript" seal) for much less.

Employers don't usually request transcripts from colleges when they're corresponding directly with the institution. Transcripts typically cost from two to seven dollars and the employers don't want to spend a lot of money if they don't have to. If they require transcripts, they'll often ask you to arrange (and pay) to have them sent directly from the school. Unless they're in love with you, they won't take your copy as proof if their policy requires transcripts. If you don't have it sent promptly, you'll probably get a call from personnel bugging you about it. There's a good chance that if you keep saying you'll take care of it but don't, they'll forget about it as clerks come and go and more recent crises steal the attention.

Most of the time, if the prospective employer does request verification of your educational credentials, he'll simply ask the school (by mail) if you have such and such a degree. In response, they get everything from single-page letters on school stationery with embossed seals to short slips of paper on which your name, degree, and date of graduation are scribbled into spaces on a photocopied form and then signed and sealed/stamped by the registrar.

No school will provide verification unless you approve it. Therefore, employers typically have you complete an authorization as you're being hired. Figure 39 presents a sample of the form they'll ask you to fill out or sign. They'll then send this to the school which will respond with a letter of verification. Obviously, when you're asked to complete an authorization form like the one shown in Figure 39, you'll enter the name and address of your phony registrar and the employer's address in the appropriate spots.

Then, when your confederate receives the form in the mail, he will respond with a verification letter.

Figure 39 presents a sample of a typical educational verification form. They come in all sizes and shapes and in all extremes of formality. Some of them come on faded photocopies and some on expensive stationery. Some are hand-typed on cheap typewriters and many are generated by computers. This variety helps the job-search liar because almost any type of forgery will be believable to the personnel clerk or recruiter who examines it.

FIGURE 39. SAMPLE OF EDUCATIONAL INFORMATION RELEASE FORM

VERIFICATION OF EDUCATION AUTHORIZATION TO RELEASE INFORMATION

I, [your name printed], Social Security Number: [the number], authorize: [the employer's name] or its agents to contact the educational institutions listed below for the purposes of verifying the information I provided on my employment application form. The institutions may release information on dates of enrollment, graduation dates, degree(s) awarded, class standing, and grades.

To the employment candidate: Please complete the following for all educational institutions you have attended.

Institution: ____________________ From: _______________

Address: ______________________ To: _______________

________________________ Degree: _______________

Institution: ____________________ From: ______________

Address: ______________________ To: ______________

_________________________ Degree: ______________

Institution: ____________________ From: ______________

Address: ______________________ To: ______________

_________________________ Degree: ______________

Signature: ________________________ Date: ____________

Please send information to:
[Name of personnel official]
[Employer's name]
[Street]
[City, state, zip]

I recommend that you use a form made from one half of a standard piece of 8 1/2-by-11-inch business stationery folded lengthwise. If you follow a minimum number of basic design principles, you should have no problems. The name of the school must be in large, bold print. Use a set of press-on letters or have the form made by a printer so the name of the school looks official. It doesn't matter if the form looks a little washed-out as many schools simply photocopy a photocopy of the form and rely on the signature of the registrar and the school seal or "official copy" stamp to vouch for its authenticity. Therefore, if you use press-on letters, repeatedly photocopy a photocopy of your final form so that any slight irregularities are obscured by the poor reproduction.

FIGURE 40. EXAMPLE OF EDUCATION VERIFICATION FORM

[Name of School]

I, Charles C. Fromfrugger, Registrar, certify that the following student: Fred Frobish Nurbelmeier, 444-44-4444,
[Name] [Soc. Sec. Number]
received the following degree(s) on the date(s) shown:

Bachelor of Science (B.S.) June 5, 1986

[This line empty]

[This line empty]

Dates of enrollment: 9/15/81 to 6/5/86

Semester hours: 123 Class standing: 157th in class of 1,127

Cumulative grade point (out of 4.0): 3.32

Not valid unless stamped in red with official school seal.

[Signature] [Date]

Once you get all of your materials together, simply send them to your confederate, all signed and sealed by you, ready to be mailed. All the confederate has to do is to type the name and address of the employer on them and send them back.

If you handle this technique with proper care, you're pretty safe. You'll have independent corroboration of your claims. If they have no other reason to doubt you, you'll never get caught unless there's some incredible quirk of bad luck.

The primary disadvantage of creating your own documentation is the expense and trouble of setting up all the forms and confederates. And, to be completely covered, you've got to set up both verification letters and transcripts, as some employers might demand that you arrange to have a transcript sent directly to them, and others may request a verification. If you don't have the materials prepared in advance, you're going to have to scramble to get it put together (unless you try the "ignore it and hope it goes away" ploy).

"EARNING" (PURCHASING) A DEGREE FROM AN ALTERNATIVE COLLEGE

There is a large number of "alternative" and "non-traditional" colleges and universities which offer many different degrees and require little, if any, on-campus study. They're called alternative and non-traditional schools because much of the "course work" in these schools consists of credit for things you've already done in life.

Clearly, if you're going to use this route, it saves a lot of work to lie to these schools about what you've done (using some of the other techniques in this book) so that you won't have to complete a lot of extra work. Regardless of the school you pick, you're going to have to do some work, and you're going to have to pay some money (from $1,000 to $2,500 for a bachelor's degree to $3,000 to $5,000 for a Ph.D.). The fees, the amount of real work, and the time acquisition of the degree takes vary from school to school.

These types of schools are not viewed as frauds (although traditional schools raise an eyebrow at them in general and consider some of them to be outright diploma mills). A few alternative schools are legitimate correspondence branches of reputable institutions. However, these versions usually require much more real course work, actual exams given by proctors who live in your city, and research papers. Some of them require that at least one or two semesters be spent on campus. Few employed people can afford to take the time to satisfy the residency requirement.

The schools listed in Figure 41 are "non-traditional" schools that don't require any residency requirements at all. Some of them are mainly concerned with making money (no harm in that!) and some of them are attempting to provide convenient but reputable alternatives to costly traditional colleges and universities. Figure 41 includes only those that offer mainstream degrees in general liberal arts and business and only those that are in this country. Most offer everything from B.A.s to Ph.D.s. The range of quality, the expense, and the difficulty of course work varies, so request their literature and make your decision based on your time, interests, and financial situation.

If you want to learn more about degree mills, alternative degrees, and Bible schools, and have time to research a larger list of schools, the two best references are *Bear's Guide to Non-traditional College Degrees*, by John Bear (Tenspeed Press) and *Guide to Alternative Education* by Educational Research Associates. *Bear's Guide* costs about $20 and can be ordered by calling (213) 822-0350. The *Guide to Alternative Education* also costs about $20, and must be ordered by mail from: 1301 Southwest 1st Court, Pompano Beach, FL 33050. The only problem with these guides is, as I mentioned earlier, almost all of their listings for these job-search lying essentials are invalid by the time the latest edition hits the streets. However, they are both excellent references for locating and selecting alternative schools from which to request information.

FIGURE 41. NON-TRADITIONAL SCHOOLS WITH NO RESIDENCY REQUIREMENTS

Beacon College
1400 I Street, N.W., Washington, D.C. 20005
(202) 898-0400

California Coast University
700 North Main Street, Santa Ana, CA 92701
(714) 547-9625

California State University, Dominguez Hills
1000 East Victoria St., Dominguez Hills, CA 90747
(213) 516-3743

Century University
9100 Wilshire Boulevard, Beverly Hills, CA 90212
(213) 278-1094

Columbia Pacific University

1415 Third Street, San Rafael, CA 94901
(415) 459-1650

Kensington University
330 North Glendale Avenue, Glendale, CA 91209
(800) 423-2495

Pacific Western University
16200 Ventura Boulevard, Encino, CA 91436
(818) 995-0876

Southland University
35 North Craig Avenue, Pasadena, CA 91107
(212) 795-5558

University of Beverly Hills
465 South Beverly Drive, Beverly Hills, CA 90212
(213) 556-0190

An additional variety of alternative schools may also be helpful for those of you who need to come up with some education. These are the "Bible schools." These can also be found in the two reference texts noted above. Because of federal laws requiring the separation of church and state, churches are free to set up whatever kind of schools they want. Bible schools run the gamut from institutions that offer rigorous on-campus, four-year college curricula which are heavy in scriptural studies, to correspondence study, to mail-order degree mills which operate under protection of church-oriented state laws. Those that are degree mills can provide a diploma, though that's not much help if someone checks with the "school." Those that offer correspondence courses are more generally useful as they may provide verification letters and transcripts upon request. Be sure to inquire, before you sign up for anything, if the school provides transcripts and verifications upon request. If they don't there's no sense wasting any money if you need a verifiable degree. If you decide to sign up for something that's going to permit you to earn a degree which is verifiable by mail, ask to see a sample transcript. If it looks reasonable, then sign up. If it's a rip-off in terms of quality, look elsewhere.

The name of the school and the type of degree you "earn" deserves a comment. Many of the Bible schools offer bachelor's in Divinity, Theological Studies, and similar religious majors. In terms of sales appeal to employers, such degree titles don't have the hard, business impression of majors in business, or normal liberal arts. If you can, try to get a typical-sounding degree so it'll sound more businesslike to employers.

The name of the school is also a consideration. Many of them are called names such as Arnold's Bible College or Arnold's Bible Institute. As an employer, I would suspect that a school with the word "Bible" in the name probably offered mainly scriptural studies and was a hotbed of religious fervor. This might repel some employers. Better, if it's possible, to select what you need from a school with a name such as Arnold's Christian College. The word "Christian" has a less fundamentalist sound to it and might be better perceived as being more mundane in the types of course they offered.

You don't need any data to support the degree you actually "earn" at an alternative school because it's not really a lie. You'll have the degree and the school will send an official-looking transcript to anyone who requests it. If you're simply using a Bible-school degree mill, you're dealing with the same data requirements encountered in the fake documentation lie.

The biggest advantage of this technique, of course, is that you won't have to lie about your education and you'll feel a lot more comfortable about your "story." You might even learn a few things in the course work. And there's rarely any risk of "exposure." The worst that anyone can say is that you got your degree at a 'non-traditional' school. You say, "Damn right, and it was a lot tougher than those diploma mills the state runs for rich people's kids."

The disadvantages are just as clear. If you're in the throes of a job search at present, you don't have the money or the time to go for the alternative education degree. This technique is best used as a strategy for avoiding problems in a future job search.

However, if you're employed and feeling bad about not having a "real" degree, maybe you'd better forget about the Caribbean this winter and enroll in one of the non-traditional schools. If you want to learn and feel proud of your accomplishments, there are many fine non-traditional schools that can help you out. Just as at major universities, you'll get out of your studies exactly what you put into them.

SUMMARY

There's one major caution which you must always follow, no matter what educational lie you're using. If you're using a fake documentation degree lie, *never* relocate to another city for a new job before your background is thoroughly approved. The danger is that the company would have paid for the move, perhaps would be in the midst of buying your old home, might owe you major relocation expenses, and would then find out that you lied to them. You could end up on the hook for the expenses, out of work in a new city, and possibly sued by the company because they'd want to recover the relocation expenses. The difficulty is that most verifications of education aren't checked until you start the job.

It's almost impossible to conceive of an instance in which straight lies and/or fake-documentation lies are completely safe for relocation situations. If you're conducting a nationwide job search with the possibility of relocation, it's far safer to develop the alternative-education degree. Then you're covered for any reference check of education. Of course, only you can make the trade-off between your situation and the risk you can live with.

Chapter Eleven

Fictitious Jobs and Employment Histories

At first glance, it might seem that creating a fictitious job requires nothing more than a little creative resume writing and a phony reference. Even a fictitious employment history might appear to be nothing more than a series of resume entries with lying references to back them up. There are thousands of job-seeking liars who believe it's that easy and who take a cavalier attitude toward the design of phony jobs. These people are taking dangerous chances as well as short-changing themselves.

There's a tendency to view a phony job as a single lie which can stand alone and operate without support. Nothing could be further from the truth. It's pretty obvious that a lie about the responsibilities, achievements, and/or compensation of an existing job must be carefully integrated into whatever truthful elements are retained in the lie system. The creation of a fictitious job might seem to present an altogether different and less strenuous lying challenge because none of the details about the job must match up with actual circumstances about a particular position or company. In effect, it almost looks like the liar has a free hand and none of the difficulties associated with lies about existing jobs. A closer look at the creation of a fictitious job shows that such an attitude is dangerous and short-sighted.

While the liar is free to develop the elements of a fictitious job in any way he or she desires, the lie system about the phony job must not only mesh with the job seeker's career progression, it must also present a richly textured and detailed story which can handle any possible question that might be asked. There must be a consistent story line which enables the job seeker to present the fictitious job as a logical step in a sequence of jobs. More than just take up a spot in the employment history of the liar, the phony job must actively create a good impression and enhance the entire resume. While the liar has a free hand in designing details about the fictitious job, extra effort must be taken to make those details fit together in a consistent and believable manner.

Just as important, the specifics of each fictitious job must be carefully thought out and designed so that the job contains all of the positive factors which employers would expect from a worthwhile candidate who actually worked such a job. As you can see, proper design of a fictitious job requires a lot of work.

The design of an entire phony employment record is even more challenging. Each job must be sequenced to develop naturally from the previous position, with a careful eye toward growth in professional skills, increases in compensation, and so on, all the while meshing with the candidate's educational record (true or fictitious) and places of residence.

DESIGNING INDIVIDUAL FICTITIOUS JOBS

There are many types and uses of fictitious jobs. The fictitious job can be with an organization that never existed or it can be in a real company for which you've never worked. It can be with a fictitious company which you're claiming is still in business or you can claim that the company has gone out of business in the interval between your departure and the present. The varieties are endless and are subject to many of the same restrictions which were discussed in the discussion of reference lying (see Chapter Nine). Once you complete your initial reading of this book, you should be able to select the type of fictitious job lie which best suits your job-search needs.

Length of Job Tenure

Any job (real or fictitious) with less than two years of tenure makes your entire resume look bad. It gives the impression that you're a job hopper. If you've only a six-month period of unemployment to cover, it's not practical to hide only that six months with a fictitious job. Even if the fictitious job looks great, employers will still be put off by the short tenure. If you must use a fictitious job to cover a short period of unemployment, it's better to drop the job previous to (or after) the period of unemployment and stretch the fictitious job to cover the dropped job's interval and the period of unemployment. This strategy makes you appear to be a more stable candidate.

If you absolutely must use the job "next" to the period you want to hide, you'll have to consider an alternative besides using a phony job. Perhaps a single time "special" consulting assignment can be created. Don't use fictitious jobs to cover short intervals. If you don't have any jobs with long tenure in your employment history, the insertion of one long-term fictitious job should be carefully examined as a way to enhance your perceived stability. Even a series of good jobs with two years tenure each aren't going to impress anyone. If you've been working for twenty years or so, you should show at least two jobs with five years of service. If you don't and you're going to be using a fictitious job for any other reason, you might as well demonstrate your stability by giving it a long tenure. If you've only been working from five to ten years, it's okay to have a few shorter jobs of two to three years in length, as it's expected that younger people will move around a bit before they settle down.

Career Growth

If you're going to take the trouble to design a phony job, you may as well make sure it's going to do everything it can. The lie system must not only stand up under fire and fill in for an experience you'd rather not admit, it should enhance your perceived value by showing continual professional and technical growth. If you're simply substituting the phony job for a bad experience in the same industry, make sure that you pump the hell out of the phony job so that it looks like you got all the experience you need to make a big jump. This is especially important if you're looking for a big salary increase as a result of the phony job.

If you don't have a firm understanding of how your technical area or industry assesses qualifications for the next big step, take a look at some career guides (a series of guides called *Peterson's Guides* is good).

Another source of the types of qualifications you should add to your experiences can be found in classified ads. Particularly helpful are those that state, "the candidate will have successfully" and then go on to list the qualifications you'll need for the job. Find the ads for the type of job you want and see what you need to put into the phony job so that you'll be considered a top candidate. After you've read about 15 to 20 advertisements for a particular type of position, you'll begin to see that there is a small number of critical qualifications. These are the ones you want to lie about.

Compensation

It's often difficult to insert a fictitious job into an employment history without modifying all sorts of compensation data from surrounding jobs. After all, the salary progression must look smooth and realistic, demonstrating the steady growth one expects from a winner.

Chances are that if you've got a problem to hide, the progression wasn't smooth and/or upward. However, be careful to consider the risks of lying about compensation for real jobs where references may be checked. The section of this chapter that deals with phony employment backgrounds presents a detailed look at how to put together a smooth and impressive compensation history.

The Company

It's not enough to simply make up a name for the

fictitious organization and hope that you'll be able to handle questions. Remember, the lies on your resume are the easiest to tell but they're not going to allow you to glide through the interview. You have to design the entire lie system right from the start so that it can hold up in any interviews as well as simply look pretty on the resume. In effect, you have to conceptualize the entire company in your mind so that you can describe everything from what the building looked like to how much money they made.

This detailed preparation does several things. First of all, if you've developed a detailed lie system and use it a lot, it will begin to seem real to you. Some of the lie systems that I've used constantly for the last five years have become so familiar that I've often had to remind myself that they're lies. There's no way anyone could trip me up on them.

Another benefit of a detailed lie system is that your fictitious job will make you consider the myriad aspects of the fake job (and all of your jobs) which might not be apparent at first. In effect, you'll force yourself to think of all sorts of other little facts which can be pumped up and/or lied about.

In constructing your fictitious job, you must consider and map out the details of the position, of the fictitious company, the employees, the products and profits, and all the other details which will build your story into a history.

Ask yourself, "how was the company set up?" Did you work for a single division with only one location or was it one of many divisions? Describe the organization chart. Who reported to the leader of your division or location? Where did you fit in on the organization chart?

What industry was the company involved in? If you're lying about having been a technical expert, such as a chemical engineer, the company will have to have had a need for your skills. In many cases, that will define the industry. On the other hand, if you're lying about being a controller, you can pick the industry with the most freedom, as job skills will be perceived by employers to transfer more easily across industries.

What products did the company make? That's going to be one of the first questions in every interview. How many different products did it make? What was the dollar volume? What about profits before and after taxes?

How many employees worked for the company? Were they all in one location or were they in various offices around the country? Be careful to consider the total dollar amount of business when you lie about the size of the company. One fellow blew an interview by inadvertently stating that the company he had "worked" for had 500 employees. He said it because it suited his immediate needs in answering the interviewer's question. Unfortunately, he had earlier claimed that the company's gross sales were 10 million per year. The interviewer questioned how a company could make so little money for so many people. Even if the entire 10 million were put into salaries, that would be only an average of $20,000 per job, with nothing for capital expenses, taxes, day-to-day expenses, supplies, etc. Needless to say, the liar had to squirm and wriggle on that one and come out looking like a fool. If you're not familiar with these types of figures for the industry you're lying about, take a look at annual reports from companies in similar industries to get some idea of ratios of employees to gross dollars and profits.

The question will come up as to the location of the company. It's best if the location is far from that of the prospective employer; no sense taking any chances on someone wondering why he can't get your "former employer" on the phone (which isn't a problem if the company is "out of business") or why the interviewer doesn't recall the street address "since I've lived in this town all my life." No sense taking any chances. Develop a mental picture of the appearance of the building and offices where you worked. Scenes from movies are helpful. You'll find that the more details you fill in, the better the story will sound and the more realistic it will seem when you think about it and tell it.

You must carefully develop the following story elements about the job itself:

1. Job title.
2. Salary grade.
3. Title and name of your boss (this must also be worked into any reference lies).
4. Employees and job titles that reported to you.
5. Daily responsibilities for you and your people.
6. Special programs and achievements of the sort that will go into your resume's achievements section.
7. The types of administrative systems (payroll, planning, performance reviews, recruiting, etc.) that the company used and which you administered for your people.

The following are some of the interview questions

which may come up and which will require you to use the above information in a creative manner. If you can't answer each of these in a spontaneous manner, you're going to come across as a less than confident candidate.

1. What kind of recommendations (references) will I get from your past employers?
2. What's your professional reputation like?
3. What would your past bosses (employees) say about you?
4. Why did you leave the job?
5. How have you been treated by past employers?
6. What single thing did you like most (least) about the job?
7. What changes would you have made in the job to make it better?
8. What about the working environment did you like best?
9. What were some of the toughest parts of the job?
10. What was your biggest frustration (satisfaction) in the job?
11. What would you have done to change things in the job?
12. What were your supervisor's best (worst) points?
13. Tell me about a typical day on the job.
14. What did your supervisor do to help you improve?
15. What single thing did you do best?
16. Did you hire/fire people?
17. How did you increase profits (sales, productiv-

ity) in the job?

18. Explain how you reduced costs (overhead, staff) in that job.

19. Describe a situation in which your management skills were put to the test.

20. How did you motivate your employees?

When rehearsing the interview questions in Chapter Twelve, be sure to include the above questions in your practice sessions. Your answers to these questions won't come up in every interview and may not ever be asked, but they could be. You can't take the chance of trying to deal with them on the spot. The dangers are particularly severe if you're lying about an industry you're not familiar with. In that case, all of the questions in this chapter should serve as a research outline about which you'll have to learn before you're qualified to lie effectively.

Be very sure, when you're developing your information, to include the necessary qualifications which you need and which are expected of someone in the position. At the same time, don't get carried away. I once interviewed a poor liar who tripped herself up by exaggerating too much. I was looking for a research psychologist with some low-level supervisory experience. The applicant claimed that she had supervised seven full-time therapists in the counseling center of a small college. Up to that point, everything she had been saying seemed believable. She had no way of knowing that I had once worked in a counseling center and was familiar with staff/student ratios. She was lying to appear more qualified as a supervisor. Too bad for her chances on that interview. Keep your lies realistic.

DESIGNING COMPLETELY PHONY JOB HISTORIES

Putting together a completely false employment background is an extreme step. You should consider it as a last-resort measure. If there's some way you can possibly use part of your actual background, use it. Constructing a job history is much like building a house on a hillside; the more connections there are to solid rock, the fewer are the chances that it will break free under stress. The more connections that your phony employment history has to actual fact, the less likely will you be to make a mistake in an interview. Always minimize your lies to the fewest and/or the smallest that will do the job.

Phony employment backgrounds are typically required for one of two purposes: to substitute a series of successful job experiences for what's been a career of second-rate or low-paying job experiences, which include possible firings and other bad news, while in search for a job in the same industry; and, more extreme, to make a fresh start in another line of work or industry when you can't afford the time or monetary sacrifices required to start from scratch. This is the most extreme form of job-search lying, but the one that obviously has the greatest benefits for a desperate liar. We'll discuss the lying needs of each of these situations separately.

Fresh Start in the Same Industry

The primary advantage of this approach is that you already know most of the technical information you'll need to sound like a reasonable applicant. This knowledge is absolutely essential to success in your lies. Every single industry, whether it's the legal profession, assembling automobiles, or lawn services, has an unbelievable number of specific terms and bits of information which an outsider can't possibly know. Most of the work methods themselves in most industries are not difficult for an intelligent person to pick up pretty fast. It's the knowledge of the jargon that presents the most problems. The newcomer doesn't usually know enough to sound sufficiently knowledgeable during the interview to get the job.

If you're staying in the same industry, you'll not only have a mastery of the jargon and the work methods, you'll understand how the industry operates, how jobs are defined, how performance is evaluated, what the products are, and so on. Your only worries revolve around building a fictitious employment history which appears sound to others in the industry.

Your basic challenge is going to be to put together a set of jobs, most or all of which are false, which shows a career progression that makes you an ideal candidate for the position you're after. Each of the individual jobs you create will have to be put together using the techniques presented in the first part of this chapter. Our concerns in this section involve setting up the proper framework into which the fictional jobs can be inserted.

Establishing the Proper Chronology

The first thing you've got to do is determine the time period which your phony job history will cover. The best way to do this is to create a time line such as that shown in Figure 42. Put the dates on the left, your age in the next column, and the activity (school or job) on the right with any notes or comments. At the bottom of the time line, note what you're going to be claiming as your current situation. Beneath that, put a dashed line and your goal.

The time line will clearly show you the time periods you'll have to "fill up" with your lies. You'll design the structure of your fictional employment background by filling in the empty spots on the time line with phony jobs.

As you can see from Figure 42, the liar must fill an 18-year job history with phony jobs. He has made the decision to claim a phony current employment situation as a consultant rather than admit to his actual job.

FIGURE 42. TIME LINE FOR ORGANIZING FICTITIOUS BACKGROUND LIES

Dates	Age	Activity/Notes
9/64-6/68	18-22	Attended college. Will leave this alone.
9/68-6/70	22-24	Need phony M.A. Will insert it here. Plan to claim part-time evening studies while working full-time at first phony job. The lie challenge: Need jobs from 9/68 to 11/86, an

		18-year period.
11/86	39	Plan to lie right up to the (current date) present with phony jobs. Will claim to be currently working as a consultant.

Target job: Engineering manager. Approximate salary 55K per annum.

If you've already got the essential education you need, your job history will have to start within three months of the date you finished school. The time line shown in Figure 42 shows that a phony master's degree, earned in night school, will be incorporated in the lie system from September 1968 to June 1970. The first phony job will also start sometime between June and October of 1968. This is a good ploy as it allows the liar to show an additional two years of experience while at the same time demonstrating the dedication of having gone to school at night while working.

Faced with the challenges shown in Figure 42, the liar decides to break the 18-year employment gap into five jobs. This will permit enough variety in jobs and promotional opportunities to demonstrate career growth to the point where an engineering manager position seems reasonable. Figure 43 presents the time line of Figure 42 with the five job intervals included.

The job tenure intervals shown in Figure 43 demonstrate a respectable amount of stability. Of course, individual tastes will affect exact distributions of time in each position. If this were your time line you may have preferred to shorten the length of time on the first position (or with the first company, which covered the first two positions) and transfer the time to future positions.

Career Development

It's important to show the correct sequence of job titles and advancement in your fictitious career. After all, it's got to show all the success and achievement the real story doesn't provide. Once you've determined the number of positions you're going to claim, you have to use the intervals to show fast-track professional development. If you're lying about the same industry you've been in, simply design your job titles to show significant advancement in each position.

FIGURE 43. TIME LINE FOR FICTITIOUS BACKGROUND SHOWING INTENDED JOB INTERVALS FOR PHONY-POSITIONS LIES

Dates	Age	Activity/Notes
9/64-6/68	18-22	Attended college. Will leave this alone.
9/68-6/70	22-24	Need phony M.A. Will insert it here. Plan to claim part-time evening studies while

		working full-time at first phony job.
10/68-11/71	22-25	3 years, 1 month. Promoted to next job in same company.
12/71-6/77	25-30	6 years, 7 months.
7/77-9/80	30-33	3 years, 2 months.
10/80-4/84	33-36	3 years, 6 months.
5/84-11/86	36-39	This will be a consulting job.

Target job: Engineering manager. Approximate salary 55K per annum.

This is the crux of careful career development for liars and non-liars alike. Too many people compromise their careers by switching jobs without moving up; they move to get out of bad situations or to take a chance in a new company. In some cases, these non-promotional moves may be essential, but they don't look good on a resume, as they ruin the appearance of stability and show no advancement.

There may not be much one can do about the hard breaks of reality in life, but it's foolish to show any less than optimum career moves on a phony employment background. Note how the time line shown in Figure 44 demonstrates a fine sense of career development on the part of our engineering liar. Each and every job change shows advancement or promotion. If, at this point, the liar had determined that another position might be necessary to make the progression through the ranks in his profession look realistic, the time line would have to be modified. An additional job could be added if enough time was available to maintain the appearance of stability. If time was not available, the liar would simply have to show a big jump, as a result of a "phenomenally lucky break" or fast advancement.

FIGURE 44. TIME LINE FOR FICTITIOUS BACKGROUND SHOWING INTENDED JOB INTERVALS AND JOB TITLES

Dates	Age	Activity/Notes
9/64-6/68	18-22	Attended college. Will leave this alone.
9/68-6/70	22-24	Need phony M.A. Will insert it here. Plan to claim part-time evening studies while working full-time at first phony job.
10/68-11/71	22-25	Electronics engineer. 3 years, 1 month. Promoted to next job in same company.
12/71-6/77	25-30	Promoted to senior electronics engineer -- project manager. 6 years, 7 months.

7/77-9/80	30-33	Engineering section chief. 3 years, 2 months.
10/80-4/84	33-36	Chief design engineer. 3 years, 6 months.
5/84-11/86	36-39	Independent engineering consultant.

Target job: Engineering manager. Approximate salary 55K per annum.

For Whom Did You Work?

The next step is to determine what types of prior employers to claim. Many of your decisions will be driven by the availability of confederates who will act as your phony references, your knowledge of your industry, information about companies that have gone out of business and can be used as former employers, and the particular requirements in your industry. For example, it's always safer to lie about having worked for smaller companies, as it's natural that no one has heard of them. It's also more believable that they might have gone out of business. However, if your industry is such that only large companies would provide the type of experience employers respect, you might have to take a chance. You'll notice that our lying engineer has avoided the most dangerous part of career design lying by using a consulting lie as the current employer. The optimum approach involves using larger, existing companies only far in the past with lying personal references portraying past supervisors whom you've kept in touch with (see Chapter Nine for techniques). In our example, the engineer would be fairly safe to claim to have worked for an existing company in the first two jobs, as few employers will have those records on hand. Better yet, a lie involving a large, out-of-business company would be almost 100 percent foolproof.

Compensation

Compensation lies about existing jobs were discussed at some length in Chapter Eight. Refer to that material before attempting to implement the techniques in this section. The challenge is to put together a compensation history which reflects steady and successful growth to the point where your current salary is 5 to 15 percent less than the midpoint of the job you're after. Figure 45 displays a work sheet of the type that you should use.

FIGURE 45. COMPENSATION WORK SHEET FOR COMPUTING EARNINGS IN FICTIONAL JOBS

Year	Position/ Title	Year- Ending Salary	Growth (%)
1968	Electronics engineer	10	---
1969	Electronics engineer	11	10
1970	Electronics engineer	12.1	10
1971	Senior elect. engineer	15.3	21

1972	Senior elect. engineer	16.4	7
1973	Senior elect. engineer	17.7	8
1974	Senior elect. engineer	19.1	8
1975	Senior elect. engineer	20.3	6
1976	Senior elect. engineer	21.7	7
1977	Section chief	28.0	23
1978	Section chief	30.8	10
1979	Section chief	32.6	6
1980	Chief design engineer	34.4	6
1981	Chief design engineer	37.3	8
1982	Chief design engineer	40.4	8
1983	Chief design engineer	43.4	8
1984	Consultant	47.9	10
1985	Consultant	50.8	6
1986	Consultant	53.8	6

Target: Engineering manager, 57.5 (midpoint), difference = 6.3 percent

List every year of your work career on the left, with the job title at year end in the next column. Then, put your annual earnings at year end in each job in the next column to the right. You start with the first job at the top and work down, increasing the compensation of the next position by an amount you select, which is put in far right-hand column. At the bottom of the work sheet, place the midpoint of the salary interval of the job you're after. In our example, the lying engineer figures that the midpoint of an engineering manager in his industry is 57.5K per year. What the engineer must do is show steady growth of 5 to 10 percent each year (as a result of merit increases), with hits of from 5 to 25 percent for promotions. As you jack up the salaries, keep an eye on the final figure at the bottom, so you don't overshoot it. Note that Figure 45 shows promotional increases of 21, 23, and 6 percent. None of the employers will ever see this type of year-to-year work sheet but you've got to make sure that your entire compensation story hangs together so that your claimed salary levels look realistic. If things don't work out and the ending salary is too low or too high, do it again, adjusting the starting compensation a little, or the increases upon promotion.

Once you've developed your lie-system framework to the point shown in the Figure 45 example, you're ready for the real work; designing the individual jobs according to the guidelines given in the earlier part of this chapter.

Geographical Considerations

Occasionally, it will be necessary to lie about previous places of residence. The most obvious need for this occurs when the job seeker has been arrested and doesn't wish to tell prospective employers about it. It's also helpful to lie about previous addresses if you wish to claim that you worked in another area of the country so that it will be more difficult for employers to conduct formal reference verifications on claimed past employers. You can't very well lie about having worked 2,000 miles away if you didn't live there. Lying about where you've lived, for either of the above purposes, is easy.

FIGURE 46. EXAMPLE OF RELEASE FOR BACKGROUND CHECK OF CRIMINAL RECORD

I, [your name here], Social Security Number: [the number], authorize [the employer's name] to contact the information bureau of law enforcement authorities to verify the facts I provided on my application regarding any criminal convictions during the last five years. I understand that information about warrants without convictions, "youth offender" convictions, and minor traffic violations will not be requested.

I understand that this release will be used only for [employer's name here] and that information will not be provided to any other sources.

Law enforcement authorities in the locations in which I have lived over the past five years may be contacted.

The cities, counties, and states in which I have lived over the last five years are:

_______to _______
Dates

_______________ _______________ _____
City County State

_______to _______
Dates

_______________ _______________ _____
City County State

_______to _______

Dates

______________ ______________ ____
City County State

______to ______
Dates

______________ ______________ ____
City County State

______to ______
Dates

______________ ______________ ____
City County State

Signature ____________________ Date ______

If you cover the reference checks, most employers won't bother with any other investigations. However, a few may conduct background or bonding investigations. Chapter Thirteen discusses these in detail. These aren't a problem as long as you lie correctly. You'll know that a background check is planned when they have you sign release forms. Figure 46 displays the form that's concerned with verifying that you don't have a criminal record. If this form appears and you've got a criminal record, you're in trouble if you tell the truth.

Obviously, if you're going to be lying, you simply fill in your claimed places of residence and nothing will turn up. Make sure that the job locations on your resume match up with the places you're claiming to have worked. This ruse works because investigators will check only local records in the places on the release form. If you have a record elsewhere, it won't show up. The one exception to this occurs in some states where you might have a serious traffic violation such as drunken driving. Many states share motor vehicle data in order to enhance enforcement. While this generally involves adjacent states only, it's a growing trend. Your best protection is to lie about having lived in states far removed from your actual places of residence.

Designing Fictitious Backgrounds in Unfamiliar Industries

The number-one principle of this type of job lie is: don't do it unless you have no other choice. I explained the reason earlier in this chapter; it's extremely difficult to learn enough to sound like a reasonable candidate in the interview (even with personnel types), much less do the job. The problem compounds itself if you've been out working more than ten years because you'll probably have to try to sell yourself as a person of reasonably senior position in the industry you've selected. It's easier to switch industries between lower-level jobs because you won't have to know as many things. Yet, simply consider how much anyone learns in only one to two years in any industry. You can't pick it up in any one book, you have to learn it on-the-job. I hate to admit it, but I can't recommend any strategy of lying which covers switching to an entirely different industry. However, there are alternatives to such a drastic change.

Typically, there are satellite industries which serve a particular industry. For example, hospitals are served by medical supply houses, pharmaceutical supply businesses, laundries, food service companies, durable medical goods suppliers, and the like. If you happened to be trapped in a lousy series of jobs in the hospital management field, you might be able to sustain a fictional story line in an alternative, but related industry. Look carefully about your own industry for career lying opportunities in associated areas. If there are absolutely none, consider staying in your own industry.

If you decide to go for it anyway, you've got to learn as much about the target industry as you can. If you're out of work and desperate, I recommend that you take anything you can get and study the target industry for about six months before you try a complex lie system. You've got to learn enough about the industry to answer every question I've presented in this book and sound like a winner. That's not something you can do in a week or two. If it's feasible, take a community college course or two in the area, or get a job as a low-level laborer or clerk in the target industry. You might even try to do some work in the target industry as a "student project" (which you lie about) so you can learn the jargon. If all of this sounds unreasonable to do while you're out of work, you're right. But it's the only way you're going to be able to switch industries safely if you're not familiar with it already. Since it's my intention to help you lie without detection, I have to present the situation accurately. Without extensive preparation, you're doomed, most likely in the interview, but almost surely on the job.

Chapter Twelve

Sustaining Your Lies in the Interview

Many authors of job-search books have observed that the face-to-face interview is the "moment of truth" in job searching. Although the purpose of this book is to use the moment for something else, there's no doubt that the interview is the single most critical aspect of the entire job search. Nobody gets hired without a personal interview and no decisions are set in concrete until the employer has a chance to see the goods in person; nobody hires a resume or voice until they also examine the ever-famous "cut of your jib." Resume and telephone lies may get you into the interview, and phony references may support the earlier lies, but the interview is the one single battle that must be convincingly won if you want to get the job. Unfortunately for job seekers, both liars and honest fools alike, most job seekers' interviewing skills are even worse than their appallingly bad resume-writing talents.

Most honest, sincere, and superbly qualified job candidates can't give a relaxed, confident, and convincing interview. Rather than concentrating on manipulating the interview to their own best advantage, most job candidates direct most of their interviewing energy in keeping their breakfast down, wiping their sweaty palms, and struggling to come up with answers to questions they never thought they'd be asked. The result is most often a nerve-wracking and unimpressive interview. And that's an honest candidate's performance!

The typical job-seeking liar, stressed by concealing his lies while worrying about how to handle questions that may uncover a hint of the truth, does even worse. I've seen the finest hand-crafted lies fall apart in interviews. They looked great on paper and sounded great on the phone, but they flopped because of poor face-to-face interview technique. It's one thing to perform on paper or on the phone, it's quite another thing to stare the interviewer in the eye and stay cool and collected while you're lying like crazy.

Fortunately for you, there's not much difference between what you as a liar are trying to do in an interview and the purpose of the skilled but honest interviewee: both of you are trying to project an aura of confidence, mastery, value, sincerity, professionalism, conformity, and courtesy. For most of us, the presentation of such qualities as "the way we are" is a lie itself. Face it, everybody is lying in job interviews in terms of the impression they're trying to make; none of us wants the interviewer to see us as we really are because nobody would hire us. This is good news because it means that job-seeking liars don't have to do anything qualitatively different from non-liars during their interviews.

Liars have to make the same unrealistic and phony impression that the non-liars are striving to make. The only differences are quantitative: the liar must do so while worrying about the content of the lies and unexpected traps while the non-liar must worry only about normal interview stress. Thus, the liar has to work a little harder (but on the same things) to project the same positive qualities.

A great deal of the added interview stress felt by the job-seeking liar can be eliminated by careful preparation of the lie system which is in use. That's why it's particularly critical for you to have answers ready to all of the questions which were presented in earlier chapters, as well as to those later in this chapter. In this chapter you'll take a look at the absolute minimum requirements for winning an interview whether you're telling the truth or not, and the problems which present liars with additional risk.

MINIMUM INTERVIEW REQUIREMENTS

The following sections discuss various aspects of interview practice and strategy which every candidate must scrupulously follow. Job-seeking liars must follow the guidelines even more carefully, as they must make such an absolutely positive impression that minor slip-ups and stress responses will seem irrelevant to the interviewer.

Preparing for Telephone Interviews

Almost all face-to-face interviews are going to result from telephone interviews. The secret for giving good telephone interviews is to be prepared. The difficulty is that you'll never know when an employer or headhunter is going to call in response to something you've sent. You must do two things to stay in control, so that you don't get caught unawares and/or compromise an opportunity by giving less than a great interview because you weren't ready when the call came in.

First of all, get an answering machine. Leave it on all the time during your job search. Buy one which allows you to listen to incoming calls without having to answer the phone; this option (a standard feature on most machines) enables you to decide whether you want to answer before they hang up. Don't bother with all of the remote message beepers and such unless you need them for something else besides the job search. Record only a very businesslike outgoing message on your machine such as:

"Hello. You have reached (area code and number). No one is available to take your call right now. Please leave your name, number, and any message when you hear the beep. Your call will be returned as soon as possible. Thank you for calling."

When you hear a call come in, you can listen and decide if you want to pick it up. If it's an interviewer and you're ready (as with a second telephone interview), pick it up. If you're not ready, you can let the machine take the message and you can research the caller's name, the company, etc., in your records before you return the call. With adequate record keeping and an answering machine, you'll never have to worry about taking a call and getting stuck because you forgot what lies you used in the cover letter and/or how much money you said you were presently making. Better yet, you'll be able to go back and read the ad before you return the call. You can then act as if you've been waiting only for their call because "your search is so selective and limited." This makes an even more favorable impression.

Meticulous record keeping is essential for the job-seeking liar. You must record all the information which will enable you to accurately determine what you said and to whom you said it, and you should organize the records in an easy-to-use format. I suggest that you organize all of your job-search materials in a single three-ring binder. Use separate sections for resume versions, cover letters, ads that you've replied to, and so on. When responding to classified ads, clip out the ad, tape it to a sheet of paper, and put it in the notebook. On the paper, make a note as to what resume version you sent with the ad, what paper it came from and the date, what cover letter you sent (if you're using different versions and/or lies), and any notes about claimed compensation. Different sections of the notebook should contain copies of all resumes and cover letters. Other sections organize information about what resume versions you've sent to headhunters or used in direct solicitation to companies. Properly organized, you can pick up the notebook and quickly locate the appropriate page for a mailing or job.

This notebook approach is particularly important when dealing with phone interviews which result from blind ads. When you answer a blind ad, you have no idea who the company is. Without warning you get a call from the mystery company which begins: "Hello, I'm Mr. Smith of Jones, Inc. We received your resume and I'd like to talk to you about your qualifications." If you've got multiple stories working, as almost everyone will if only lying about compensation, you're going to be at a distinct disadvantage unless you can match the ad with the caller. Once the caller mentions where the company is and what it does, you shouldn't have any problem matching the company to one of your ads. This is, of course, easiest if you let the answering machine take the call and then do your research before you call back. In some cases, you might not be able to locate the exact ad as several may seem about right. In that case, slip the appropriate sheets out of your book and read all of the ones that appear close. Then call back and ask, in the initial conversation, where they placed the ad and about when. This additional information should make it easy to match the ad and then handle the interview with finesse. Once you become adept at it, you'll find that you can usually handle all of this in real time, taking the call and accessing the necessary information at the same time. But until you've had a lot of practice, there's no sense trying to be a superstar and taking a chance on messing up even a single phone interview.

If you're on the phone talking to the interviewer and you're suddenly not sure you've got the right ad, just interrupt and say that "the front doorbell just rang. Could you excuse me for a moment?" You can then research for another minute or so. You can always simply disconnect them in the middle of one of your sentences, as if there's phone trouble. You'll then have several minutes to do more research. Leave the phone off the hook while you read, as it'll prevent them from calling back.

If the prospective employer calls, and you accidentally take the call because you're expecting a personal call and you're not prepared or willing to duke it out with a phone interview, excuse yourself with a flattering lie such as, "I'm thrilled that you called but I can't talk right now. I was halfway out of the door on my way to a guest lecture at the community college and I'm cutting it close right now. Can I get back to you tomorrow/later today?" You'll then be able to call back when you're ready to work the magic on them.

Specific techniques for answering questions and handling the content of phone interviews are identical (except that visual cues don't have to be controlled) to those involved in face-to-face interviews. We'll discuss these techniques later in this chapter.

Personal Appearance

The subject of proper attire for interviewing gets a lot more attention than it needs. Proper personal appearance is critical but the expectations of interviewers are very basic and straightforward. You don't have to be a fashion expert to figure out what to wear. Interviewers expect candidates to dress in a way which demonstrates that the candidates consider the interview, the company, the interviewer, and the job very important to them. That's the basic bottom line in dressing for interviews and for the work in business in general. If all the interviewer knows about you is the resume and a few words on the phone, he's going to rapidly begin to fill in the gaps of his knowledge from the moment he lays eyes on you. If you're dressed in a professional, respectful, and tasteful manner, that's the type of impression he'll begin to form instantly. This initial expectation of his will then color everything you say positively.

Study after research study demonstrates that people who dress up and look neat and sharp are trusted more than less tastefully dressed people, are assumed to be more sincere, are thought to be more educated, and are assumed to be more successful and intelligent. It may be phony and it may be plastic but that's the way it is. If you're lying, you can't afford not to do everything possible to foster the most favorable impressions in everyone you meet.

To make the proper impression, you must dress slightly more conservatively than the norm for everyday work in the same organization. For men, this means that if suits are the norm everyday, the smart applicant wears a dark blue or black, conservatively cut suit. One should never wear browns or greens or bright-colored suits, and never a sport coat and slacks instead of a suit. Ties are absolutely mandatory for all interviews. Even if you're interviewing for a laborer's job, you must dress up slightly. Perhaps a suit might be overdoing it, but a tie and sport shirt would be appropriate as they would represent "slightly more conservative" attire than the everyday norm for the job.

For the majority of job-search liars who will be working in office environments, suits or their equivalents for women are mandatory. It's not necessary to always wear a three-piece suit but in very conservative industries such as banking and insurance, a three-piece suit is almost mandatory, except in summer. For women, white or pastel blouses with suits or a skirt and jacket are mandatory. Bright colors and patterns should be avoided, as well as bright or gaudy jewelry. Suits and skirts/jackets should be dark blue or black, as for men. Ties or bows (neck only, not in the hair) can be used but should be a coordinated color and conservative in pattern and shape. Women must present a businesslike appearance but must also present just enough femininity by means of accessories to tap into interviewers' favorable feelings about women in general.

Male interviewers expect all women to be slightly feminine, even at work, because of associations with wives and mothers; in most men, there's an underlying, subconscious expectation that all women are "good" and nice. Clothing that makes a slightly feminine appeal creates a favorable impression in most men. Clothes that are too masculine don't appeal to this subconscious positive expectation. It works with women interviewers as well, because they'll identify with other women in business. Clothes that are too feminine (frilly dresses, loud colors) tend to appeal directly to less favorable (for business) stereotypes about housewives or female movie stars -- that is, associations with less "powerful" women such as those who are housewives.

For both sexes, jewelry should be kept to a tasteful minimum. Shoes should be conservative and well polished. Certain accessories are essential for making an impression of success and confidence. A good quality briefcase or attache case is essential. Women should not carry a purse into the interview, but the attache only. A good quality pen and pencil set, kept in the jacket pocket and used to make notes, lends an impression of preparedness and success. A small appointment book, whipped out from the attaché to check dates for follow-up interviews, the date when you can expect to get a decision, etc., again shows that you're prepared and professional.

Preparing for In-Person Interviews

Each and every face-to-face interview must be treated as the rare and sacred opportunity that it is. You'll get few enough of them for all of the ads you'll answer and the legions of headhunters you'll talk with. Once you have one scheduled, take pains to get ready for it and ensure that nothing goes wrong. Some of the things which will promote a calm and problem-free interview are:

1. Make sure you know how to get to the interview. If you're not sure, call the company (not the person you're going to see) and get detailed instructions.
2. Have a map of the area unless you know it extremely well.
3. Prepare all of your clothes the night before.
4. If you're going to the interview from home, leave an hour early to allow for all of the routine disasters that can occur. If you're leaving from work, make sure you take extra time. If you arrive late, you've blown it.
5. Don't show up more than 15 minutes early at the interviewer's office. You don't want them to think you've got nothing else to do.
6. Try to learn a little something about the company before the interview. Many books will tell you to do a thorough research job on the company, but most candidates don't have the time. If you can,

pick up an annual report or go to the library and check out the *Million Dollar Directory* or *Dun and Bradstreet's Directory* (ask the librarian). Check local directories if the organization is a very small one. Often, you can learn a great deal by simply reading the company-related stuff found in the waiting room, and then mentioning some little item in the interview. It doesn't take much to sound like you've taken a lot of trouble to look into it. If you find something at the library, photocopy a page or two and make sure you take it out and refer to it at some point in the interview so they'll know you took the trouble to look them up.

7. Immediately before going into the building, read the ad or other data about the job from your notebook and review your lie system in your head.

8. Have extra copies of your resume and a copy of your reference sheet ready if you decide to present it during the interview rather than mailing it later with the thank-you letter.

Interview Behavior

When you walk into the building where the interview will take place, you must have your interview facade in full operation. Don't turn it off until you get back outside. Before, during, and after the interview, you must:

1. Be unfailingly polite to everyone.

2. Smile whenever you greet or walk up to someone. Keep a smile in your voice and make sure that you smile at the interviewer at appropriate points such as when he or she makes a pun or when a question is asked and you answer, "Say, that's a good question (smile)!"

3. Shake hands with everyone to whom you are introduced. Limp wrists and fingertip shakes are bad news. Men and women alike must receive a firm, palm-to-palm handshake.

4. Never play with jewelry or hair. Keep your hands in your lap or take out a pad of paper and pen and pretend to be taking notes if you must, but don't fidget with your hands. Don't twitch your feet or tap your fingers. If you've got these nervous habits, rehearse with a friend and have him point it out. Better yet, tie a bell to your feet when you rehearse; the immediate feedback of the noise will stop the unwanted motions. Never chew gum or smoke, even if it's offered. Don't accept a beverage or coffee (it could spill).

5. If a lunch or dinner is part of the interview, order only the neatest, non-messy, and easiest to eat foods. Stay away from trendy stuff and stick to basics. Do not drink any alcohol under any circumstances, even if offered; you can't afford to compromise your ability to react to dangerous questions.

6. Body position and movement are an extremely important interview tool. Always sit up very straight and don't fiddle with your hands, hair, or jewelry. Keep your hands resting in your lap and use them to make small gestures as you talk. By not moving around, you'll seem less nervous and more stable, composed, and in charge. If you sense the interviewer warming to you, begin to lean closer to his desk. This is a particularly good move when coupled with phrases such as "Look, let me be honest with you" or "I'm glad to hear you say that. Here's how I feel." In social situations, people move closer as

feelings of intimacy develop, as they begin to feel empathy with someone, or if they like someone. Your moves toward the interviewer, after a decent interval, will signal your acceptance of the interviewer and lead the interviewer to "like" you more without knowing why. All of these things usually happen subconsciously but you can use them very consciously. If you're a male interviewing with a male, a pat on the shoulder or arm when you're leaving can be very effective if the interview has gone well. A two-handed handshake is also good for male-to-male interviews. Women should never attempt any other "touches" other than a formal, "man style" handshake (palm-to-palm with firm grip, not a caress with a few finger-tips).

Nod your head occasionally when the interviewer speaks and smile when he completes a topic. Always look the interviewer straight in the eye as much as you can. These looks will demonstrate attentiveness, sincerity, and honesty. Most interviewers don't think people can "look you in the eye and lie" so they'll be doubly impressed by whatever you say if you do look straight into their eyes. Don't use a continuous glare; break your eye contact occasionally to glance about the room, particularly when you're pretending to be in deep thought. After some practice, you'll have ready answers to everything, but it's a good idea to pretend to think about an occasional answer as the interviewer will be flattered that he came up with a good question.

7. Be particularly sensitive to the interviewer's preferences toward your demeanor and responses. If you're giving an answer to a question and the inter-

viewer starts to fidget, you're taking too long; make your future answers shorter. If the interviewer is continually asking you to elaborate, make your initial responses longer. If the interviewer is very serious and somber, stay very formal. If the interviewer is more genial and wants to be more relaxed, act more relaxed (but remain detached and objective).

The First Few Moments of The Interview

The first few minutes of the interview will determine 95 percent of the impression you make. Nobody will ever admit it, but almost all hire/not-hire decisions are made in the first three minutes of the interview. They'll decide from the way you talk, smile, walk, look, and move whether or not they'll hire you. After that, you can make a mistake that'll change their minds, but it's almost impossible to reverse an early no-hire decision. Therefore, it's absolutely critical that you conduct the first few moments of the interview with skill and carefully planned purpose. When you first meet the interviewer, smile, shake hands, introduce yourself, and don't hurry in your answers or comments.

There are a number of steadfast rules which a smart job seeker follows in every interview. They're even more important if you're lying. Follow them and you'll reduce any chances of a problem.

1. Never say more than you have to. The easiest way to get any lie system in trouble is to embellish it on the spot. The more you say in response to any question, the greater your odds of generating a further question which may be unexpected. Answer all questions completely but then

stop and smile. If they want more information, they'll ask.

2. No matter what happens, be positive and confident. You must never, in any circumstance, let on that you are depressed, surprised (except for good surprises such as, "I'm really surprised at the level of technology you have here!"), caught unawares, having difficulties, or having doubts.

3. Never be tempted to give an honest answer to questions about what you "really" want out of a job or "why you're looking." The only acceptable answer to either of these questions is that you're eager for more challenge, opportunities for growth, and a more stimulating work environment.

4. Let the interviewer run the show. The worst possible impression you can make is to try to overpower the interviewer and take control of the interview. This is sometimes a difficult rule to follow when you're working with a complete idiot, but you don't have any choice. If you attempt to force the interviewer to talk about what you need to say, he'll resent your aggression and lack of respect. If it's not going well, work as craftily as you can to say what you need, but don't push. There is an incredible number of bad interviewers who only like to hear themselves talk. If you get one of these, smile a lot, flatter him, and look incredibly interested; you may get invited back even though he didn't interview you (he's not really interviewing anyone so the most pleasant candidate is going to get selected).

5. Don't jump to any conclusion. Many liars ruin otherwise great interview performances by trying to out-psyche the interviewer. It's a dangerous game. If

you're not sure what he wants to hear, be generally positive and non-committal. Your assumptions and all of your behavior must be sculpted on a rock-solid set of traditional values: family, flag, capitalism, and so on. Assume only that they want hard work, honesty (ha!), and loyalty.

6. Have a ready explanation and plan which explains everything you've ever done. If you've paid attention to the earlier chapters in this book, you're lies will be comprehensive and solid. But that's only half the battle; everything else in your life must appear just as solid and well planned. The interviewers are looking for people who appear to be in charge, organized, and powerful. If you let on that much of your life experience has consisted of reactions to problems, unexpected setbacks, and luck, you'll make a bad impression on the typical interviewer. Although that's how almost everyone's life works, nobody admits it during interviews. In essence, you must have a lie system developed for even the truthful aspects of your life. This lie system must create a facade of purpose and careful planning to explain how you got where you are.

7. Allude to a great family life which supports your work. There must be no problems anywhere in your background or present situation. If they ask about family background, they're trying to see if your family life is statistically representative of the profile they like. The best profile is having a father who was a physician and a mother who was an attorney. There's no way they'll ever be able to find out the actual truth unless you tell them, so lie about it. The family was close and everyone worked hard.

8. Spread around a lot of praise for everyone you've ever worked for. This makes you look like a team player and someone who won't make trouble when you join them. It also makes you look like a winner who's not afraid to share the glory.

9. Never argue or disagree with the interviewer, even if he is wrong. Always smile and agree with everything he says. Then, always agreeing and smiling, tell him why he is wrong. For example, the interviewer says, "You don't seem to have the type of in-depth project experience we need." You say, "You're right, I can see why it appears that way. However, when I was with (etc., etc.)." You then proceed to demonstrate how the actual situation is exactly the opposite of his idiotic assumption but you never tell him he's wrong. It makes the entire interview go better.

10. Never admit that you don't have a qualification. No matter what happens, don't come out and actually admit that you're lacking of a required qualification or credential. Of course, if you've carefully prepared your lies and you know the industry, you shouldn't be caught by surprise too often. On occasion, an inept interviewer will *extemporaneously* embellish the job requirements, generally because he or she doesn't understand the position (this most often happens with personnel officers). He'll seize on something you say ("Well, at Zigbottom Steel, we had state-of-the-art blast furnaces") and come back with an idiocy such as, "Well, that's a problem because all of our blast furnaces are twenty years old. You might not be familiar enough with our equipment." Chances are that the issue is immaterial but it's a delicate trap.

If you argue or try to point out his ignorance, you're dead. If you try to explain, you're also dead. So you say something to the effect, "That's a very astute observation (he'll love it if you can do it with a straight face). However, the newer models incorporate all of the more basic manual features, and we were all required to have in-depth operating experience and training in them as well (smile)."

More Questions You Should Be Ready to Handle

Some of the earlier chapters presented questions which might be asked and for which you'll have to have answers if you expect your lie systems to operate smoothly. There are additional questions of a more general nature which will invariably come up and which will have to be handled smoothly, whether you're lying or not. Check through the following list and make sure that you have an answer for each of them. The section following this one will outline the proper method for developing answers which will stand up under the stress of an interview.

1. Tell me about your home life (when you were growing up).
2. What did your father/mother do for a living?
3. How were you influenced by your upbringing?
4. What's your family like?
5. What type of discharge did you get from the service?
6. Does your spouse object to your working long or late hours?
7. Is frequent travel a problem for you?
8. Would you have any problems with relocation?

9. What kind of transportation do you have?
10. Have you ever had credit problems?
11. Have your wages ever been garnished?
12. Do you own your own home?
13. What jobs did you like when you were a child?
14. What's your personal net worth?
15. Do you get alimony (child support)?
16. Do you find it difficult to work with men (women, blacks, whites, gays, etc.)?
17. Where were you (your parents, spouse) born?
18. How involved are you with your children?
19. What is your spouse going to say about this job?
20. Is your recent divorce a problem?
21. Are you planning a family?
22. Who's taking care of your children while you're at work?
23. Do you plan to get married?
24. Why aren't you married?
25. What kind of shape are you in physically?
26. Do you have any trouble keeping up with men (younger people)?
27. When did you get your first job?
28. Do you have any trouble getting to work on time?
29. How good is your health?
30. Do you get sick often?
31. When was your last operation?
32. What new goals have you set for yourself lately?
33. Where do you plan to be in five (ten) years?
34. If you could start your career over, what would you do differently?

35. What are your long-/short-range objectives?
36. Are you happy with your career progress to this point?
37. How come you're not further along in your career?
38. What self-improvement programs are you working on now?
39. What other jobs are you trying to get now?
40. Are you planning on more education?
41. What do you see as the best opportunities in your field?
42. Why are you trying to change careers at this point in your life?
43. What motivates you?
44. What types of people do you like/dislike?
45. What do you think causes some people to fail in (job title)?
46. Describe your closest friend and tell me how you and he/she differ.
47. Describe how you work under pressure.
48. Do you think stability is more important in a job than challenge?
49. What types of friends do you have?
50. How would your friends/enemies describe you?
51. What's your temper like?
52. What is your major strength (weakness)?
53. What is your biggest achievement (failure) in life (recently/last job/last five years)?
54. With what kind of people do you find it difficult (pleasant) to work?
55. What do you do to get along with difficult people?

56. Tell me something which supports your claims of being a self-starter.
57. Describe what you mean by success.
58. What do you get out of work besides money?
59. What would you do if you didn't have to work?
60. How do you react when you're criticized by a supervisor?
61. Are you sensitive to criticism?
62. What does cooperation (teamwork) mean to you?
63. How important is money (service to man) to you?
64. Describe how you feel in a group of people.
65. Describe your decision-making abilities.
66. What do you do when you make a mistake?
67. What are your hobbies?
68. How do you spend your free time?
69. Describe your personality (yourself).
70. What do you do best (worst)?
71. What's your opinion on women (alcohol/gays/etc.) at work?
72. How do you feel about abortion (religion/extramarital sex)?
73. What was the last book you read (movie you saw)?
74. What was the last thing that made you really angry?
75. Who is your hero?
76. What qualities do you admire in a leader?
77. What makes a good employee?
78. Describe your leadership qualities to me.
79. How long will you stay with us?
80. How many hours per week should a person

put in a job?

81. How do you feel about company policies?

82. How long will it be before you make some major contributions here?

83. What unique contributions can you make?

84. Are late hours a problem?

85. You're overqualified for this job. Why do you want it?

86. Well, what do you think of our little company?

87. This place is a pressure cooker. Can you handle it?

88. Do you think you want (can do/would like) my job?

89. Are you going to be out to take your boss's job?

90. Are you willing to relocate to anywhere the company needs you?

91. Do you like to travel?

92. Do you like big or small companies?

93. How much money do you want?

94. Why do you want to work for us?

95. What is it about this job that interests you?

96. What do you think (your field) is all about?

97. You've been moving around (with one firm) for so long, what makes you think you'll fit in around here?

98. How long do you think it's reasonable to wait for a promotion?

99. What do you know about our company?

100. Why should we hire someone who we're going to have to train in our way of doing things?

Several things should be clear to you from the above list of questions. First, many of them are illegal. That doesn't help in the interview situation because if you get angry or tell them that they're asking illegal questions, they'll drop you like a bad background report. What you must do is answer any and all questions in accordance with the earlier presented guidelines for interview content. Never get upset, never argue, never decline to answer, and always be positive and enthusiastic. Remember, to you, nothing is a problem for long because life is one big, happy set of challenges which you're eager to overcome.

DEVELOPING YOUR INTERVIEW SKILLS

There are no magic secrets to developing good interview technique. It takes carefully prepared lie systems, a clear understanding of what you'll encounter, and then hard work to make the proper responses a habit. The first thing you'll have to realize is that there's no substitute for the experience you'll gain from actual interviews. No matter how much you practice, it's not quite the same as the real thing. Take every opportunity to interview that you can get. No matter how bad a prospective job seems, no matter how shoddy the organization is, or how incredibly rude or ignorant the phone interviewer is, never turn down a face-to-face interview. Even if you know you can't take the job and wouldn't take it even if you were starving, go for the interview. Even if you have two other firm offers and you're going to take one of them, go for the interview. After a few months of interviewing, you'll think you've heard every stupid question, met every type of totally ignorant personnel manager, and been subjected to the rudest behavior possible. You'll be wrong. After only a few months of interviewing, you'll continue to learn something in every interview.

Each interview will teach you a little more about the darkest side of man's potential. Such exposure is invaluable; it'll help you develop incredible skills for keeping a straight face when they tell you the salary, extemporaneously orating on any topic at the drop of a question, and kissing up even the most limited intellects with finesse. In addition, you'll increase your skills in assessing the stupidity level of the interviewer in the first few minutes, you'll improve your ability to embroider fictional past experiences, and you'll further develop your repertoire of "canned" responses to stock questions. Most important of all, you'll become a little more at ease with each successive interview. After enough practice in real world situations, you'll become a confident and relaxed liar. Few people can reach this stage of performance without extensive practice, so don't ever turn down an opportunity to interview.

Before you attempt any interviews, practice your answers to all of the questions in this and earlier chapters after you've developed your lie systems. I recommend that you use a tape recorder at least and a videorecorder and VCR if you can. With the camera or tape recorder running, read the question out loud and give your answer as if you were in an actual interview. Don't take short cuts and don't give it less than a 100 percent effort; you want these sessions to represent as closely as possible what you'll be saying in a real interview. When you've gone through about ten questions, stop the recorder, rewind, and then listen to/observe your responses. If you're typical, you'll be appalled at your mumbling, pauses, verbal garbage ("uh," "er," "you know,"), tension-ridden voice, desperate searches for the correct word, and so on. If you're using a videotape camera, you'll be even more shocked that you didn't look very masterful, you squirmed around a lot, you fidgeted, and generally did a bad job. Believe me, you're typical of most interviewees who think they're pretty good. Most people give terrible interviews but they've never had an opportunity to see how they really do and get some honest feedback. If you use the tape recorder or camera method of practice, you'll improve your performance at least 200 percent in only a few hours.

AFTER EACH INTERVIEW

As soon as you complete each interview, by phone or face-to-face, take a moment and make a brief note as to any questions that you didn't handle well. Do this as soon as you leave or hang up, as you'll forget many small problem areas if you put it off. Put a section in your record book for these questions so you'll be able to write them down immediately. Later, review the problem areas and practice your answers with the recorder or camera. Once you've been stumped or surprised by a question, it'll never happen again on that or a similar question if you rehearse an answer for five to ten minutes.

Be sure to send a follow-up thank-you note to the interviewer after each and every phone and face-to-face interview, unless he unequivocally told you to forget it (no sense wasting the time, unless you plan to go back to the company again later).

Also, be sure to make appropriate notes about each completed interview in your record-keeping notebook. Use the back of the sheet or add sheets if you need to. The notebook must contain everything about a job, so don't skimp on keeping it up to date. Attach any business cards you obtain to the sheets as well. If they call back, you'll be able to refer to everyone by his correct title and name; this will impress everyone as to your interest in the position.

IT'S ALL IN THE WRIST

This chapter, particularly in its presentation of a lengthy list of possible interview questions, may give the impression that interview content and what you say is the most important element in handling interviews successfully. The chapters on lie systems might reinforce this impression. Don't be misled.

The content of your lies is secondary to the way you present them (at least in the interview -- you've still got to back many of them up with data and references). If you lie with confidence, with clarity, and with the proper tone of respect, courtesy, and professionalism, you can get away with almost any lie you care to tell in the interview. The lie systems are important only so that you can support your lies in an effective manner should the need arise (as it often will).

In terms of successful lies, presentation style, and not content, is 95 percent of the challenge. The difficulty, of course, is in developing the panache to present yourself in a polished manner. If you follow the guidelines I've presented in this chapter, and if you practice at least five hours, you'll be in the top five percent of all candidates in terms of your presentation of yourself, lying or candid. If you practice more, you'll be even better. If you can make the commitment to put in the long hours and hard work to develop your interview technique, there's nothing to stop you from becoming one of the best job-seeking liars in the world.

Chapter Thirteen

Job-Search Liar Obstacles

The primary influence which discourages job seekers from lying is not simply guilt and moral conflicts. If desperate enough, anyone can overcome his moral compunctions and learn to lie well. Yet, even if you have no conscience at all, you might be reluctant to try the types of lies you need because you're worried about being caught by employers. A healthy respect for employers is certainly not out of place; the last thing your job search needs is for you to take the situation lightly and try to use a pack of poorly designed and cavalierly executed lies. You have to be serious, convincing, and businesslike in every step of your job-search lying.

On the other hand, you must base your planning on a realistic appraisal of exactly what you're up against. Too much respect for the employer's lie-detection skills may deter you from using the types of lies your job search requires. If you know what you're up against and design your lies accordingly, your odds of success will be maximized. Therein lies the purpose of this chapter: to discuss the various techniques which employers use to verify and check applicants' claims. We'll look at the various obstacles and traps which employers use to investigate applicants, and we'll discuss the ways these techniques work, the areas which are particularly risky for certain lies, and how you can best take advantage of and elude employers' detection systems.

At first glance, it might seem that the odds are in favor of employers when it comes to ferreting out and exposing job-search liars. Yet, if you've read this far, you've probably begun to realize that the typical employer's recruiting and selection system isn't as precise or as well organized as you assumed before you read this book. Employers do a lot of things to ensure that they get the best person for the job. As you've seen, there's no comprehensive methodology in use which guides the design and use of employers' selection systems. Many of the things which are done in the selection and verification process are done simply because "somebody thinks it's a good idea," or "it's always been done this way," and/or, "I read an article in *The Personnel Manager's Monthly Journal and Gazetteer* which said that all the biggest companies do it this way." As a result of this confusion, there's no one system of interviewing or resume analysis designed to discover liars. In fact, interviewing is one of the aspects of the selection process which actually works in favor of a skilled liar. If you watch your lying steps, you have little to fear from the standard elements of the recruiting and selection process.

It's much the same way in terms of the specific things which employers do in order to uncover fraud and dishonesty, both by employees and applicants. Many of the verification and detection schemes are used because the personnel people believe they work, because they were used before, and/or they're part of "our policy." You've already learned, in Chapter Nine, how to falsify references. You know that reference checks aren't a problem. The same is true with most types of lies and most things that various employers use to detect liars and/or verify that applicants are who they say they are; the careful liar faces a minimal risk if he knows the dangers and avoids them.

The specific elements of selection and/or lie detection systems which we'll discuss in this chapter are:

1. Resume Screening
2. Telephone Interviews
3. In-Person Interviews
4. Formal Reference Verification (FRV)
5. Personal Reference Verification (PRV)
6. Background and Bonding Checks
7. Aptitude and Skills Testing
8. Psychological Testing
9. Lie Detectors and Voice Analyzers
10. Government Security Clearances

These ten processes, techniques, and activities subsume just about every aspect of the job-seeker/employer interface. If you fully understand the methods and traps of each of them, you'll be well equipped to successfully implement your lies. In the sections which follow, we'll discuss how each of the techniques work, the specific dangers, if any, they present, the best way for job-search liars to deceive them, and the odds of getting caught when using the various lie strategies that have been presented.

RESUME SCREENING

There's little for the job-search liar to fear from the initial resume-screening process. As mentioned in Chapter One, screeners are looking for a neat and businesslike presentation, a sense that the candidate has the minimum qualifications, and whatever individual preferences he may have. No screener is actively looking for lies or signs that a candidate may be shamelessly pumping up his credentials. As long as the resume is carefully prepared and appears professional, anything that's on it will be believed. This is because a good resume is 100 percent of the candidate's presentation at that time; there's no other data available to counter the initial impression made by the resume.

Dangers to the Job-Search Liar

There are few dangers at this early point for the job-search liar if the resume is carefully prepared. However, if there are any typos, misspellings, poorly chosen words, or inappropriate jargon, an attentive resume screener is going to toss the resume in the reject pile. That's not the same as being discovered as a liar but it's a lost job opportunity nonetheless.

Figure 47 presents the odds of getting caught by various employers' tactics when using each of the ten principal job-search lie systems. The odds are shown in terms of expected numbers of people out of 100 who would be discovered in the lie. The odds are estimated on the assumption that the job-search liar has carefully prepared and executed the lie system. As Figure 47 demonstrates, the odds of being caught through resume screening are very small.

FIGURE 47. PERCENT PROBABILITY OF LIE STRATEGIES BEING CAUGHT BY PROSPECTIVE EMPLOYERS' LIE DETECTION MECHANISMS

A	B	C	D	E	F	G	H	I	J
1. Resume Screening									
-	-	-	-	-	-	-	-	-	-
2. Telephone Interviews									
-	-	-	-	-	-	-	-	-	-
3. In-person Interviews									
-	-	-	-	5	-	-	5	10	10
4. Verifying Employment/Education									
-	-	15	-	20	25	-	-	-	15

5. Reference Checks									
-	-	-	10	-	5	-	5	5	5
6. Background, Bonding Checks									
-	-	5	-	-	20	-	-	-	20
7. Aptitude, Skill Tests									
-	-	-	-	10	-	-	-	-	-
8. Psychological Tests									
*	*	*	*	*	*	*	*	*	5*
9. Lie Detectors, Voice Analyzers									
*	*	*	*	*	*	*	*	*	*
10. Government Security Checks									
-	-	-	-	20	20	-	-	35	80

Lie-Strategy Key:

A = Pumping up every fact
B = Altering job details
C = Altering compensation
D = Altering references
E = Creating education
F = Altering job dates
G = Dropping job
H = Creating consulting job
I = Creating fictitious job
J = Fictitious background

* = Other considerations apply; see text.

TELEPHONE INTERVIEWS

If the resume makes the "cut" at the screener's desk and the hiring manager (if he sees the resumes) doesn't veto the candidate, the next step is often a telephone interview. Larger companies will often set up an initial in-person interview with nothing more than a short phone call which is made to determine that the candidate is still interested. These aren't formal telephone interviews, as they have no screening function. If the job is out of town or the interviewer doesn't want to waste a lot of time and money with in-person interviews with a lot of losers, the phone interview will be used for preliminary screening.

Dangers to the Job-Search Liar

The interviewer will be doing one or both of two things: first, getting more details for things that aren't crystal clear on the resume, and second, trying to get the candidate to say the things on the resume in his own words. The first purpose holds no threat for you now that you've read Chapter One and know how to put together a great resume. The second purpose is more critical. If you're lying about an area that you don't know very well, a skilled interviewer may be able to discover some areas of weakness or confusion. For example, you might claim to have been a manager of an accounts payable department. The interviewer may ask, "So, tell me about the division of labor in your department and the number of people who reported to you?" If you haven't given that particular aspect of your lie system much thought, you'll hesitate a little, perhaps hem and haw, and there goes the interview. Don't ruin your chances by sending out resumes which tell lies that you haven't completely developed into lie systems. If you incorrectly assume you'll have plenty of time to think about what you're going to say before you get into the face-to-face interview, you could be surprised by a grueling and lengthy phone interview. I've personally had phone interviews which have lasted over an hour and which have covered my background twice. The caller may have been an idiot, but if I hadn't had my story straight, I would have come across as a poor candidate. The only way to be sure you're prepared is to carefully follow the rehearsal and practicing suggestions given in Chapter Twelve.

Figure 47 demonstrates that the odds for exposure, assuming careful preparation, are less than one in 100 for all lie strategies when telephone interviews are handled properly.

IN-PERSON INTERVIEWS

In addition to the detailed information provided in Chapter Twelve, I just wish to emphasize that the principal purpose of the in-person interview is to determine whether the candidate satisfies the very subjective expectations of the interviewers. Interviews are not conducted to objectively assess technical qualifications or determine work skills. Most frequently the interview is merely a forum in which the interviewers assess whether or not the candidate will "fit in" with their interpretation of the organization's personality. Clothing styles, level of confidence, and careful attention to the sensitivities of the interviewers are the most critical factors which must be attended to by the job-seeking liar (as well as by non-liars).

Dangers to the Job-Search Liar

The well-prepared, practiced job-seeking liar faces little more risk than an honest candidate. If the candidate is at ease and can present a confident, respectful facade to the interviewers, there's little to worry about. The primary danger of the in-person interview is inadequate advanced preparation of the lie system and resulting stress responses which are perceived by the interviewer. This is the same danger which exists in the telephone interview but here it's even more critical. As we saw in Chapter Two, physiological reactions to stress are readily apparent to observers. Even if they're not interpreted as indications of lying, they may be seen as evidence of a lack of confidence. On the phone, your worried look or slight flush after an unexpected question will not be seen and you may be able to keep the surprise or worry out of your voice.

During the in-person interview, however, any such slip will be all too apparent. The average interviewer will then question you more closely about your technical skills, education, and so on, as he attempts to reassure himself that he's not about to make a mistake by hiring you. Once the interviewer gets on the scent of a potential problem, he'll stick with it. If you're not prepared, more careful, in-depth, or more extensive questioning of your weakly prepared lies may uncover further inconsistencies in your story. If that occurs, you'll probably turn into a quivering mass of shot nerves and perspiration-soaked clothes. Then, you'll feel depressed, defeated, and even if the interviewer wasn't suspecting anything, you'll talk yourself into ruining the rest of the interview ("well, I've blown it already so why should I even try to be nice, energetic, or convincing?"). Of course, if the interviewer is sharp and you make an obvious slip or can't handle a question, he will be on you like a pit bull, digging for what will be interpreted as a possible lie. Once that happens, even if you recover and handle it beautifully, the briefly suspected lie will taint his opinion of you and the interview is lost to someone else with whom he is comfortable. The moral here is to scrupulously prepare and practice your job-search lies to perfection.

Figure 47 shows that there's a 5 percent chance of being caught when lying about phony educational credentials. This risk is related to the fact that the interviewer may ask a question about your "education" which you can't answer ("so, give me a brief synopsis of the types of case studies you evaluated in your senior-year management classes"). No matter how well prepared, you may just come across an interviewer who, by blind chance or cunning, asks a question you can't handle. There's also 5 percent risk in lying about consulting jobs, for the same reasons.

The risk of capture is 10 percent for both fictitious jobs and completely false backgrounds. The risk derives from both the possibility of being asked an unexpected question and doubts raised in the interviewer's mind by less than scrupulous lie designs. No matter how good, there's always a risk that someone will know enough to trip you up, especially if you use actual schools and/or businesses as the basis for some of your lies. The risk is usually small, especially when you consider the intellectual impoverishment of most personnel office employees and the unsuspecting nature of people in general, but there's always a chance.

FORMAL REFERENCE VERIFICATION (FRV)

FRVs, covered extensively in Chapter Nine, of employment or education are mail or telephone checks with claimed past employers or educational institutions which are conducted to determine whether your claims are true. In most cases, the prospective employer asks you to sign a release during the interview or as you're being processed into the job. It's sent to former employers and schools who respond with verification information. Without a release (see Chapter Nine for examples), most employers and schools will release no data.

Dangers to the Job-Search Liar

A careful job-search liar faces only very small dangers from employment or education verification. Figure 47 demonstrates that there's a 15 percent risk when altering compensation. This risk exists only for liars who use their actual past employers as references *and* the employer provides compensation data as a matter of policy. Of course, if you don't use actual employers who follow this outrageous violation of individual privacy, you face no risk. There is a larger 20 percent risk of exposure when using phony educational credentials. In every 100 job-search liars, 20 will make serious mistakes in designing or buying their phony transcripts or diplomas. If you're careful, the risk is lower. The largest risk when using this strategy occurs with lies involving altered job dates. This is because almost all employers will provide actual dates when verifying past employment. The risk isn't 100 percent because not all employers will check, not all past employers will respond correctly (or at all), not all will notice discrepancies, and some won't do anything.

One time, when I was being processed into a job, I happened to get caught in a date-change problem when the clerk noticed a discrepancy between the true dates I put on the bonding form (we'll discuss bonding later in this chapter) and the lying dates I had used on my resume. I had to complete a statement card for each discrepancy. I figured that I was dead but nothing ever happened (and I was being hired to work as a manager in the personnel department!). This type of freak exposure doesn't happen often. The real risk is from using actual employers as references who do respond to inquiries. You avoid this problem when you use phony organizations.

For the same reason, there's also a 15 percent risk of discovery when using fictitious backgrounds. It may be necessary to use a real company as a reference in the past to build credibility. While this is usually safe because old records are usually not available, there's always a chance of something unfortunate happening. Part of the risk also derives from the negative impression that might be caused by less than perfect phony references or an interviewer's doubts because he never heard of even one of your phony companies. If you're using all phony companies and references, a sharp interviewer/screener may wonder why he's never able to get a reference from someone who still works at one of the companies on your resume. As mentioned in Chapter Eleven, it's a good idea to eliminate this type of doubt by using at least one existing company as a past reference (if you've got an accomplice who will help you). The odds of discovery as a result of this general type of suspicion aren't great but they exist.

PERSONAL REFERENCE VERIFICATION

Reference checks are the phone-to-phone contacts between the employer and the contacts the job seeker identifies as past supervisors. Most often, reference checks will be made by the hiring manager, as he will want to talk personally with the candidate's past supervisors. As discussed in Chapter Nine, these telephone conversations are generally short and not very specific about job details (which is why it's so easy to lie and use phony references).

Dangers to the Job-Search Liar

As shown by Figure 47, the odds of discovery when using phony references are low. If properly instructed (provided with the resume version you're using and given some advance warning), phony references generate a minimal risk of discovery. The risks shown in Figure 47 are the inherent risks of having to use less practiced liars as references. Despite the best intentions of lying well, there's always a chance that one of your confederates will make a blunder. If you prepare them ahead of time, the risk is lowered, but errors are still inevitable. Some won't be noticed but a perceptive interviewer may get suspicious if there are inconsistencies.

BACKGROUND AND BONDING CHECKS

Background and bonding checks are two of the most overrated techniques which employers use to verify that job seekers are telling the truth. They're sloppy techniques which will generally discover criminal records and widely known bad habits (such as excessive drug use which the neighbors know about) but they're notoriously poor at uncovering routine, job-seeking lies.

Bonding checks are background investigations which are conducted prior to the issuance of a bond, which is much like an insurance policy on an employee's honesty. If an employee is going to be working with large amounts of money or working with equipment that could cause significant damage, the employer has the employee bonded, which means that insurance is purchased to cover some proportion of any losses that might occur if the employee were to steal money or damage property. Before a bonding company issues the bond, it investigates to make sure the employee or candidate is trustworthy, not a convicted felon, and the like. A background investigation entails the same type of investigation but isn't followed by the issuance of a bond.

When a background investigation is requested by an employer, the employer provides the investigation outfit with all of the employee's data from the job application, including Social Security number, past employers' names and addresses, school attended, and so on. Typically, the applicant will have completed a Formal Reference Verification release form (such as that shown in Chapter Nine). These completed and signed forms are photocopied and given to the investigators. References (the names of individuals who are claimed to have been former supervisors) are usually not given to the investigators. The investigation company then may do a number of things. They attempt to call all of the past employers and schools to verify employment information and education. They check with the Department of Motor Vehicles in each state the applicant lived in. They check police records of each area in which the applicant lived. They may have investigators visit the applicant's neighbors (past and present) and make inquiries about habits, drug use, etc. They do this by going to the neighbors' doors and asking questions about you. They're looking for anything anyone may know about drug use, legal or financial problems, and the like.

Sounds pretty impressive, doesn't it? Don't worry about it. Employers' infatuations with background investigations result from their beliefs that the investigations are scrupulously and carefully conducted by daring, intelligent, private-eye types, much like the detectives on TV. Fortunately for job-seeking liars everywhere, what really goes on is something else altogether. In actual fact, the investigations are conducted by low-paid investigators who aren't always high school graduates. The lack of more formal education often means that these individuals aren't all that effective at making telephone inquiries and/or in face-to-face interviews. They don't know how to really dig for information when they're talking to people.

Even better, most of the investigators are underpaid and on a production schedule, which means that they have to complete a minimum number of investigations each day. This results in shortcuts, outright lying about having checked, and a great deal of missed data. The entire process works in favor of the job-seeking liar. I've gotten four jobs which required at least a background check and two of them required a Department of Defense top-secret security clearance (more on this later in this chapter) and I was lying shamelessly about various aspects of my resume every time. Not once was anything flagged as a problem.

Let's look at an actual report prepared by the nation's largest background-investigation service. Figure 48 presents a verbatim transcription (only the names and critical numbers are changed).

FIGURE 48. ACTUAL BACKGROUND-CHECK REPORT

Account No.: 444-44
Date: 1-5-89
Name: John Liar
Address: 21 Forked Tongue Drive, Los Angeles, CA
Position
Applied for: Manager
Date of Birth: 11/07/46
Soc. Sec. No.: 444-44-4444

SCOPE OF BACKGROUND CHECK. Two locations, two sources, seven years. Criminal court records.

EMPLOYMENT RECORD. 6/75 to 1/3/83. Jeff Department Store, Blue Hills Manor, New York, New York. The subject was formerly employed with this department store. We are in the process of obtaining employment details, and they will be supplemented.

EDUCATION/SPECIAL SKILLS. The extent of the education is not known to the sources contacted.

MANAGEMENT OF PERSONAL FINANCES. Worth is placed at 100K consisting of equity in the home he is buying and personal possessions. Lifestyle is consistent with his income and he meets his obligations promptly.

HEALTH HISTORY. He is described as an active healthy person with no impairments and no past injuries.

ALCOHOL/DRUGS. He will take one to two cocktails at a social gathering but otherwise does not use alcoholic beverages. He does not use drugs.

COMMUNITY STANDING/HONESTY/INTEGRITY. He is married and has two children and lives in a middle-class residential section, and he is buying a home in the 42K range. He has a good personal reputation and standing in the community. He has been at his present address for a short time. His former address is 445 Macken Drive, in a multiple unit. He is well regarded and is an honest individual.

PUBLIC RECORDS. Yahoo County records were checked and found to be clear. New York City records were found clear.

Dangers to the Job-Search Liar

As the example shown in Figure 48 demonstrates, these background checks don't amount to much. Most of the information is hearsay and opinion. The people who conducted the check were careless, overworked, and couldn't have cared less. Unless a neighbor is out to get you (and tells the investigator that you use drugs and/or beat your spouse), you won't have any problems. The only real danger is exposure of a criminal record. If you're operating with that type of handicap, it's best to avoid employers who do background checks or who bond their employees. Of course, it's fairly easy to get around this problem if you follow the advice given in Chapter Eleven about changing your claimed place of residence if you had a problem there. Nobody can discover a criminal record on you if they ask the police about you and you never lived there. Few employers check criminal records on their own (I've never heard of any company doing such an independent background check but there are probably companies around that do).

In terms of risks, Figure 47 demonstrates that the

two biggest dangers occur when you're faking entire jobs and/or backgrounds, and/or changing dates. The dates are a problem because most employers will verify dates if asked. The phony jobs and backgrounds can be a risk if nothing can be verified. The best bet is to use phony jobs that involve now out-of-business phony companies which were "small" so that it seems natural that the investigator has to check with the individual who used to own it or run it. If you use a large and/or real company, he'll call or write to the personnel department instead of any phony references you might have set up as "past supervisors." For example, even if your brother were owner of a business with 200 employees and agreed to be a "past supervisor" of yours, the investigation company isn't going to call him to check on your employment there; they're going to call his personnel department. The people in personnel wouldn't know about the ruse and you'd be sunk if they correctly reported they had no record of you.

The bonding check is similar to the background check. When a bonding investigation is conducted, the employer will usually have you sign a release form which gives the bonding company permission to ask for data about you. Typically, the form will have the bonding company's name on it and there will be a place for you to list former employers. The fact that the form asks for phone numbers demonstrates that most of the "investigation" will be done on the phone. If you've set up decent lie systems, you'll have no more problems with the bonding check than with a background investigation.

One clever way to get around a bonding form (or

even a background check) is to *not* lie on the release form. Most of the time, you'll be interviewed on the basis of your resume or job application. The bonding form (and most background investigation forms) is not usually completed until you're about to be hired or are just coming aboard. At that point, nobody much cares about what's on the bonding form except the bonding company. You can simply fill out the bonding form with the truth on it and hand it in. If it's a big employer, nobody will have the time to check to see if the bonding form and the application match.

Of course, there's always an exception. As luck would have it, I actually encountered one such exception when I was lying my way into a job in a bank in Denver. In this bank, one of the clerks was assigned to check applications against the bonding forms. Luckily, all I had done was changed a few dates (lengthened two jobs by a year to blot out a termination) and I was able to verbally dance my way out of it. Most companies aren't as thorough. Of course, it goes without saying that if you're telling big lies and someone spots different company names on the two forms, you're out the door before you really get in.

APTITUDE AND SKILLS TESTING

Aptitude and skills tests aren't as popular as they once were, primarily because many minorities don't score well on them. As a result of not wanting to be sued by the government for discrimination, many companies who used to administer these tests have given up the practice. In any case, they're not much of a threat to the job-seeking liar. In almost every case in which aptitude and skills tests are used, the tests are pretty much general assessments of intellectual functioning in which the applicant answers questions that assess general verbal and mathematical skills. Either you do well or not, regardless of whether you're lying.

Common tests that are used for general intellectual assessment of employees are the Wesman Personnel Test, the Wonderlich Personnel Test, and the Porteus Maze Test. There's no strategy that will help you do better on these tests other than being more knowledgeable, smarter, and/or more relaxed. If the employers are convinced that a certain score is mandatory, you'll be rejected if you don't make the cut. That's small solace if you don't make the cut, but it has nothing to do with detection of your lies.

Dangers to the Job-Search Liar

The one area which might cause a job-seeking liar any trouble would be a specific achievement test in a given specialty area, as with a French test for someone claiming to be a French translator. Of course, if you are capable in the technical area, such tests should prove no more difficult for you than they would be for the honest job seeker. If you don't have the skill or knowledge required to do the job, you shouldn't be lying about it anyway as you'll fail on the job.

A related but not as critical area of risk (as shown in Figure 47) involves your scores on such tests and claimed educational credentials. If you score very low as a result of stress or confusion, the employers might wonder how you could also be a college graduate, assuming that you were claiming to have a degree. It wouldn't make much difference at that point, however, as they'd probably reject you for a low score without a thought at that point. They wouldn't give the test if they didn't judge by the results.

PSYCHOLOGICAL TESTING

Psychological testing consists of pen and pencil or performance tests (such as puzzles), and are used to make judgments about various traits of the candidate. Measured traits might range from decision-making skills to performance under stress, to how comfortable the candidate is when working as a team player. Several large companies use batteries of psychological tests to assess management and/or executive candidates. For lower-level employees, often only one or two tests are used, generally because some people in the personnel department think they understand psychological trait research as applied to personnel selection. They rarely do but that lack of knowledge doesn't stop them. The psychological tests are combined with a variety of aptitude tests such as those discussed above in order to give the employer a well-rounded, detailed picture of the candidate's style of managing and his general capabilities.

Dangers to the Job-Search Liar

Insofar as a job-search liar is concerned, there's little danger of being exposed as a liar simply as a result of the psychological tests themselves. Yet, there is a potential problem in one area, and it's one that all job seekers, honest and lying, face from certain psychological tests. There are some tests that are used to estimate the basic honesty and dependability of candidates. In almost every case, these tests are misused and misinterpreted by unskilled, unlicensed personnel who have no training in the complex theory and meaning of the tests' results. Therefore, it's necessary to give you some warning.

The tests most commonly used for these purposes are the Minnesota Multiphasic Personality Inventory (MMPI), the 16 Personality Factor Test (16PF), the California Psychological Inventory (CPI), and the Guilford-Zimmerman Temperament Survey (GZTS). These tests have anywhere from 200 to 566 true/false or agree/disagree items. Look for the name of the test or its initials above somewhere on the answer sheet or on the test booklet itself. There are a few other lesser known tests which are used for the same purposes. If there are questions about how you're feeling, about what's going through your mind sometimes, it's the same type of test. For example, if a question asks, "Sometimes I feel so angry I could break things," it's a test similar to these. When you're taking these types of tests, be very careful to adhere to the following guidelines:

1. Never admit any criminal acts, such as petty shoplifting as a youth, and never admit that you've been in trouble with the law. That type of response is automatically categorized into a score which will make you look like an employment risk.

2. Never admit any nagging physical problems such as headaches, regularity problems, sweating a lot, and the like. These responses will be used to estimate if you are a possible abuser of sick time or a possible workmen's compensation claimant.

3. Don't try to make yourself look too good. Most of these tests have what they call "lie scales" and "fake good" scales. They're composed of questions about things which are not flattering but aren't bad, such as picking your nose (unless it's a job in a restaurant!), worrying about how you look, being interested in sex, and so on. Don't admit to every item that's slightly negative but don't deny them all, either. If the question is about something that your family knows about you, it's safe to admit. If it's something that even your spouse or significant other would be shocked to know about, don't admit it.

4. Be as consistent as you can. All of the tests have another type of lie scale which consists of the same questions with slightly different wording. The theory is that if you're trying to give a phony impression, you may forget what you said earlier and you'll give a different answer to essentially the same question. Too many of these reversals will make you look like you're hiding something.

There's a simple technique which can help you deceive such tests. Once, before I was trained as a psychologist, I took the 16PF for a sales job. I knew that salespeople were supposed to love parties, groups, and social events. I established a mental picture of what a typical salesperson would say and I answered every question in that manner. I got the job (I also had to quit because I hated it; so much for lying about a job you can't do).

5. Never admit a fear of people, a worry that you're going to hurt someone, that someone is "after you," or that you have thoughts that are too terrible to talk about. If you would be inclined to answer posi-

tively to many of these things, you probably have a few problems (unless someone is truly after you). In that case, I would recommend that you get some professional help after you get the job; don't use the testing situation with an employer to seek help.

Of course, given the large number of improperly trained people out there who are using these tests for the wrong purposes, there's always a chance that you'll be rejected for no sound reason at all. There's nothing you can do about such rejections, just as you have no defense against interviewers who assess candidates on the basis of their hair color. Follow the above guidelines on the psychological tests and you'll do as well as the next person.

There's one additional area of personnel-world quackery which has raised its ugly head in the last few months: remote-control testing over the phone. There's one company that sells a remote-control testing service to employers which uses push button telephones. The employer dials the number of the service, punches in a code number and hands the phone to the applicant. The applicant listens to a computer give instructions and then answers a list of true-false questions by punching the buttons on the phone. The people who came up with this nasty little bit of pseudoscience claim that applicants have too little time to lie and that the test is therefore very accurate in identifying potential problems. They believe that people will tell the truth to the phone more often than to the interviewer. The entire test is only about 30 questions, from which they claim to be able to make accurate personality and honesty assessments. Not likely, but that won't stop employers from using it. It's a big hit already because it's a new gimmick. Just follow the guidelines here and don't admit anything you couldn't tell your mother.

There's one more test that you're bound to run into if you interview enough. It's called the Myers-Briggs Type Scale Indicator. It's a test that characterizes people into one of 16 basic personality types. The Myers-Briggs has become all the rage in the last few years as a self-assessment instrument for workshops in management development and consciousness raising. Unfortunately, although it's an interesting test to take just for curiosity's sake, it's not a valid predictor of job success. This hasn't stopped many companies, some of them quite large and many in the hospitality industry, from using it alone to screen people for management positions. You'll recognize the test because its name is plastered all over the front of the test booklet. If you run into it in the hospitality industry, the employers are looking for people who have personalities described by the four-letter code of ESTJ. You can fool the test into thinking that you're an ESTJ by answering all questions as if you have the following characteristics:

1. You love to be around people and social events much more than being alone and reading.

2. You'd rather do something, anything, rather than sit and wait or think about something.

3. You're always the center of attention and know what's going on.

4. You like to get things over with and done so you can move on to other concerns; you love to make decisions fast.

5. You don't like a lot of theoretical namby-

pamby and philosophizing; you tell it like it is and that's the way you want to hear it.

6. You're self-confident and in charge of all situations.

There's a very similar test, a derivative of the Myers-Briggs called the Keirsey Temperament Sorter which assesses the same personality types. It can be found, along with detailed information on the 16 personality types which it measures, in a book entitled, *Please Understand Me* by David Keirsey and Marilyn Bates (published by Prometheus Nemisis Book Company of Del Mar, California). The same type of rules apply to fooling this version. If you think you've run into this type of test, buy the book and prepare yourself for the next time.

LIE DETECTORS AND VOICE ANALYZERS

The theory behind lie detectors and voice analyzers is that they detect the minute physiological changes which are caused by the stress of lying. Lie detectors monitor respiration, galvanic skin response (GSR) which is changed by sweating, pulse rate, blood pressure, and leg movements (twitching). The examiner asks the candidate a list of questions, some of which are control questions used to establish the response patterns which accompany truthful answers. The more critical questions are the content questions which attempt to get at the critical issues. Most often these issues have to do with criminal activity, stealing from employers (is there anyone out there who hasn't taken a pad of paper and a few pens?), and the like. Presumably, the liar will feel more stress when he has to lie, will show some physiological responses, and will be identified by the highly skilled lie-detector technician. Voice analyzers, newer and not as commonly used, claim to be able to do the same thing by graphically displaying the frequency and pitch characteristics of the vocal chords under the same type of questioning.

Unfortunately for crime fighters and employers everywhere, lie detectors and voice analyzers are not reliable. That's why evidence based upon them is not allowed in courts of law. Different examiners routinely give different judgments on the same set of data. The error rate (who's lying versus who's telling the truth) in controlled studies with highly trained lie-detector specialists is sometimes as high as 70 percent and is never lower than 10 percent. Even under the best of conditions, one out of 10 people will be incorrectly identified as a liar or will be assessed as truthful when he's lying. Most often, the error rates are in the 20-to-50-percent range. Unfortunately for many job seekers, personnel office personnel don't know all the facts and tend to accept lie detector data without question. This means that you may be forced to take a lie-detector test if you want to be hired (or keep your job, such as when frequent check-ups are made by store chains to control theft).

Dangers to the Job-Search Liar

Lie detectors and voice analyzers don't pose a particular problem with any specific aspect of lying. There's nothing you can do about the fact that the whole process is unreliable. In fact, the very unreliability of these techniques can be used in your favor. If you confound and confuse the results sufficiently, the examiner will most often pass you, as he will be reluctant to admit that the situation was too complicated to understand. The way you do this is by randomly generating physiological responses that have nothing to do with any stress responses which might be related to your lies. If you can generate physiological changes to some truthful answers such as "Is your name Joe Jones?" the pattern of physiological changes when you're lying won't be so evident.

It's easy to generate spurious physiological responses. For example, if you contract your sphincter muscles and bear down on your abdominal muscles much like you're trying to have a bowel movement, you'll generate an increase in blood pressure. Do this every third question or so (don't show any visible signs of what you're doing). If you know you're going to be tested in advance, tape a broken thumbtack with about 1/8 inch of point left to the side of your big toe. Every third question or so (not the questions on which you're straining your abdominals), squeeze your toes together until it really hurts. This will change your GSR because you'll sweat a little more in response to the pain (you won't notice the small amount it will take to change the GSR). There will be a tremblometer attached to your leg or free arm (one arm will have a blood-pressure cuff attached). The tremblometer is supposed to measure your nervous twitching. Subtly tap your foot (or arm) or tense it up tightly (it'll shake a little) in response to every third or fourth question. Try to keep it pretty still and relaxed in between.

You can also generate some physiological changes as a result of your mental stage. Whenever you're giving a true answer, scream out in your mind "NO" as loud as you can and try to think of all the ways in which your answer could be wrong. For example, if the investigator were to ask you, "Is your name Joseph Jones?" and that was true, you'd answer "Yes," but at the same time scream out "NO" in your mind, use one of the above physiological tricks, and then think to yourself, "to my friends, my name isn't Joseph, but Joe." Do the reverse with lies. When you give a lying answer, think to yourself, quietly, "that's the truth as I know it," and remain calm.

Of course, the best defense is to practice telling your lies as much as you can. You'll find that as you tell them over and over, the truth becomes faded and hard to remember. That's what happens to fishing stories over time, remembrances of past sexual conquests, and recollections about youthful sports achievements. If you say the lie often enough and embellish it with enough details to give it life, you won't even believe it's a lie anymore after a while. That perception, plus the above techniques, will get you through lie detector tests as effectively as the truth (which doesn't necessarily work most of the time, either).

Voice analyzers are much more unreliable than lie detectors (if that's possible). The abdominal tightening exercises, the thumbtack trick, and the internal mental games all work well with voice analyzers. Use them in the same manner.

GOVERNMENT SECURITY CLEARANCES

If you're getting a job with a defense contractor or

with a government agency which is involved with defense work, you'll have to have a clearance of some sort. Clearance levels run from Confidential to Top Secret.

The mere mention of an investigation for a government "top-secret security clearance" conjures up visions of exhaustive and detailed analyses of every aspect of your life. Conjured visions are one thing, but the reality is something else. Most government security clearances are conducted by phone. The people who do the investigations are government employees, civil servants, who work for a government agency. They're a lot more intelligent and educated than the people who work for civilian investigation companies and they have the force of the law on their side. They also know that if they screw up, there's a chance, however small, that they'll get caught and will be fired or fined. So they tend to do their jobs a little better than civilians. They also tend to get better information than civilian investigators, aside from their skill levels; when they call and tell people they're "with the DOD (Department of Defense), doing a background check for a security clearance for John Doe," most callers or face-to-face interviewees take it very seriously.

Yet, most investigations are a joke. Why? Because the number of security-clearance applications is so high that the investigators are swamped. They're months behind, they make careless errors, they overlook things, they let small details that "look okay" go by without checking them, and so on. If you're a bona fide American citizen with no relatives living overseas and with all sorts of respectable data on your application (and the applications are immensely long and detailed, including the address for every place you've ever lived), most of the stuff you put down isn't going to be checked. They'll call the employers on the phone but that's it. If you've set up your references correctly, it'll work well.

If you're simply dressing up your resume, changing a few dates, shamelessly pumping up each job's importance, the investigators couldn't care less. They don't care if you're a job-seeking liar, they're concerned with whether or not you might be a potential security threat. If they think you're using drugs, having money problems (such as gambling debts), have serious sexual problems (sheep and the like), relatives living in communist countries, and so on, you're going to be checked over more carefully. These types of problems indicate that you might be susceptible to blackmail. Without any indications of that sort of trouble, nobody is going to care or even check on such things as a few changed dates. Even if it had all of the above problems, there's a chance that the application would go through anyway. Every year, the press is full of stories about how top-secret security clearances have been given to foreign spies with foreign names, people who have criminal records (this is an automatic exclusion if known), and people who are heavy into drugs and all the neighbors knew it but nobody asked them.

I've saved the best for last. *You don't even have to lie to get the clearance!*

I've been granted two top-secret security clearances with all sorts of lies about dates, job duties, and so forth on my resume. The trick is that my security application contained the absolute truth and nothing but the truth. If my employers had looked at the security application, they would have had heart attacks and thrown me out the door. Fortunately for me (and them, too, I suppose; who needs a heart attack?), the security forms are confidential government documents that aren't passed around. If you type them up yourself (insist on it, saying that it's easier that way), nobody will ever see them if the company is following procedures. Most often, you'll submit them to the security office and they'll put them in a sealed envelope in front of you and off they go. The personnel department will never see them.

Of course, in one company where I submitted my forms, they violated the procedures and had one of the secretaries type them up. But she didn't really care what was on them and had never seen my resume anyway! In that situation, only monstrous lies such as those concerning education (as in showing none on the security forms but claiming a Ph.D. on the resume) would be obvious. So, there's really no need to lie on the clearance forms in 99 percent of most cases.

Dangers to the Job-Search Liar

As the above implies, the job-searching liar doesn't have much to worry about in terms of government security-clearance investigations. Figure 47 demonstrates that the only risks are in the areas of changing dates and fictitious jobs and careers. These risks are not because of the lie itself being discovered, but because the deceptions, if big and/or numerous enough, may make it appear as if you're trying to hide something. If the investigator thinks that maybe you're trying to hide a year or two that might have been spent out of the country, you're in trouble. Of course, all the employer will be told is that your clearance was denied but you'll be out of a job if you need the clearance. Obviously, the biggest risk of arousing that type of suspicion occurs if you're trying to pass an entire phony career and you don't do a good job. In that case, you've got an 80 percent chance of discovery. The risk from changing dates is only 20 percent and only applies if you're changing a lot of them and really moving the time around. If you're simply tightening things up by six months here and there, it's no problem. And remember, most of the time, you don't even have to lie!

If you're trying to hide a criminal record or dishonorable discharge from the service, you'll probably get caught. They do a fair job of checking criminal records because it's especially embarrassing if they miss one and it's discovered later. They do check FBI and local police records. And, outrage of outrage, they don't even give you a break if you're honest and admit that you've been in jail or had problems in the Army. So much for not lying. If you're dealing with serious handicaps such as those just mentioned, avoid defense contractors.

SO WHERE DOES THAT LEAVE YOU?

You might have one of two reactions to the materials presented in this section. The first is that things can't be so easy for the job-search liar and that I must be wrong. The opposite reaction is, of course, joy at finding out that the employer is at the mercy of almost any lies. Both of these reactions are incorrect and dangerous.

Believe me (I'm not trying to get a job from you, am I?), the situation I've described is accurate. In fact, given the distribution of intelligence among personnel types and their associates, I've probably been overly charitable in assessing their skills and precision. I'm not concerned that you believe me because I want you to like me; I want you to lie successfully so you can get the job you need. The problem is that if you falsely perceive that employers hold the upper hand in ferreting out liars, you'll be reluctant to try the types of lies you need. For many people, a moderate amount of lying will go a long way. Carefully planned lies, boldly executed, are almost impossible for employers to detect. Don't be held back by unrealistic fears, especially now that you know the real story.

On the other hand, don't get cocky about what I've told you. Almost every one of the worst military defeats in history occurred because one side took the other side lightly. Crassus, Anthony, Custer, Chelmsford, and Hitler were all devastated because they underestimated their opponents and/or took them lightly. Don't believe that you have the upper hand when dealing with employers. They are always in charge and you must lie to them carefully and with a fair amount of respect. It's not the precision of their arsenal of techniques you have to fear; it is the ability of even the most stupid person to perceive uneasiness, lack of confidence, and/or a slipped phrase that will defeat you.

If you execute your job-search lies carelessly

because you think you've got the system beat, you'll make mistakes and the interviewers will notice them. Then, unprepared and caught off-stride, you'll become flustered and fall apart. Don't let it happen. Respect employers and interviewers. They're not good liars, they're often not very smart, and they're not particularly threatening in appearance. But they're always dangerous foes of the job-seeking liar. Respect them and survive the interview to get that job and lie again next time!